NO ROOM FOR DOUBT

A True Story of the Reverberations of Murder

ANGELA DOVE

BERKLEY BOOKS, NEW YORK

THE BERKLEY PUBLISHING GROUP
Published by the Penguin Group
Penguin Group (USA) Inc.
375 Hudson Street, New York, New York 10014, USA
Penguin Group (Canada), 90 Eglinton Avenue East, Suite 700, Toronto, Ontario M4P 2Y3, Canada
(a division of Pearson Penguin Canada Inc.)
Penguin Books Ltd., 80 Strand, London WC2R 0RL, England
Penguin Group Ireland, 25 St. Stephen's Green, Dublin 2, Ireland (a division of Penguin Books Ltd.)
Penguin Group (Australia), 250 Camberwell Road, Camberwell, Victoria 3124, Australia
(a division of Pearson Australia Group Pty. Ltd.)
Penguin Books India Pvt. Ltd., 11 Community Centre, Panchsheel Park, New Delhi—110 017, India
Penguin Group (NZ), 67 Apollo Drive, Rosedale, North Shore, 0632, New Zealand
(a division of Pearson New Zealand Ltd.)
Penguin Books (South Africa) (Pty.) Ltd., 24 Sturdee Avenue, Rosebank, Johannesburg 2196,
South Africa

Penguin Books Ltd., Registered Offices: 80 Strand, London WC2R 0RL, England

The publisher does not have any control over and does not assume any responsibility for author or
third-party websites or their content.

PRINTING HISTORY
Berkley trade paperback edition / March 2009

Library of Congress Cataloging-in-Publication Data

Dove, Angela.
    No room for doubt : a true story of the reverberations of murder / Angela Dove.
       p. cm.
    ISBN 978-0-425-22588-2
  1. MacDonald, Jacque.   2. Mothers of murder victims—California—Biography.   3. Parents of
murder victims—California—Biography.   I. Title.

   HV6533.C2D6 8   2009
   362.88—dc22
   [B]

            2008047589

PRINTED IN THE UNITED STATES OF AMERICA

10 9 8 7 6 5 4 3 2 1

For Debi
and those who loved her.

FOREWORD

When Jacque MacDonald asked me to write her story, I was honored. Jacque's daughter, Debi, was murdered in her home in Modesto, California, in 1988, while her own little girl slept nearby. Debi's murder had baffled investigators. They told Jacque there was nothing more they could do. Everyone encouraged her to get on with her life. Instead, Jacque tracked down the killer herself, saw him brought to justice, and started helping other families who faced the same obstacles. I have never known anyone who became so single-mindedly determined to win a losing battle, and then won it. From the moment she approached me, I wanted to tell Jacque's powerful and uplifting story.

However, I knew that taking on this project would be difficult for me. Jacque's monumental journey lay in stark contrast to my father's. Debi had been married to my father, Harold Whitlock, for five years at the time of her murder. She was my stepmother and the mother of my baby sister, Jessica. Debi's murder had devastated our family, and in order to tell Jacque's story, I would have to revisit those terrible events. I agreed, ready to face the nightmare of the past.

Instead, I stumbled onto a new aspect of the story—one I found just as devastating.

While researching the facts surrounding Debi's case, I discovered the huge body of evidence linking my father to her murder. I learned things about my dad that literally brought me to my knees. Only now, years after his death, could I understand all the things I sensed in him: his guilt, his inability to forgive himself, and the self-destruction that eventually ended his life. Today Jacque MacDonald is hugged tearfully by strangers, applauded by politicians, and speed-dialed by police departments across California's Central Valley. Today my father is dead. No telling of these events can get around this fact.

"No room for doubt" is a phrase I picked up during an interview with Modesto Homicide Sergeant Jon Buehler. "It took nine years to solve Debi's case," Jon told me, "but Jacque always believed it would be solved. And she made us believe. There was never any room for doubt."

This conversation took place at a time when I hoped to tell Jacque's story but avoid revealing how Debi's death affected anyone else. However, there is no way to compartmentalize murder. Its reverberations ripple across lives, across miles, across time. So Sergeant Buehler's phrase became something of a mantra for me as well. I could not allow any misgivings to deter me from telling this story—the full story—with unflinching honesty.

Because I have tried to be sensitive to those involved in these tumultuous events, certain names and circumstances have been altered. Where people's recollections have differed, I have had to choose between versions or try to merge the two. Other times I had to condense several occasions into one. I have endeavored to portray the truth of events, relationships, and characters as I understand them.

During the last year it has become clear to me that we can never really know another person. We have only our perceptions, colored by our beliefs and biases and experiences. We live with one foot in fiction, taking what we know about a person and creating the rest. Each of us necessarily decides our own truth.

This book is my truth.

I would like to thank all the people who have assisted with this project, particularly the Modesto Police Department and those officers who shared with me their personal and professional experiences of Debi's case; the Stanislaus County criminal court and clerk's offices, including Michael Tozzi; Merced District Attorney Larry Morse and Sheriff Mark Pazin; Margaret Speed and the victim/witness offices of Merced and Modesto; Daryl Farnsworth and the editorial staff of the *Modesto Bee*; Comcast Cable executive Barbara Rodiek; Oxygen channel producer Deborah Dawkins; California Congressman Dennis Cardoza and his staff; California Assemblywoman Cathleen Galgiani and her intrepid aide, Robin Adam; the staff of the Modesto city museum; Modesto historian Colleen Bare; Jacque's many friends and fellow survivors, as well as her family, whom she credits for all her successes; the friends and family of Debi and my father, who shared both their joy and pain; my agent, David Fugate; former Penguin editor Katie Day; editor Andie Avila; and my readers Ginny Barrett Patten and Bob Clark. I am enormously grateful to my husband, Ira Dove, and our children, my mother, and my sister, without whose blessing and patience I would not have written this book.

I will always be thankful to Jacque for inviting me on this journey, and to those who supported me along the way. Jacque MacDonald inspires people to be braver versions of themselves. That gift has carried me through this project.

INTRODUCTION

It was absurd that the sun was shining.

Jacque MacDonald stood by the mausoleum, surrounded by her loved ones. Her husband, Dennis, was there, along with her surviving daughter, Karen, and son-in-law, Cliff. Jessica was there also, Jacque's beautiful three-year-old granddaughter. How much did Jessie, tapping her shiny new shoes, understand? How much did any of them understand? Of course Jessie thought her mother would be back soon. Didn't they all cling to that fantasy? Call it denial. Call it desperation. But the thought that Debi would be among them again was more real than being without her.

Jacque's body reverberated with a kind of palpable nothingness. How could emptiness be so filling? It overflowed, rippling out of her. It swallowed the mourners, the press, the cemetery. It ate up the whole world.

Five days ago Debi had been alive: a wife, a mother, a sister, a daughter. There were so many future possibilities for her. In one violent moment, they had evaporated.

Jacque couldn't bring herself to think of the end of Debi's life. She pushed it back down into the dull void. But even now she could feel the restlessness. The anger. Rage. It was coming. Her internal radar guaranteed a catastrophic storm headed her way. Would she be caught up in it? Would it leave her in ruins? Could she ever rebuild?

She held the small, ornate box in her hands. It was so light, yet it was the heaviest burden she had ever carried. This was all that remained of her firstborn. Debi's life, her aspirations, her future—they were all ashes now. Drowned in blood, consumed by fire, and returned to the hands of the woman who had carried this child inside of her, who had walked the floors during the nights of colic and had slipped coins from the tooth fairy under her pillow.

Jacque's thoughts drifted. She hated her dress. She'd bought it at the last minute because Debi's sister had been adamant that everyone wear blue. It was, after all, Debi's favorite color.

Jacque was aware of whispers, sobs, prayers. But none of it made any sense. She didn't hear the ceremony. There must have been one. She vaguely remembered a priest taking the box from her, touching her gently as if he were taking the real Debi away from her. Someone else had done that days ago. The priest's words were directed at her, but they were too far away for her to understand. They joined the pulsing nothingness, swirling away in the winds of the approaching storm.

Somewhere, another mother was burying her child. Everything around Jacque was a pantomime, but that other mother was real. If Jacque could, she would reach out and touch her.

The funeral service was over. People said their words to Jacque, hugged her and cried on her, not realizing she wasn't there. Eventually she was alone. A ghost mother. Her eyes traced the lettering on the new bronze plaque: Deborah Anne Whitlock. Somewhere inside of her, thunder rolled.

"Well," she said to the memory of her daughter. "What the hell am I supposed to do without you for the rest of my life?"

People now recognize Jacque MacDonald. They've seen her on TV, hosting her show or accepting the National Crime Victims' Service Award from the United States attorney general. They've heard her on the radio. ("She's British, right? Wasn't her daughter murdered?") They remember seeing her on *20/20*, or *America's Most Wanted*, or *Jerry Springer* back when his show had some class. Perhaps they read about her daughter's case in *Newsweek*, or *People*, or some tabloid. Maybe they saw her last year on an Oxygen channel special.

If these same people live near California's busy Highway 99, they might recall the billboard of her daughter's face smiling down on their morning commute, promising a reward for any information about her murder.

Cameras seek Jacque out at victims' rights rallies. Short, fiery, her London accent lending her an air of refinement, Jacque can always be relied upon for an engaging quote or a thoughtful reflection.

What the cameras don't see, of course, is underneath. Within that petite frame is a storm of unrelenting anger. The electrical charge it generates fills up her delicate frame and leaks out of her, fueling those around her.

"I'm not a hero," she repeats for the umpteenth time. "I'm just a mother whose daughter was murdered. And now, I'm fighting back."

ONE

Phone Calls

Jacque MacDonald surveyed her kitchen with satisfaction as she carried the cleaning rag to the laundry room. This was going to be an exciting visit. It was the first time Dennis's mother, Brona, had been to their new house, and they were eager to show it off. Though they had been married for over six years, Dennis and Jacque felt like young newlyweds in their first home. And the house looked perfect, if Jacque did say so herself.

It was March 25, 1988.

Dennis had waited a long time to find the right woman, and Jacque had stormed into his life in a way that only an Englishwoman with fiery red hair can pull off.

This was the second marriage for Jacque. After the disastrous end of her first marriage, she had vowed never to trust another man. But air force officer Dennis MacDonald had a kind and giving spirit, and his soft voice and easy smile won her over quickly. "Besides," Jacque laughs whenever she tells the story, "I always have been a sucker for a man in uniform." She had wandered the base near Merced looking for her girlfriend who worked there. The day was growing hot, and Jacque felt herself drooping like the plants left too long unattended on the officers' patios she passed. The front door of a nearby house opened with a creak, and a man's voice called out, "Are you lost?" Jacque turned to see an officer she had met the night before at a local bar and jazz club. He recognized her, too, and invited her in for a cold glass of orange juice. They had been together ever since.

Jacque and Dennis felt they had spent too much time waiting and dreaming about *one day*, but never acting on those dreams. They were married only a year after they met. And now, six years later, they had built a beautiful three-bedroom home in Burnsville, Minnesota, which was close to Northwest's Minneapolis–St. Paul hub but removed from the traffic of the city. Jacque felt at home immediately in the place. As a pilot's wife, she was alone for days at a time. It was important to her to have a home where she felt comfortable and secure while Dennis crisscrossed the skies in various 727s.

Although she loved the house and town, Jacque wished Burnsville were closer to California. She and Dennis had moved away when Dennis had become a commercial pilot two years ago, but Jacque's daughters still lived in the Central Valley. The oldest, Debi, lived in Modesto with her husband, whom everyone called Howie, and their three-year-old daughter, Jessica. Karen, only eighteen months younger than Debi, was married to Cliff and lived in nearby Merced with their three-year-old daughter, Megan.

Jacque missed her daughters and granddaughters terribly, but her claustrophobia kept her feet firmly on the ground. Debi and Karen understood their mother's anxiety, rolling their eyes with a smile whenever Jacque referred to an airplane as "a small tin box hurling through the skies." The sisters planned to bring their little girls to visit their gran in two months. Jacque could hardly wait to see them.

Jacque glanced at the leaden clouds framed by lace curtains in the kitchen window. The Minnesota winters were harsh for Jacque who, although she grew up in the chill damp of London, had acclimated to the California sunshine during the intervening years. Now, she mused, she had traded the rain clouds of her childhood for the snow clouds of her grandmother years.

Mackie ran into the room, her small black nails clicking on the white tile. She looked up at Jacque expectantly, her mustached snout quivering excitedly. Jacque laughed. "You don't care that it's cold out there, do you?" Mackie yipped and pranced around her, and Jacque stooped to pet her. She loved this miniature schnauzer that had slept contentedly in her lap during the long ride across country in the moving van.

Jacque walked to the hall closet to get her coat, hat, and gloves. She clipped Mackie's leash onto her collar, and the little dog half tugged her out the door and into the chilly Minnesota morning.

As she made her way through the neighborhood, Jacque could feel the excitement of approaching spring. The crocuses were sending out tender shoots that promised color enough to banish even the foulest winter gloom. Neighbors smiled easily, chirping hellos across slushy front lawns and silently agreeing that they would soon be shoveling the last of the winter snow.

Dennis and Brona arrived home that evening at about six o'clock. Dennis walked to his wife and leaned down to plant a kiss on her cheek. While he carried his mother's bags into the guest room, Jacque lit the gas burner below the teakettle and made Brona comfortable on a plush white chair accented with tiny roses. "I want to hear all about your trip," said Jacque, "but let me give Dennis his phone messages while I'm thinking about it." She headed toward the back of the house, barely glancing at the family portraits lining the hall.

Dennis was in the master bedroom already loosening his regulation tie. Northwest had begun painting the tails of their aircraft red during the Second World War to make the planes more visible during harsh northern weather conditions. Now the color was used for ties on the pilots, scarves on the flight attendants, and as accents on the 1920s circular logo, a halo around a pair of golden wings.

Jacque smoothed Dennis's navy blue uniform jacket, which lay neatly across the bed's rose-covered comforter. Friends always teased Jacque that even without her accent, the rose-patterned fabrics throughout the house would give away her British upbringing.

Jacque came up beside her husband and tucked her small frame under his arm. He hugged her warmly. "Hi there, sweetheart. How was your week?"

"I'm just glad you're back," Jacque smiled. "You had a call today."

"Who?"

"The chief pilot. He said you should call him once you got in."

Dennis's posture straightened. It was unusual for the supervisor to call a second officer at home. "That's odd. I better call back before dinner."

A low whistle sounded from the front of the house. "That'll be the tea. Would you like a cup?" asked Jacque.

"No, I'll get some later."

Back in the kitchen, Jacque poured tea for Brona and herself, placed the cups and some biscuits (she never could bring herself to call them *cookies*) on a tray, and headed into the living room. She turned to her mother-in-law.

"I'm so glad you could come. Would you like to see the house?"

Jacque gave Brona a quick tour. Then, their tea ready, the two women sat on the couch and quickly lapsed into small talk.

Jacque lost track of the time; otherwise she might have wondered why a simple call to the chief pilot was taking so long.

Dennis entered the room sometime later, his face ashen. Something was very wrong. Jacque stood up, walking toward her husband. "What is it?"

Dennis looked at his wife, bafflement in his blue eyes. "It was Cliff," he said, referring to the husband of Jacque's younger daughter, Karen.

This didn't make any sense at all. What did her son-in-law have to do with Dennis's chief pilot? "What?" Jacque asked in confusion. "I thought you were calling the chief pilot." Then comprehension dawned. Cliff had called the chief pilot, trying to get in touch with Dennis. He had wanted his news delivered to Jacque by her husband, in person. The chief pilot had served as a go-between.

"Oh my God." Jacque's breath caught in her throat. "Something's happened to Karen."

"Sit down," said Dennis.

Her legs wouldn't have obeyed the order to sit, even if Jacque had given it. "Just tell me."

Tears welled in his eyes as he placed his hand on hers. "It's Debi."

Confusion crested anew in Jacque's mind. Why would Cliff call about Jacque's older daughter? True, her daughters were best friends and lived only thirty miles apart, but why wouldn't Debi's husband, Howie, call if something were wrong?

"What happened?" Jacque whispered.

"Debi's been killed." His voice cracked. "Somebody cut her throat."

Jacque's memories of that night are sporadic and incomplete. She remembers being outside, walking aimlessly. She remembers standing outside a neighbor's door. She must have knocked. The door opened, and the man's quick smile faltered. "My daughter is dead," she said, and the sound was like somebody else's voice from far away. She remembers Dennis's warm hand gently coming to rest on her shoulders then, his soft voice both apologetic and placating as he turned her from the neighbor's door and back toward home.

Jacque's friend and coworker, Cathy Wood, had planned to come by Jacque's house that night. Born and raised in Ireland, Cathy had made some traditional sweets and promised some to Jacque. She helped her kids with their homework, finished eating dinner with her husband, and then called Jacque. She picked up on the first ring, and Cathy asked if it was a good time to come over.

"Oh!" Jacque seemed a bit surprised. Perhaps she had forgotten.

"Ah," said Cathy. "Are you going out to eat with Dennis's mum, then? I can always come over later."

"No, no. That's all right. It's just that I've only just now found out that my daughter was murdered."

The kids were putting dishes in the dishwasher. Surely Cathy misheard through the clatter. "What did you just say?"

"My daughter, Debi. She's been murdered."

Cathy thought her friend had to be joking. She didn't sound upset at all. On the other hand, it wasn't like Jacque to joke about something so horrible.

"Jacque, are you serious?"

"Yes, Dennis just found out. I just . . . I . . . ." Her voice trailed off into helpless silence.

"Oh, Jacque. I'll be right over."

Cathy knew both of Jacque's daughters from her long conversations with Jacque over coffee after work and from the pictures throughout Jacque's house. She had looked forward to meeting them and their little girls when they came to visit in a few weeks.

Cathy arrived at the house within minutes, her curly hair frizzed with the evening's humidity. Dennis opened the door and stood aside to let her pass. "Thanks for coming so quickly."

"Of course." Cathy gave him a quick hug. "How is she?"

Dennis didn't answer but nodded in the direction of the living room. Inside Cathy found her friend sitting on the couch, staring at the carpet. Only her hands moved, clasping and unclasping of their own accord.

"Jacque?"

Jacque turned toward her and smiled faintly. "Oh, Cathy. Hello." She was clearly in shock.

Cathy rushed toward her friend and hugged her, crying. "I am so sorry. So, so sorry."

Within minutes, the doorbell rang again. Jacque hardly stirred as the house filled with friends. At some point, Jacque's minister arrived and tried to counsel her, but his words fell on deaf ears. Finally, he clamped a strong hand on Jacque's shoulder and announced, "You should rejoice! Your daughter is in heaven now!"

Jacque blinked and looked at this man as if she had never seen him before. For the first time since the phone call, her face registered shock and anger. "My daughter is dead," she hissed, "and I am not going to be happy about that." The room fell silent. Jacque's eyes were bright with rage, and the minister quickly left. Jacque, her armor of shock finally compromised, slipped away from the room of family and friends and the knowledge that they shared.

Jacque remembers none of this. One moment Dennis was leading her away from her startled neighbor's front door, and the next thing she recalls is her body in motion, rocking. Knees pulled to her chest, she cowered behind her bedside table. Rocking, with no eyes on her, stifled noises tore at her throat.

Later, Dennis came to her. In the eerie silence of the house, he lowered himself beside the nightstand. The house was eerily silent. "Come on, sweetheart. You need to rest." He gently lifted her onto the bed.

There are no more memories from that night.

Like Jacque, I received the news of my stepmother's death from a telephone call. I had flown from the San Francisco airport to Savannah, Georgia, the day before, where I planned to spend spring break with my mother and her sisters. We were to celebrate my eighteenth birthday the following day.

I was in my aunts' guest room, honoring the first morning of vacation by refusing to get out of bed. The room's dark paneling and thick carpet deadened the noise from the rest of the house, and the heavy drapes fought valiantly against the invading southern sunshine. The digital clock radio showed eleven a.m., but I was still on Pacific time. I stretched luxuriously and rolled over, determined to stay put until my stomach started grumbling.

I became aware of my mom and her sisters, Cyndy and Alecia, whispering in the hallway. They were probably planning some prank. Any minute now they would burst into the room and launch into an impromptu song and dance routine featuring lyrics about my laziness. I come from a goofy family that loves laughter, and it wouldn't be the first time someone's late slumber had been sent up in song.

Mom opened the bedroom door and stood uncertainly in the doorway. My expectant grin faded. "Angela, your dad's on the phone. You better get up and talk to him." Her voice was shaking slightly, and she had a look in her eyes that I had seen only when I was in danger.

"What's the matter?" My feet were already on the carpet.

"You better let your dad tell you." Mom started to say something else, then thought better of it. She settled for "I want you to know that everything is going to be all right." She was trying to soften a blow, and the knowledge of her intent made my chest seize up so that I could hardly breathe.

I headed into the hall and cut left toward the kitchen. Alecia, a younger version of my mother, stood in the hallway. Her brow was furrowed in concern, and she pointed silently toward the back of the house. I understood. Wheeling around, I walked to the back bedroom, the one Mom was using. I grabbed the phone from the bedside table.

"Dad? Something's wrong, isn't it? What happened?"

My dad cleared his throat. "Yes, honey. Something is wrong." It was the first time he had spoken to me in weeks, and he had even called me *honey*. This had to be really bad news.

"Is it Jessie?" Her name caught in my throat. I loved my three-year-old sister as if she were my own child, and I didn't know what I would do if something had happened to her.

"No, Jessie is OK."

I started crying then. I'm not sure why. I was so relieved. My sister was fine. Whatever else had happened, I could take it. And yet, even as the pressure in my chest started to subside, I felt my mother's hand rest on my knee and realized she was seated beside me on the bed. My aunt Alecia was in the doorway, looking on with pity and uncertainty.

"Honey, Debi is dead."

I still see this moment in every detail. And like Jacque, I don't remember much at all for the next several hours. There are a few moments when I fought my way up for air, but mostly I was caught in the undertow.

I remember thinking that Debi had been killed in a car accident during her long commute to work, and Dad saying, in a kind of hesitant way, that "someone" had killed her.

"You mean someone killed her on purpose?" I asked. *Why on earth would anyone want Debi dead?*

"It appears so." He went on to tell me he had found her at home, that someone had killed her in the house when he was out. He also said the investigators would be calling me later that day. "They're trying to figure out who might want to do this," he explained, "so just answer them as best you can."

Suddenly his voice became very edgy. "Do you know if Debi had any enemies? Did she have any . . . I don't know . . . fights with anyone? Any arguments?"

"Not that I know of."

"I need you to really think about it, OK?" My father seemed desperate. Then again, wouldn't any man be desperate to find out who had just murdered his wife?

I didn't understand the significance of his panic. How could I? There was so much he wasn't telling me. I didn't know Debi had been killed two nights ago. I didn't know where my father was when she was killed. I didn't know he had spent most of the previous day in police custody. And I didn't know he was the prime suspect to his wife's murder.

TWO

The Last Night

Jacque MacDonald's older daughter was built very much like her. At thirty-two, Debi Whitlock was petite with reddish brown hair and bright eyes that always held a hint of her next smile. She met her challengers head-on, but she was so bubbly that her opposition wouldn't realize for quite a while that they had been soundly beaten. If they caught on at all.

As the investigators pieced together the last day of Debi's life, the picture it made was fairly nondescript. She had spent a scheduled day off from her relatively new job as assistant manager of the Sears store in the Merced Mall. She dropped her daughter, Jessica, off at day care and spent much of the day cleaning house and running errands. She took movies back to the video store. She returned library books and checked out new ones. She carried clothes to the dry cleaner. Around noon she met her husband for lunch at a nearby restaurant. She picked up her daughter from day care in the late afternoon and apparently headed directly back to her house.

In one of Modesto's newer middle-class neighborhoods, 1504

Dalton Way was a ranch-style house that sat in the middle of a nicely mown and trimmed lawn, replete with an automatic timer that cut sprinklers on and off during the early morning hours. This was the kind of neighborhood where people were doing well and expected to do even better. The area was sandwiched between cheaply built duplexes and apartments toward town with nicer developments farther north and west.

Debi pulled her Ford Taurus directly into the garage using her electronic remote to open the exterior door. She didn't bother to close the door again. The Whitlocks habitually left it open during daylight hours whenever anyone was home.

By the time Harold Whitlock arrived home at 5:15 p.m., Debi had already changed into a comfortable, well-worn sweat suit. Debi always dressed nicely during the day, even on her days off, and it was pure joy to come home and get comfortable. She chose turquoise pants and a shirt with alternating stripes of turquoise and white. The coroner would later call them green.

Harold walked from the garage into the house via the door connecting the garage to the kitchen. Inside the door was a message board with thumbtacks on it. Debi's key ring was already there, decorated with an acrylic butterfly, its body a golden plate engraved with her name. Harold hung his keys next to hers.

"Daddy!" Jessie cried out, running to him.

"Jessie!" he called back, stepping over the scattered remains of his daughter's forgotten tea party. "Did you have fun at Evelyn's today?"

"Uh-huh." Jessie ran back to the living room as quickly as she had come. Her father heard the voice of Snow White coming from the television.

Debi walked into the room carrying a laundry basket piled high with clothes. She propped it on the bar as she eyed the plastic dishes on the kitchen floor. "JJ, you need to come pick up these toys!"

"I busy!" Jessie called back.

"Well," Debi laughed. "I guess I know where I rank!"

Harold glanced up from the stack of new library books he was perusing. "Maybe if you had an entourage of dwarfs?"

Debi wrinkled her brow. "No, I don't think it would be worth it."

"Yeah, I know what you mean," he said, his eyes scanning a book jacket. "All that singing."

Their conversation thus far was civil and child-centered. Maybe that's as good as it could get right now. Debi wondered how it had reached this point. She and her husband were cordial strangers living in the same house, crowded together with resentments they harbored and words they would never say. Never mind. At least they were working on it now. Lunch had been a step in the right direction, Debi felt certain. How could they make decisions about the future if they couldn't even have a conversation?

Shaking herself from her thoughts, Debi picked up the laundry basket again and walked into the garage, turning right to load clothes into the washer. When she returned to the kitchen, Harold reminded her about the bachelor party he was hosting. She seemed to believe him. For her part, Debi reminded him that she had to open the Merced store the following morning, which meant she had to leave by 5:30 a.m.

"Oh, I'll be home before that," Harold said, his expression souring. "I don't particularly want to go."

"You're in charge," Debi reminded him. "I think you'd be missed."

Her husband laid down the stack of mail he was thumbing through and wandered into the kitchen. "It's a party at a bar," he said dryly. "Do people really need directions on where to go from there?" He opened a cabinet door and took down a jar of peanuts. "Step one, order drink. Step two, swallow." He popped the lid off the jar, emptied some nuts into his hand, and tossed them in his mouth.

Debi laughed. In spite of their problems, Howie always could make her laugh. He had a quick, laconic sense of humor that continually surprised her and bore witness to an intelligence that she only wished he would use more often.

Stifling a sigh, Debi went back out into the garage to the standing freezer. Inside, bags of frozen vegetables were organized by color on the shelves, and the racks on the doors were lined with individual-serving-sized freezer meals: meatloaf on the top, turkey in the middle, and pepper steak on the bottom. It looked like a home shrine to Freezer Queen. Debi made her selections and came back into the kitchen.

Harold Whitlock glanced disdainfully at the boxes as Debi placed them on the counter near the microwave. "Ah! Another fine, gour-met meal!" he exclaimed in mock enthusiasm. It was something he had always teased her about. Debi's only talent in the kitchen was making chocolate chip cookies. Otherwise, she was a disaster. She wouldn't chop vegetables for fear of cutting herself, and her mashed potatoes were a lumpy nightmare. Still, the cookies redeemed her.

"Hey, at least I eat," Debi replied. She stopped there. She always did.

Still in his suit from work, Harold went back to the master bathroom to shower and change before the party. The bedroom had that same perfected conformity evident in the freezer. A picture of Harold and his daughters sat at one corner of Debi's dresser, and a picture of Jessie and her cousin Megan, wearing matching dresses, sat at the other. Centered between the two was a mirrored tray with five glass perfume bottles evenly spaced across its surface and a small crystal box containing some pearls and a few pieces of costume jewelry. Debi's bedside table was bare except for a lamp whose mate was on Harold's table, and a Judith Krantz novel from the library. The room smelled of lemon furniture polish.

Harold walked over to his chest of drawers and emptied his pockets onto its surface: a packet of Salem Lights, assorted coins, and a white cotton pocket handkerchief. After his shower, he transferred everything back into the pocket of his jeans. Harold always wore suits to work, rain or shine, but tonight was a decidedly casual affair.

Walking back into the kitchen, he grabbed a beer from the refrigerator and carried it to his chair in the family room. He tapped a cigarette out of the pack and lit it, listening as Debi drew a bath and Jessie threw bright plastic toys into the tub. Harold grabbed the television remote control and turned on a rerun of M*A*S*H.

In the preliminary trial hearing, Harold initially said he left home for the party at 7 p.m. Soon after, he put the time at 9 p.m.

Much later that night, Harold Whitlock perched on a barstool at Ortega's Cantina, a Mexican restaurant and bar owned by the very prolific Ortega family. Regulars knew it simply as Ortega's. The restaurant on the right side of the building was well-lit and airy, and the waiters (many of them adult children of the owner) bustled back and forth with efficiency and pride. But by now the restaurant had closed, its entrance roped off so that patrons had to turn sharply left at the front door and walk down a ramp into the cool darkness of the bar. The music tonight was loud, and a few people gyrated on the dance floor across the room.

Not long ago, this whole area of town had been orchards. The mall was the first big structure to replace the neatly laid rows of grapevines. The only remaining clue to the history of this land was the big neon sign in the parking lot: Vintage Faire Mall.

Soon the nearby almond orchards were cleared to make way for the businesses that always spring up around malls: restaurants, movie multiplexes, nail salons, and big box stores. People with the same names carved onto Modesto's oldest burial markers and historic buildings bemoaned the disappearance of the town's agricultural past. But Modesto was now the fastest growing city in the state, and all those people commuting to and from the Bay Area needed houses and manicures and paper towels packaged in bulk. By most people's standards, a new prosperous Modesto was arising from the old canal systems and dusty fields.

In the same way, Harold Whitlock was trying to build himself into something bigger and more successful. Once a poor boy from Virginia, the grandson of a railway worker, he had decided to leave his troubled past behind. He would erase the last traces of the boy abandoned by his alcoholic father, the adolescent once labeled "incorrigible" and shipped off to boarding school at the local preacher's behest. Instead, California provided a new start, a place where he could use his hard-won charms and his basketball player physique to compensate for his lack of higher education.

He had seen a glimmer of his potential during his high school years at Oak Hill Academy, where he and his girlfriend, Diane, had graduated as covaledictorians. Two years after graduation, the president had offered him a position at the new alumni office, and he had been tempted. Now married to Diane and a new father, the offer proved that he was no longer the troubled young boy who had once burned a neighbor's shed to the ground. He had won the respect of respectable people, and that meant more than he could ever express.

At the same time, he felt he could accomplish so much more. His wife's mother and stepfather had moved to California and spoke highly of the area. They had also agreed to help out with child care while Harold and Diane began taking college courses.

And so Harold had moved his young family across the country. He and Modesto had found each other, and together they would become more prosperous than anybody had ever imagined.

Harold began in an entry-level position at Sears in 1976, determined to prove himself. He made friends easily and impressed supervisors with his rigorous work ethic. His efforts were rewarded with raises and promotions, and soon he was named department manager for Housewares. He bought Diane a new set of dishes, then a new house to put them in. He congratulated himself, knowing that he would soon be in store management. He just needed the right edge to get there. He had to spend more time with the right people, and as luck would have it, he knew where to find them.

Ortega's was the unofficial after-hours watering hole for the Sears up-and-comers. Harold had avoided the bar scene most of his life, always aware that, as he put it, "If cheap booze was a religion, I'd come from a family of saints." So it came as a shock to his wife when Harold started going out with the guys after work to have a few drinks.

"But you hate bars!"

"Yeah, but that's what it takes to get ahead. I see how the game is played, and I'm going to play it. Trust me."

Diane looked at him, still the boy she'd fallen in love with, but trying to be so much more. He wanted more for himself and his family. She couldn't fault him for that.

"Listen," he said earnestly, answering the look in her eyes, "there's no way I'm going to turn into my father."

"I know you'd never be like that, Rocky," Diane said softly.

"And I watched what Granddaddy's drinking did to Grandma Ruby, too. How many times did he pawn her ring for liquor?" He shook his head. "That woman was too good for him. He'd pawn her ring one month, then buy it back when the railroad paid him. The next month, he'd pawn the shotgun."

Diane knew all about the shotgun. It was in the closet now, not so much for protection as it was a talisman against the past.

During the next several years as she watched Harold slide into alcoholism, Diane would think back on this conversation and marvel at what fools they had both been.

By March 25, 1988, Ortega's Cantina was Harold's social headquarters. It was directly across the street from Sears and a short drive from his current job as a department manager at Best Products. In this dark, moodily lit room, Harold Whitlock had made friends, schmoozed coworkers, shed himself of his first wife, and romanced his second. He had disavowed the name Harold (the only thing he'd ever gotten from his father) and his family nickname of Rocky. Now he was Howie. "Happy Howie," his closest friends sometimes called him. He knew every one of the Ortega brothers, their wives, their children. He and Debi were particularly close with Jerry Ortega and his wife, and the two couples, along with Bob and Doris Kramer, enjoyed frequent barbecues at one another's homes.

There was over a decade of good memories in that room, but tonight Harold Whitlock did not appear happy at all. Liquor was flowing, and the guys from work had achieved that immature raunchiness that every bachelor party held at a bar somehow reaches. That was to be expected. But someone had crossed the line, and Harold was furious. As he later admitted on the witness stand, "One of the employees made an off-color remark that I took exception to, and it just upset me."

Anyone who knew Harold Whitlock well would understand that those words belied a much darker reality. Although he was a loyal friend and could always be counted on to help a person in trouble, he also had a long memory for anything he perceived as betrayal or insolence. He had ended friendships and even family relationships over the wrong comment or a misjudged action. Harold Whitlock's anger was not something to be taken lightly.

Near midnight, Harold walked to his truck and revved the engine, making his tires squeal as he exited the big parking lot.

Twenty minutes later, Debi was dead.

The investigators had pieced together much of Debi's last evening at home up until my father left the house, but they needed me to fill in the rest. Although my father had told me to expect a call from the detectives working the case, I did not realize the importance of this interview. I certainly didn't realize the effect my story would have on my family, the investigation, or the eventual hearings about Debi's murder.

The investigators were cordial and professional, well-versed in talking to people who had experienced the worst life could throw at them. They told me their names, which I immediately forgot, and they tried to ease me into the interview with some basic background questions. I confirmed that I was seventeen years old and a senior at Fred C. Beyer High School in Modesto. I was the natural child of Harold and Diane Whitlock, and yes, Debi was my stepmother. Was.

My parents had moved to California from their home state of Virginia when I was two. They separated when I was nine, and my father began dating Debi shortly after their divorce. During that time my mother raised me, but I visited Dad and Debi on the weekends. Mom stayed in California long enough to finish putting herself through school at nearby Stanislaus State College. She also obtained her certificate in public accounting. Then, five years after my parents separated, she moved the two of us back to Virginia just before I started high school.

I returned to Modesto to visit Dad and Debi for the summer prior to my junior year. While there, I took a summer school class at the high school across town in my old school district. I hooked up with some old friends and made new ones. Most importantly, I met my baby sister, sixteen-month-old Jessie.

I didn't think about it while I was talking to the investigators, and wouldn't have mentioned it anyway, but my father had initially hidden Debi's pregnancy from my mother and me. Debi wrote to me shortly after I moved back East, telling me the exciting news. "Your father and I are so happy. I know your father loves you very much, and he hopes this baby will be as sweet and special as you have always been." I had to take Debi's word for it. My father never discussed it with me.

I had mixed feelings at the time. On the one hand, I hated to think I would be so readily replaced. I had hardly left the state, and before my father had a chance to miss me, he would have a replacement child (a prime example of the self-centered logic of a fourteen-year-old). On the other hand, as I read Debi's letter I felt somewhat sorry for her. I was sure she didn't know about the day Mom and I were loading the moving van to head back East. My father had arrived at my mother's house unannounced, jumped from his sports car, and begged her not to go.

"It's too late for this, Rocky," Mom told him tearfully. "What do you want from me? You left five years ago. Go home to your wife." She spat the final word at him. We had only recently learned he and Debi had been married for over a year.

Dad hung his head and mumbled something, but my mom cut him off. "You made your decision! In fact, now I know that you had already made your decision when—" She broke off, fighting tears. "Why did you ask me to take you back right before you married someone else? What is wrong with you?" Without waiting for an answer, my mother ran to the house.

He stayed for about an hour, helping load the truck in absolute silence. Then, just as abruptly as he had arrived, my father hugged me awkwardly and left. He didn't say good-bye.

Dad's actions that day reaffirmed my mother's belief that she was making the right decision by moving away. Later we realized that scene had occurred while Debi was five months pregnant.

Upon returning to Modesto two years later to visit Dad and Debi, I finally got a taste of being a big sister. And in a word, I was smitten. Jessica Jacqueline Whitlock (whom Debi had hoped everyone would call JJ) had soft curls and mischievous dimples. And, like her grandmother and namesake, Jessie was petite and gregarious. I fell under that toddler's spell immediately and knew it would break my heart to live three thousand miles away from her.

I plucked up my courage and asked Dad and Debi if I could live with them long enough to finish high school. They both seemed pleased and immediately said yes. Debi was particularly supportive. She always looked for ways to strengthen the tenuous relationship between my father and me. Besides, they both said they could use the help with Jessie, and I was only too pleased to give it.

The detective on the phone brought me back to our conversation. "Your grandmother on your mother's side also lives in Modesto, is that correct?"

"Yes." Since my mother and I had returned to Virginia two years ago, Nana had been thinking about doing the same. But then I moved in with Dad and Debi, and she decided to stay in the area long enough for me to graduate.

"Yes," repeated the detective, "and lately you've been primarily staying at your grandmother's residence?"

I knew where this was heading. I had moved out of my father's house a few weeks ago and had been staying with my grandmother ever since. This was a painful episode in my relationship with my father, and I had no intention of talking about it. Besides, I didn't think it had any bearing on their investigation.

"That's right," I said carefully. "I shared time between Dad's house and my grandmother's house. Lately I've mostly been staying with my grandmother."

"Oh? And why is that?" He tried for a tone of casual interest.

I weighed possible answers. "Well, it's my senior year. I'm studying for finals, and I'm the editor of the yearbook. I'm at school a lot, and my grandmother's house is only three blocks away." I bit my lip, waiting to see how this answer went over.

There was a pause, then the other detective took the lead. "Angela? I was just wondering how you would, uh, characterize your relationship with Debi."

"We got along fine," I said with all honesty.

Even when we lived in the same house, Debi and I didn't cross paths all that often. Once she received her promotion and became a regional buyer at the Hayward office, Debi was out of the house before I awoke and many days didn't get in until after dinner, when I was doing homework. Debi often had a day off during the week, but I was at school, or babysitting for another family, or hanging out with my friends. We, along with Dad, shared care of Jessie, and the happy little girl comprised most of our common ground.

I didn't relate this to the detectives. Why should I explain that Debi and I had a kind of silent partnership? We knew the rhythms of each other's lives, and shared a love of reading and similar tastes in clothes. We were friendly, but we weren't particularly friends. Outside of the child we both adored, we never discussed much of anything. We both had our problems with my father, but without ever saying the words aloud, we had agreed never to discuss those, either.

"And how would you characterize your father's relationship with Debi?"

Red flags went up. "What do you mean?"

The first detective cut in again. "We're just interested in what their home life was like. You know, did they get along all the time, or most of the time? Did they argue?"

"Doesn't everybody argue sometimes?"

"Sure they do." The second detective gave a practiced chuckle.

"Well, I guess they mostly got along." I wasn't about to say any differently. Dad could tell them what he wanted to about their recent marriage problems. It wasn't my story to tell.

The interview turned toward my last meeting with Debi, and it didn't take too long for me to understand that some of what I had to say was tremendously important to the Modesto Police Department. The detectives began walking me very slowly through the night of March 24. This was only two days ago, and I felt confident in my memories of the evening.

I had been excited about my plans to spend spring break with Mom and her sisters in Savannah. At approximately 10 p.m. my best friend, Kelli Clark, and I arrived at Dad and Debi's house. We knocked on the front door since the garage, usually open during the day, was already closed for the night. (I no longer had keys to the house and wouldn't have used them if I did, a fact I did not share with the detective.)

The house was mostly dark, except for a few lamps shining up front. After a short delay, Debi unlocked the front door and opened it. She was wearing her purple robe.

"Sorry it's so late," I said. "Time got away from us."

"That's fine," she said. "I was still reading." At the end of her hectic day, Debi loved to curl up in bed with a romance novel. "I didn't pull down a suitcase since I wasn't sure what size you needed."

"Then I'll just go check out your fine selection," I replied in mock seriousness. Because Dad and Debi both worked retail, we often took turns pretending to be finicky or gullible customers, and the counterpart high-pressure salespeople.

Debi laughed, taking the bait. "I'm sure you'll find something just right for your needs. Let me know if I can help you in any way!" She flashed a patented, high-wattage smile. I laughed and headed through the kitchen toward the garage.

I came back into the kitchen shortly carrying a suitcase. "Got it. Sorry again about the time. We'll let you get to bed." I knew Debi's commute meant she had to be up early on weekdays.

I didn't tell Debi at the time, and I didn't tell the investigators now, but the truth was I had chosen to wait until I thought Dad was asleep, or at least reading in his room, before I arrived. We had had a falling-out less than two months prior, prompting my move into my maternal grandmother's house across town. My father and I had hardly spoken since. Kelli knew I dreaded seeing him, so she had volunteered to go with me to get the suitcase. Now, talking to the detectives, I believed that my relationship with my father had nothing to do with Debi's murder. I omitted any reference to it.

That night at my father's house, suitcase in hand, Kelli and I headed toward the door.

"Wait!" Debi called out. "Don't leave without giving me your flight schedule. Especially if you want anyone to be at the airport to pick you up." She laughed her big, hearty laugh. "Of course, maybe you'll like living at the airport."

Kelli joined in. "You could buy some tacky T-shirts, catch up on the tabloids . . . Maybe find out about Bigfoot's baby."

"OK, OK," I said, throwing up my hands in surrender.

Debi grabbed the notepad and pen from beside the phone on the kitchen bar while I pulled my airline tickets from my purse. I read off the information, and Debi jotted down dates, times, and flight numbers.

The investigator interrupted me. Where was Debi standing? Could I see the notepad as she was writing on it? Could the notepad be seen from the hallway?

I hesitated. "The hallway? No." They must be confused about the layout of the house. "Debi was on the kitchen side of the bar, and Kelli and I were on the living room side. No one was in the hallway."

"You could see down the hallway?"

"Yes."

"Were any doors closed?"

I thought back. "The master bedroom and my sister's room."

"Wait. You couldn't see your sister's room from the bar, right?"

So they did know the layout of the house. "No. I went back there."

There was a brief pause, and the detective asked me to continue my narrative.

While Debi was still writing, I said, "I'm just going to give Jessie a quick kiss before I leave."

Debi looked up from her notepad. "Well, OK," she said, "but be quiet. Your dad is already asleep."

There was a choking noise from the phone line. "Could you repeat that?"

"She told me my dad was asleep already."

"Have you spoken to you father about this?"

"About him sleeping? I don't know." Our conversation was such a blur that I didn't know exactly what I had said.

"OK, so Debi told you your dad was asleep. You're certain?"

"I'm certain." I could still remember the relief I felt to hear that I wouldn't have to face him that night.

"When we talked to Kelli earlier, she didn't say anything about that." The detective's words sounded like a challenge.

"You talked to Kelli?"

"Yes, and she didn't mention Debi saying that. Is there any chance you could be mistaken?"

"Not a chance." Debi's statement may not have resonated with Kelli, but it certainly did with me. I had practically cheered at Debi's pronouncement.

The detectives finally asked me to continue. I told them that I had headed down the hallway then, past the partially closed door of the dark master bedroom. Turning right, I quietly opened Jessie's bedroom door. This room functioned as home office and bedroom, with a wooden desk on the right and Jessie's white twin bed and dresser on the left.

With eyes still accustomed to the bright track lighting above the kitchen counter, I paused in the doorway of my sister's room. In the darkness, I relied on the sound of Jessie's deep, rhythmic breathing to locate her. I also heard my father's breathing coming from the room next door.

"Wait!" The cop on the phone interrupted me again. "You heard breathing? Are you positive?"

"Yes, I'm sure." How was I ever going to get through this if they kept interrupting me? "I didn't want to turn on any lights, and the two rooms are right next to each other." I remembered standing in the near total darkness, picking out the long breaths of my father in the next room and the slightly shorter breaths of my sleeping sister. I silently recalled groping my way through the darkness until I felt Jessie's comforter on the bed, then her tiny leg underneath. I planted a gentle kiss on my sister's forehead and stood for a moment, my hand stroking her soft curls, listening to her easy sleep. As I had done so often when I lived in the house, I sent out a quick prayer for her well-being. Since I had moved out six weeks ago, I had missed this little girl terribly. I worried about the stress in the family and its effects on her. But the break with my father wasn't going to be put aside anytime soon. The hurt was too deep this time.

"Did you close the door again when you left?" the officer asked, prompting me to continue.

"I think so." I remembered trying to close the door quietly, more afraid of waking my father than my sister. I walked quickly back down the dark hallway to rejoin Debi and Kelli in the front of the house. Kelli held the suitcase, and she and Debi were trading good-byes. I bade Debi a good night and said I'd see her in a week.

The investigators asked me to go over a few things again: the breathing, the garage door, which lights were on in the house. But I kept thinking about how anxious I was to leave that night, how I hurried outside after Kelli because I was afraid Debi was going to try to talk with me about my shattered relationship with my father.

Debi saw a problem as an invitation to roll up her sleeves and get to work. But my father and I were a different breed, and Debi couldn't understand the stalemate between us. Ours was a relationship she had tried to nourish throughout her years with my dad, and I believe she took it personally when our tenuous connection snapped.

I thought back to her phone call to me shortly after I moved out of the house. "Just leaving, without a word?" she chided me. "That wasn't a very good way to deal with the situation, do you think?"

"I left a note."

"A note. Well that doesn't solve anything, does it?"

I told her I didn't want to talk about it.

"I picked up on that," she said with gentle sarcasm, "but if things are bad, you don't just walk away from them."

If I had known Jacque better at that time, I would have recognized where Debi's directness came from. Years later, I would hear Jacque say almost the exact same thing, only she would be talking about the stalled investigation into Debi's murder. However, as a smart-aleck teenager being called out by her stepmother over the phone, I had bitten my tongue to keep from bringing up Debi's own recent talk about divorcing my father and the brief period of time weeks ago when she had moved out. Wasn't that walking away from a bad situation? However, I knew they had been trying to patch things up. Debi was back in the house and had scaled back her hours at work. They'd even had me babysit recently so that they could go have dinner together. And in spite of my defensiveness, I realized Debi cared about my father and me. She honestly wanted us to have a good relationship. I also knew that was becoming increasingly unlikely.

On the last night I saw Debi, I toted a borrowed suitcase down the front steps and followed Kelli into the driveway. Debi looked after us, then shut the front door and engaged both locks. Lights began going out in the front of the house, and we loaded the suitcase into the hatchback of Kelli's red Nissan.

One of the detectives cut in. "Were there other vehicles in the driveway?"

I thought about that for a minute. "No. I don't think so."

"What about your father's truck?"

I tried to remember. From the passenger's seat of Kelli's car, I had noticed that Dad's blue truck was missing from the driveway. Debi had said he was home. Oh well. As with all truck owners, my father's friends were always borrowing the vehicle to move furniture or haul lawn and garden supplies. Or maybe Dad had sold it. It was not uncommon for my father to sell one car and buy another on a whim.

"No, my dad's truck wasn't there," I answered the detectives. "But, um, can I ask you a question?"

"Absolutely."

"When did—I mean, wasn't Debi killed yesterday?"

"Our medical examiner says she died about two hours after you girls left. It appears you were the last to see Debi alive."

THREE

The Morning After

The Whitlock house was quiet in the dark, early hours of March 25, 1988. Grainy light appeared through the sliding glass door to the backyard, barely distinguishing the shapes of juniper bushes and lava rocks around the small carp pond. The soft hiss of a neighbor's automatic sprinkler system filtered into the house.

Shortly after 5:30 a.m., Modesto's 911 emergency operators received a call from the Whitlock house. "Yes, I need help," Harold Whitlock said. His breathing was shallow, and his voice was shaking. "I just got home. There's blood everywhere. I—I think my wife is dead. Please send someone. Oh, God, hurry."

"Is there anyone else in—"

"Oh God. My little girl. I forgot to check on my little girl. Hang on a minute, OK?"

The operator was already placing a call to the first response team at Modesto Fire Department by the time Harold came back on the line to say that his daughter was asleep in her bedroom.

"Sir, I'm requesting assistance for you now. I need you to stay on the line. Is your wife breathing?"

"I don't think so. I—oh my God. Please hurry."

"Sir, please calm down. Just stay on the line."

He didn't.

Moments later, the wail of a siren shattered the early morning quiet. The headlights of a Modesto fire engine shone briefly through the Whitlocks' small kitchen window, making a misshapen rectangle of light scurry from the refrigerator across the back wall. The siren let out a last, dying cry that leaked out across the neighborhood. Jolted from sleep, neighbors began fumbling for light switches and robes.

From the truck's passenger seat, Captain Tom Brennan took in the scene: dark house, light in the kitchen window, garage door open. A tall, thin man came walking out of the garage, his hand raised.

"The guy's outside," remarked Engineer Michael Kraus, shutting off the truck's engine. "You think he's the husband?"

"I guess."

"Then where's the wife?"

Dispatch had sent for the fire department response team from Station 4, the closest of Modesto's eight stations. The call had been a "difficulty breathing/stop breathing" code for an adult female at this residence. Dispatch had given them no indication of foul play.

Brennan and Kraus, friends with over a decade in the department together, had brought along firefighter Gary Lopez. Lopez was the new kid, only twenty years old, fresh out of training, and looking forward to the heroic excitement that his big brother had bragged about down in the Los Angeles County FD. And Gary was a quick study. In the backseat, the kid was already grabbing his first aid kit and jumping down from his seat.

Now the husband was walking toward the truck, shielding his eyes from the light. Kraus flicked off the headlights and opened his door. Lopez was already talking.

"Are you Mr. Whitlock?"

"Oh my God. My, my wife—"

Kraus walked around the truck to join them. "Sir, where is your wife?"

Harold Whitlock put his hands over his face, then rubbed them over his forehead and into his graying hair. "Ahhh—ahhh . . ." He was babbling, incoherent.

We're probably too late, Brennan thought, surveying the scene from the truck. If the wife was still in distress, the husband would likely be with her inside; his presence in the driveway indicated that she had lost consciousness. At the very least.

Brennan reached for the driver's side door. Suddenly, his radio crackled to life.

"Captain Brennan? Report your 2-20."

Brennan reached for the radio. "Just arrived on scene. We haven't checked the victim yet. The husband is outside, so I'm guessing the wife might have stopped breathing altogether." Through the windscreen, Brennan saw Kraus still trying to talk to the husband while Lopez ran toward the garage. Dispatch came back on the radio.

"Be advised that call may be an assault."

"What do you mean? I thought it was a stop breathing call."

"Situation is uncertain. The husband's call was garbled, but we think he said there was blood, that his wife may be dead. Proceed with caution."

Damn. The kid, Lopez, was already in the house. Brennan jumped from the truck and walked quickly toward Kraus and the husband.

"Mike? I need you inside with Gary."

Kraus stopped midsentence and looked at his superior officer, eyebrow slightly raised.

"Better get inside," Brennan repeated. Kraus nodded and hurried through the garage.

"Mr. Whitlock, I'm Captain Tom Brennan. We're gonna do everything we can to help your wife. Can you tell me what happened?"

Harold Whitlock was pacing, his eyes bloodshot. The sounds coming out of his mouth could not be called words.

Inside the house, Gary Lopez clutched his first aid kit and called out, "Mrs. Whitlock? Modesto Fire Department! Do you need assistance?"

There was no sound.

He was standing in the kitchen. Dark cabinets surrounded him. A bar opposite him separated the kitchen from a formal sitting room. To his right was another opening leading to a sunken den. Lopez walked toward the den and glanced around. Empty. He turned on his heel and walked back through the kitchen, cutting around the bar and turning left toward the bedrooms.

"Ma'am? Where are you—"

Gary Lopez stopped in his tracks as suddenly as his breath caught in his throat.

The woman in the hallway was lying spread-eagle, feet facing him and head pointed toward the master bedroom. Her face was covered by a bloody shirt, and her chest was exposed and perfectly still. Her arms stretched above her. A large butcher knife rested against the inside of her bare thigh.

Like a solar flare, the image etched itself into Gary Lopez's memory.

She had to be dead. Still, he forced his feet to move toward her. He bent at the waist and touched his hand to her ankle. It was cool. She had been dead for awhile.

Mike Kraus's voice made him jump. "Hey, Gary? You need any—Jesus Christ!" Kraus had just entered the house and come around the bar when he caught sight of the woman's body.

"She's dead, Mike," Lopez mumbled. "She's . . ." He didn't even know what to say.

Kraus was next to him. He bent down and touched the woman's foot, an instant replay of Lopez.

"She's been dead a few hours."

Lopez grunted an agreement. Who had done this to her? And was he gone?

Sheer terror ripped into Lopez's stomach. He was very aware that he was in an unsecured house with only a first aid kit for protection. "We gotta get out of here."

Still gripping his kit, Gary Lopez practically ran from the house. He gulped the cool air in the garage to steady his stomach, then called to his supervisor.

"Captain? We gotta call the police."

Captain Brennan looked toward Gary Lopez and saw the panic in the young man's eyes.

"It's bad," Lopez said, looking over toward the husband. No wonder the guy was freaking out. "Real bad."

"We'll need homicide." That was Mike Kraus, emerging from the garage just behind Lopez. He put his hand on the young man's shoulder. "Knife attack. Lots of blood. She's been dead for a few hours."

Lopez looked over at Harold Whitlock, worried that a husband hearing those words might collapse. Instead, Harold Whitlock seemed oblivious. He was still pacing, mumbling, clutching his hair in his fists.

Captain Brennan walked back to the truck and made the call. "We've got a homicide here. Possible knife attack. You better notify PD."

The radio crackled. "Roger. What's the situation on the husband?"

Interesting question. The captain had been trying to get Mr. Whitlock to string together more than two words, but to no avail. The guy was obviously in distress. Was this a distraught husband who had just discovered his wife murdered? Or was this a man coming down from a homicidal rage? Hard to tell. But knives were messy, and Whitlock seemed clean. Come to think of it, he looked as if he had just showered.

"I'm not sure. Just get someone over here."

Brennan replaced the mic and walked back toward the house. Where was the ambulance? They had been dispatched simultaneously. He noticed Gary Lopez was working with the husband now, trying to get him to calm down. Kraus was standing nearby. Brennan caught his eye.

"Did you look around?"

"Not really. Just checked the wife. She's cold."

Brennan considered his options. Should he have two men with the husband, who might be the killer? Or should he have backup in the house? Three guys with no more protection than some sterile gauze and a strong sense of duty. And he had to make the call that could endanger all of them.

"OK. I'm going in the house. You stay out here with Lopez and the husband. And be careful, Mike. We don't know what his situation is."

"Got it." Mike Kraus looked steadily at Brennan. "She's in the hallway, and it's bad. I've never seen anything like it."

"OK."

Brennan walked through the kitchen, down the steps into the den. A faint breeze came in through the open sliding glass door, but the room was devoid of homicidal maniacs. He circled left and went up the steps to the sitting room, glancing behind a small love seat as he passed. From this direction he could see down the length of the hallway. An open bedroom door next to the body spilled early morning sunlight into the interior of the hall, a grainy spotlight on the nightmare on the carpet.

Brennan swore under his breath.

Forgetting about the danger of a lingering assailant, the captain moved forward and knelt beside the body, checking the temperature of her foot. There was no need to try to locate a pulse.

A faint noise caught Brennan's attention, and he jumped to his feet. Someone else was inside the house. He placed his back against the wall and called out, "Modesto Fire Department! Is anyone else in the house?"

He peered into the bedroom to the right of the victim's body. It contained the same rust colored carpet as the hallway, a full-size bed, and a sweater chest against the far wall. A closed window, drapes pulled back, proved to be the source of light. He checked the double closet, but it contained only a few summer dresses.

Leaving the room, he continued down the hallway and noticed directly beside the master bedroom a closed door, which had initially been hidden from view as the hallway curved around to the right. He made his way toward the door cautiously, stepping around the body as best he could. Holding his breath, Brennan firmly gripped the knob and pushed the door open forcefully.

Along the right wall was a worn, wooden office desk with two stamped envelopes and a banker's lamp on top. Across from him was a wooden dresser with ceramic drawer pulls and a few stuffed animals across its surface. Beside that was a twin bed, a cluster of stuffed animals, and a small girl in pink pajamas sitting up and looking at him with undisguised curiosity.

In that instant, the entire scene changed for Tom Brennan. Filters normally in place while he was on duty suddenly crumbled. He'd felt it before, whenever he was called to the scene of an accident and discovered it involved children. He looked protectively at the small girl whose hair was tousled with morning curls.

"Hello, there," he said, removing his hand from the doorknob and trying somewhat successfully for a relaxed, friendly grin.

"Hi." The girl seemed perfectly at ease.

"I'm Captain Brennan. Are you OK?"

"Uh-huh." She pointed toward the bedroom door. "My mommy's out there."

Brennan's mind raced. *Dear God, she's seen her mother. Maybe even watched as it had happened. And yet, maybe . . .*

"What do you mean, honey?"

The little girl picked up a stuffed rabbit beside her. The doll had floppy, polka-dot ears and a flowery purple dress. It looked new—probably an early Easter present. The girl made the rabbit jump up and down a few times. "My mommy's in the kitchen. She's making my breakfast."

Her simple faith in a world that no longer existed crashed into Tom Brennan with the force of a well-placed punch. This girl's mommy would never make her another breakfast. She just didn't know it yet.

From outside came the sound of brakes. That would be the ambulance. Patrol officers wouldn't be far behind. He had to get the girl out of here. Brennan looked around the bed. He shouldn't remove much from the room, but it was cold outside. More importantly, he needed something to cover her eyes. He saw a small blanket curled up by the girl's pillow.

"What's your name?"

"Jessica."

"Well, Jessica, is this your blanket?"

"Uh-huh."

"I'll tell you what. I'm going to take you outside to see your daddy, OK?"

"OK. Can Bunny come?"

"Sure. But it's kind of cold, so I think you and Bunny should get under this blanket, OK?"

He scooped the little girl from the bed and threw the blanket over her head. She seemed uncertain about the blanket, but Brennan needed her to wear it.

"Jessica? You just hang onto Bunny and keep her warm, and we'll be outside with your daddy in just a minute."

He felt the girl's grip tighten on her rabbit as he gathered the ends of her blanket close to her body. He didn't want her to be able to see anything. Carefully he carried her out of her bedroom and across the body of her mother, bracing himself against the wall to keep his balance. He noticed there was another print on the wall. A partial handprint. Stamped in blood.

Gary Lopez was still with Harold Whitlock, who had finally begun to talk. He said he had just arrived home, and Gary noticed that as Whitlock lapsed once again into agitated silence, Mike Kraus had nonchalantly wandered over to Whitlock's pickup truck and touched its hood. About that time the ambulance arrived, and Lopez had asked if Whitlock wanted to be checked out by the EMT. Whitlock said no. Kraus had walked over to the ambulance to talk to the driver, probably to tell him the location and state of the body. Based on personal experience, Lopez silently agreed that no one should walk into the house unprepared.

Lopez turned at a noise in the garage and saw his captain holding a blanket with two small bare feet protruding from the bottom. He stood amazed as Brennan stopped in the driveway and began folding back the blanket until it revealed a small girl. And a purple rabbit.

"Wow. Is that your daughter?" Lopez asked Whitlock.

"Yes," he answered in a strangled voice, then turned away from her, his back shaking.

Captain Brennan headed toward the ambulance, passing Kraus and a medic on the way. He saw Kraus do a double take at the sight of the child, but that conversation would have to wait.

In his arms, the girl was looking at all the unusual vehicles. "Jessica? Your daddy has to talk to some people right now, but he's right over there, OK?" She turned to look and nodded. "How's about I show you this ambulance? It's got some pretty cool stuff inside."

Now that she'd seen her father, the girl seemed unfazed by all the hubbub. She turned her attention to the ambulance. "What's in there?"

"Oh, lots of stuff. Let's see if there's a driver here. They know all about ambulances."

Sure enough, one of the crew rounded the side of the vehicle just as Brennan arrived.

"Hi!" said Brennan, catching the man's eye and concentrating on keeping his attention. "This is Jessica. I just brought her out of the house with a *blanket over her head* to keep her warm. I told her that *her daddy is busy right now*, but that you've got some interesting stuff in the ambulance. Why don't you show her how you *run a basic* on people to make sure they're OK?"

The EMT guy was pretty quick on the uptake.

"Sure. Hi there, Jessica. I'm Kevin. Who's that you're holding?"

"It's Bunny," said the little girl, craning her neck to look inside the back of the ambulance.

"Do you think Bunny would like to look around?"

Brennan put the girl down on the floor of the ambulance and said, "Jessica, I'm going to go help these people, but Kevin's got some neat stuff to show you. You just call me if you want me to come back, OK?"

"We're fine, Captain," said Kevin with a smile. He turned his attention back to the little girl, looking her over with a practiced eye. He picked up a small blood pressure cuff. "Hey! I want to show you this funny bracelet."

"Bunny, too?"

"Sure, Bunny can help."

Captain Brennan turned away from the ambulance and took a deep breath. The sky was now silver and brightening all the time. A neighbor from across the street was standing uncertainly in front of his house. The PD could handle that.

The fire engine was on the street, and the ambulance was beside it. A black-and-white patrol car had arrived, and the officers were talking to Kraus and Lopez a short distance from the husband. Mr. Whitlock had walked over to the far side of the driveway and was seated on some railroad ties that bordered a large planter area sporting a few sparse palm trees and an expanse of decorative bark. Brennan walked toward his crew.

"—was when I walked over and felt the truck," Kraus was saying. "It was warm."

An officer turned toward Brennan. "And you found a kid inside? But no one else?"

Brennan nodded. "The daughter. Jessica. The EMT is checking her out now, but she seems fine. She has no idea." He looked toward the ambulance, then continued. "I noticed inside that the back door was standing open a little. It's a glass door leading out to the patio."

The officer made a note. "OK. We'll take a look."

Twenty minutes later Tom Brennan, Mike Kraus, and Gary Lopez were on their way back to the station. They rode in silence. No radio. No discussion. Once they pulled into the garage, Lopez climbed out of the rig and shut the door. He walked into the station house, not bothering to speak, and headed toward the break room. There was a small television set on the counter next to the

Coke machine. As he fumbled in his pocket for change, he heard music. Someone had turned the channel to MTV. The music video now playing was an old song used in Robin Williams's recent movie, *Good Morning Vietnam*. Lopez heard Louis Armstrong's voice sing out in a contented growl,

> *I see skies of blue, clouds of white,*
> *The bright blessed day, the dark sacred night,*
> *And I think to myself, what a wonderful world.*

Gary Lopez felt his muscles tense. It was not, in fact, a wonderful world. It was a world where people did extraordinarily horrible things to each other. As the young man grimly fed quarters into the drink machine, he knew for certain that the image of Debi Whitlock's desecrated body and this song would be fused together in his mind for the rest of his life, coming for him when he least expected it.

Back at the Whitlock house, a brown Buick sedan pulled up at the front sidewalk. Harold Whitlock turned from the detective interviewing him and walked quickly toward it. A large man in a navy jogging suit unfolded himself from the driver's seat and stood shaking next to the car, holding onto the roof for support. Tall, fortyish, with wavy brown hair, the man watched silently as patrolmen strung yellow tape along the wooden beams of the front stoop. Then he saw Whitlock approaching. The man loosened his grip on the car and walked around the hood. He was already crying when Harold reached him.

"No!" wailed the man, catching Harold into his massive arms. "It's true! I didn't think it was true until I saw you."

Bob Kramer was Harold Whitlock's best friend. In fact, the

two men shared a friendship that was all but brotherhood. Bob had known the Whitlocks for over a decade—had introduced them to each other after providing emotional support to both of them as they divorced their first spouses. Bob and his wife Doris were Jessica's godparents, and the two families saw each other almost every day. It was Bob who had rechristened Harold Whitlock "Howie," a moniker that led many to believe that the man's name must be Howard. Bob's nickname for Debi, Little Red, was something the fierce redhead would only allow Bob to call her.

Doris Kramer got out of the passenger's side door. Of this husband and wife team, Bob felt his way through life while Doris relied first on reason. She was kind and friendly, but years of marriage to Bob had trained her to take the lead in high-pressure situations. She noticed Harold's demeanor—shaken, speechless, almost immobile—and patted her stricken husband to release his hold. Bob pulled back, wiping his eyes.

Doris blinked back tears as she gave Harold a quick hug. She had questions, but now was not the time to ask. "Where's Jessie?" she asked.

Harold nodded toward the ambulance, and Doris turned to see the girl's curly head peeking out the back door. Jessie was watching Bob with some concern.

"You haven't told her?" Doris asked, still eyeing the girl.

"I—" Harold gulped for air. "I can't. Not here." He looked around as more cars arrived. "Not like this."

"I agree," said Doris with a nod. She straightened her shoulders and forced a slow, steady breath. Jessie was watching her now. Doris smiled and waved. "Hi, honey," she called out.

"Hi, Aunt Doris! Come see this!" Doris could make out a stethoscope around the little girl's neck and a bunny sporting several new bandages clasped in her arms.

"She's in her pajamas," Doris observed.

"They don't want me to take anything out of the house," Harold answered.

Bob blew his nose loudly into an already-distressed pocket handkerchief. "Fine, I'll get her clothes."

"Nobody's allowed in," said Harold.

Bob's watery eyes flashed red. "Screw that. She needs some clothes." He started to stomp toward the house, but Harold grabbed his arm.

"No, Bob. They're just doing their job."

"Howie's right," said Doris. "We can get her some clothes. And some breakfast. Let's just get her out of here."

Bob wasn't backing down. "It's just a pair of pants and a shirt. I know right where they are."

"No!" Harold shouted, and Bob froze. Harold lowered his voice again, his eyes wild. "Even if they'd let you in, I won't. No one's going in. No one else is going to see her like that."

Harold closed his eyes and forced his open palms hard against them. He looked like Oedipus about to blind himself after viewing the worst image imaginable. Doris placed her cool hands around Harold's wrists and gently pried them away from his face, forcing him to look at her. "We're taking Jessie to our house. If you need a ride later, call us." She emphasized the word *us*.

An officer wandered toward them, but Doris maintained her grip on Harold's arms. "Listen to me. Jessie will get through this. We all will. Bob and I are here for you, and we love you. Come over as soon as you're finished. You're staying with us now."

She hugged Harold briefly, then turned and walked toward the ambulance. "What you got there, Jess?" she called.

The officer reached Harold and Bob. "You're Mr. Kramer?" he asked, looking at his notebook.

"That's right. Who the hell did this?"

"We don't know, sir, but we're working on it."

"Well, you find the bastard," said Bob, "and you put him in a room with me and Howie. We'll take it from there."

"I understand, sir. We'll do our best. You're going to take the little girl?"

"Yes," Bob managed. "She's our goddaughter." He burst into new sobs as Doris returned with the girl. Doris addressed the officer.

"We'll have her at our house, and we can leave you our address if you need it."

The officer shook his head. "That won't be necessary, ma'am, thank you. Mr. Whitlock already gave us that information. We'll be in touch."

"I'm sure you will." She put her arm on her husband and said meaningfully, "Jessie says she could use some breakfast, and I thought we might go buy her a special outfit. What do you think, Uncle Bob?"

Bob's attention was fully turned toward his friend. "Do you want me to stay?"

Doris cut in before Harold could answer. "I don't know that that's the best thing in this situation." She turned toward Jessie. "Daddy has to stay and talk to these men for awhile. You get to hang around with me and Uncle Bob today, OK?"

Harold turned toward his daughter. "Jessie, you go with Uncle Bob and Aunt Doris for awhile. I'll see you at their house later." Then he turned away from her.

Doris buckled Jessie into the backseat, her mind whirling. This was not good. Doris had noticed the way the detectives were looking at Howie, looking at Bob, judging all of them. Did they consider Howie a suspect? How much did they already know?

Harold Whitlock had called the Kramers in a panic less than

an hour ago. They could hardly piece together what he was saying: he had been out all night, then come home to find Debi dead. Murdered. What should he do?

During the last few months, Doris had seen Bob's pain as his best friends' marriage dissolved. Now Debi was dead. How would big-hearted Bob handle it if Howie was charged with her murder?

A half hour later, Crime Scene Manager Dick Ridenour was assembling his troops. All five members of the Modesto PD Robbery/ Homicide division were now on site, and it was his turn to act as CSM. Some people said heading up the scene was the easy part: log your hours up front, write up some reports, and sit back while the lead detective did the rest of the work. But Ridenour knew better. He'd played both parts many times in his eleven years on the force, and he knew that the way the scene was handled was a tough game to play. It was you against the future defense attorney, and she was going to know every mistake you made. In fact, she was relying on you to make mistakes, because it made her job so much easier. The attorney called the game "due process." Dick Ridenour called it "letting the bastard walk."

The men assembled around him, some carrying plastic foam cups of coffee, some grabbing the time outside for a nicotine fix. No one had been inside yet; they were waiting for a judge to sign a search warrant. Hopefully the DA would show up with it soon. However, Ridenour had talked to the first responders and patrol guys, and the latter were now finished roping off the house. Identification Technician Denise Ducot, the only female on scene, was anxious to get inside so she could shoot video and stills before the rest of the team started working.

"OK, I need someone to take the husband's statement. Bill, you're gonna take this case?"

Detective Bill Grogan nodded. "I've got the wiener," he said with utmost seriousness.

A few of the guys grinned in spite of the circumstances. A few months back, one of the guys had brought in a small, inflatable Oscar Mayer wiener that was now passed from desk to desk in Robbery/Homicide. If the toy was on your desk, you were up to take lead on the next case. Once you had your case, the wiener went to the next guy. It was often remarked upon, with many wry smiles among this all-male unit, that the wiener was all-powerful.

"Congratulations, Bill," said Ridenour blandly, jotting notes in his workbook and then flipping back to the previous page. "Looks like there's some confusion about Mr. Whitlock's alibi. Let's make sure we nail that down and start tracking it. Also, I understand the scene is pretty messy in the hall and bedroom, so watch where you're walking. One of the fire department guys said the back door is open." He pointed to the right of the driveway. "This alley runs along the back of the house."

"Think our perp exited that way?" This came from Grogan's partner, Fred Vaughn. His expression was serious. Having a partner with the wiener was almost as bad as having it yourself.

"That's my guess, Fred. Fire guys said he left a signature on the wall next to the body, too."

"Sure it's not the husband's print?" asked David Rhea.

"He said he didn't touch any blood," said another officer. "Of course, he also told me he was at an all-night party, or maybe sleeping. Now he remembers he was banging his girlfriend."

"She any good with a knife?"

There were a few chuckles.

Ridenour cut in again. "Guys, we don't know what went on in there, and if we think we do, we're just going to get sloppy."

"We're here to open doors, not shut them, right, Dick?" said Elvin Tomlinson. It was a saying they'd all heard from Ridenour.

"I'm sure Bill would appreciate our not getting sidetracked, since it's his case," Ridenour conceded. "More importantly, it's my scene and my ass on the line." He ignored a comment about his ass being in good hands. Graveyard humor came with the badge. If you couldn't take it, you were in the wrong line of work.

"DA," Lucian Beltran announced.

The guys turned as one to watch as Stanislaus County District Attorney Tom Brazelton drove up. He waved a paper at them: the search warrant. Ridenour turned back to the officers around him. "The game is on, gentlemen. And lady. You all know what we're up against. So let's suit up. Give Denise a chance to shoot some footage before you move anything; she'll give you the all clear when she's done with an area." He snapped his notebook shut and glanced up at the growing throng of neighbors and reporters coming together on the sidewalk. "Jim, you're handling the press?"

Sergeant Jim Watson nodded an affirmative. As a rule, the sergeant was the media contact until the case was well under way.

Ridenour continued. "And can someone talk to the masses, please? They'll know it's a homicide once the gurney comes out. May as well tell them. We need to know if anyone saw anything, heard any screams—"

"—or any arguments about a mistress—"

"Yes, yes. Let's stay focused. Bill, you want to take the husband downtown, or give him to Fred?"

The detectives filed inside the house, feeling the near-electric charge of being at a homicide scene. Officer Ducot's flash was already casting a strobe over Debi Whitlock's body. The detectives grew somber and reflective as they caught sight of her.

Harold Whitlock was at the kitchen table, giving a rudimentary statement that would later be typed at the station. The detectives eyed him suspiciously, prompting their intuition to tell them whether or not he was their guy. Wife dead, daughter alive, mistress in the picture—determining his guilt shouldn't take long, once they had some prints to match.

Ridenour wandered through the house taking notes and fielding questions. The knife by the victim had already been bagged to protect any prints it might carry, and Whitlock had identified it as belonging in the knife block next to the kitchen sink. Another knife, also bloodied, lay in the sink. Someone would bag that soon enough. Right now, the hot spots in the house were the body, the master bedroom, and the back door.

As Fire Captain Brennan had surmised from his walk through the house, the back door was apparently opened by the killer or killers, as connoted by the smear of blood on the drapes. Further investigation outside would reveal drops of blood on the concrete patio.

Sometime later, Ridenour and Grogan met in the garage. It wasn't an arranged meeting, but they both felt compelled to talk, crime scene manager to lead detective.

"I don't envy you this one, Bill," Ridenour said, his voice hushed by the violence inside the house.

"What do you think?"

Ridenour had seen a level of bad news that didn't often make it to the agricultural mecca of Modesto. Back in the seventies, and barely out of his first year in homicide, Dick Ridenour had worked a double homicide that ended up taking him all the way to Las Vegas. A contract killer by the name of Elbert Easley had been hired by a California businessman to get rid of his partner. Easley had taken out the partner and his wife, Reiner and Sigrid Junghans, by binding them hands-to-feet with wire, stuffing rubber balls into their mouths, and stabbing them over one hundred times with an ice pick. Modesto's famous "ice pick murders" were perhaps the most brutal homicides to occur in Modesto since the pioneer days. Shortly after his conviction for those murders, Easley signed a confession stating that he and two accomplices had burned down a Nye County, Nevada, brothel called the Chicken

Ranch. According to Easley's confession, printed in the Las Vegas *Sun* on July 30, 1979, the hit had been planned by the owner of another local whorehouse. Fourteen prostitutes nearly lost their lives in the fire.

That had been Ridenour's welcome to the homicide unit. Since that time, he'd drawn some of the worst homicides, and he'd handled them well. He didn't brag about it, but it was something his coworkers knew at all times, and they respected him for it.

Ridenour stood in the Whitlocks' pristine garage, struggling for the right words. "This guy. The guy who killed Debi Whitlock. He was trying to tell us something."

Grogan nodded. "The knife."

"The knife," Ridenour agreed. "The knife is interesting, propped up against her inner thigh. And there's the way he took his time positioning her."

"Some of the guys think maybe he dropped the knife. Came out of his rage. Maybe something else interrupted him."

Ridenour was shaking his head. "No. I don't think so. You don't prop up a knife when you're in a hurry. I think there was something going on. Something more. In his head. It was like he killed her, and he killed her, and he killed her again. Then he dragged her into the hall, stripped her, probably defiled her—we'll know soon enough. And then left the knife there. Right there. Who is he posing her for? Himself? Us? He obviously hated her. He wanted everyone to know."

Grogan was quiet for a moment. Unlike Ridenour, who thought aloud, Grogan was probably the quietest person on the team. "Unfaithful husband?"

"I gotta admit, it seems likely. Nothing's missing but the woman's purse. The guy didn't even take her ring. The daughter is untouched. Nothing is disturbed, overturned. The husband himself said the doors were always locked, so I'm guessing she let this person in or he had his own key, then he left through the back alley. But we can't be sure yet. We've got to keep our minds open until we get the print and blood match."

Grogan nodded. "I agree. But the guy keeps giving different alibis. And supposedly he's acting weird about the truck."

They turned toward the blue Ford. It had a beat-up white cover over the bed. Cursory glances showed no evidence pertaining to the crime, and a more thorough investigation of the truck's interior would have to wait until some of the officers were finished inside.

"We'll check it out," said Ridenour. "But if it's not the husband, this could take a while."

Grogan smiled—or close to it. "Maybe."

Ridenour rolled his eyes. "Oh, right. I forgot who I was talking to." Grogan had a reputation for catching lucky breaks and for being in the right spot at the right time. It's not that he wasn't a competent investigator. He was. But he was also one of those people who win raffles and radio contests without effort. Add the probability of Harold Whitlock's guilt to Bill Grogan's endless string of luck, and this case could be wrapped within a day.

FOUR

The First Week

Bad news travels fast. Across the Central Valley, radio stations were disrupting their sleepy Saturday morning programming with the horrifying announcement. Unsolved murders were practically unheard of in this agricultural area. At the time, Modesto averaged fewer than ten homicides per year, most of them easily traced to enemies or murderous lovers or spouses.

Modesto was still relatively unknown to people outside of the Central Valley. Residents had to supply references: "You know, Modesto? We're ninety miles southeast of San Francisco, about an hour from Yosemite. Have you ever heard of Diamond brand nuts? Gallo Winery?" With the high-profile murder of Deborah Anne Whitlock, Modesto began to develop a new reputation in the mind of the nation. This redefinition would continue through burgeoning gang violence and the infamous murders of Chandra Levi and Laci Petersen. In fifteen years' time, residents would no longer have to reference the larger agricultural industries of their booming city. But they would remember that time wistfully.

It was no accident that Debi and her sister Karen lived so near each other, or that their children were so close in age. The sisters had always been exceptionally close and almost laughably different. Debi, the older of the two, grew up fearless, determined, and full of mischief. Because she had the same diminutive build as her mother, Debi was often considered "fun" and "cute," a reputation bolstered by her infectious laugh. People were often surprised by the steely determination underneath.

Karen was the more domestic of the two. Debi's life was so busy as she pursued her career that Karen took it upon herself to do the Christmas baking for both families. There was always a "Debi" section in Karen's summer vegetable garden, full of the tomatoes and zucchini that Debi loved but didn't have the time or green thumb to grow.

Inseparable as children, the sisters hoped to see the same sisterly bond grow between their daughters. They went through their pregnancies together, big round bellies protruding as they stood side by side. Every six months they photographed their little girls in matching outfits. Together, the sisters planned a life where their girls would be constant playmates. But those plans never materialized.

On the morning of March 25, Karen hadn't watched the morning news shows, hadn't listened to the radio on her way into work at the Merced County Sheriff's Department. She had too much on her mind: she had secured part of the afternoon off so that she and Debi could take their daughters to have their semiannual portrait taken at the Sears store where Debi worked. Then they would all go out for ice cream.

Karen was ticking through her plans for the day as she pulled her car into the parking lot. The morning was chill, and she buttoned her sweater as she stepped from the car. She checked on the two pink dresses draped across the backseat, smoothing them so they wouldn't wrinkle.

Once inside the building, Karen made her way back to her office. People exchanged good mornings with her; none of her coworkers had connected her to the homicide they'd heard about all morning. Karen worked in her office for a while, then walked the long corridor to the common area of the sheriff's department. As she drew closer, she heard her own name whispered in hushed urgency.

"—so depending on what Karen and Cliff will need, I can help take care of their daughter."

"Well, we don't know for certain yet. Hopefully Cliff is finding out."

Karen rounded the corner into the break room. "Finding out what?"

Within minutes Karen was walking, dreamlike, toward the dispatch office. She banged on the locked door, heard the lock disengage, and pushed it open. Her husband sat by the telephone. He was silent, his expression troubled.

"Mary said Debi has been injured. What's going on? Where's my sister?"

Cliff looked up, pale in his deputy's uniform. "I don't know yet. I'm waiting for a call back from Modesto PD."

"But someone was murdered in Modesto? It can't be Debi. She's working in Merced today."

The phone rang. Given the circumstances, the ring should have been ominous. But it wasn't. In real life, it never is.

Cliff listened silently for what seemed like a long time. Fighting a pervading sense of doom, Karen walked back into the hall and closed the dispatch door. She kept walking, her feet carrying her back and forth across the worn linoleum of the hallway. Down to her office. Back to dispatch. Then down the corridor again. She was some ways away when she finally heard Cliff's voice talking to her supervisor, explaining that there had been a family tragedy, and that he and Karen would be out of the office for a few days. Then suddenly Cliff was in the hallway, pulling up short because his wife was there, panic and pleading in her eyes.

"Is it really Debi?" Karen asked.

Cliff couldn't say the words. Not to her.

It couldn't be true. Why would somebody kill Debi? Confusion gave way to rage. Karen hadn't realized her purse was in her hand until she flung it against the opposite wall, shouting, "No!" Just as suddenly, the anger was gone, replaced with a hollow grief that robbed her of her strength even to stand. She sank to the floor.

On a coworker's desk, the radio droned on, "—identified as Deborah Anne Whitlock, who, police say, was stabbed to death in her Modesto home. Again, we'll have more on this story as it comes in. Now, back to the music."

At the Sears store in Merced, manager Steven Bloomberg had unlocked the exterior doors to the store at precisely 9 a.m. His assistant manager, Debi Whitlock, was uncharacteristically late, and he asked another employee to unlock the door connecting the store to the Merced Mall.

Making his usual walk-through, greeting employees and making certain the floors and racks were tidy, Steve heard a faint click over the intercom and realized that his secretary had forgotten to turn on the prerecorded music. Now, instead of hearing a mix of light rock and easy listening, he heard her voice paging him to the office.

"Regional's on the phone," she said as he came into the administrative offices.

"Thanks, Janice." He walked toward his office. "And can you get some music playing out there?" He pushed the door partially closed behind him and reached for the phone.

"Good morning. This is Steven Bloomberg."

"Steve?" It was Jack, his regional manager.

"Hi, Jack. What can I do for you?"

During the next thirty seconds, the wrecking ball of reality laid ruin to his future plans. He put the phone down and stared at it.

"Janice! Get security in here. Now!" With shaking fingers, Bloomberg rifled through the Modesto phone book to locate the number of the police department. He fumbled the phone, depressed the receiver, and dialed again.

"Yes, can you tell me if it's true that Deborah Whitlock was murdered last night? Has her husband been arrested?" He licked his dry lips as he listened, closing his eyes as the woman on the phone said there had been no arrest. Bloomberg heard Janice in the other room, paging security. He walked around the desk, the phone cord stretching behind him, and shoved the door closed with his foot. "Listen," he said to the police operator, "I have information about the murder. I know who did it. Who do I talk to?"

Most of the homicide team was still at the Whitlock house. Bloomberg's call was patched through to an officer who said he'd take the information.

Bloomberg bit his lip, thinking hard. How much should he say? "Listen, I'm a friend of Debi Whitlock's, and you guys need to arrest her husband. I know he killed her."

"I see," said the officer, "and who exactly are you?"

"My name is Steven Bloomberg, and I'm the manager of the

Sears store in Merced. I am—I was Debi's boss. And she told me her husband was going to kill her."

"OK, Mr. Bloomberg. I'm not at liberty to talk about the case, but I'll forward your information along to the officers in charge."

They were giving him the brush. "Wait! Is Harold Whitlock in custody?"

"I really don't know, sir."

"I have to know!" Bloomberg practically yelled. "I have reason to believe he's coming after me next."

Finally, the officer sounded genuinely interested. "And why is that, sir?"

Damn. They'd know soon enough anyway. Bloomberg took a breath. "Because Debi Whitlock and I were seeing each other. Romantically. And he knows it."

"You're saying you were having an affair with the victim?"

"Yes. And her husband knows it!"

"And can I ask, sir, where you were last night?"

"What?"

"I said, where were you last night? Can someone verify your whereabouts?"

Bloomberg opened his mouth, closing it again when he could think of nothing to say. *Oh my God. A murderous madman is coming after me, and now the police are going to arrest me for Debi's murder.* "Listen," Bloomberg said, fighting panic. "I was alone last night. I don't have an alibi. But I'm telling you, Harold Whitlock murdered his wife, and I can guarantee you I'm next."

The officer on the phone retained a tone of skepticism as he took down Bloomberg's contact information. They had just hung up when security arrived at Bloomberg's door. He wasted no time filling them in.

"We've got a situation, and I need your help. Debi Whitlock has been murdered. Probably by her husband. And he very well may show up here. I'm going to have to call a management meeting, but I need you guys watching every entrance to this store. Call in backup if you have to. Just watch for him. His picture's on Debi's desk."

As security left, Janice came to his office door. Her eyes were wide and tearful. "Is it true? Debi Whitlock's dead?"

Bloomberg nodded. He recognized in her a grief he could not yet feel but he knew would come. Right now, terror had center stage. "It's true, Janice. Please keep that to yourself for right now though, OK? And page the managers to come to my office—no, the break room. I should be the one to tell them, unless some of them already know."

The meeting in the break room was short and sorrowful. Some of Debi's close friends were completely overcome with grief, and Steve gave them the rest of the day off.

Having dismissed his department managers back to their positions, and the sad task of telling the other employees the news, Steve turned to the one employee left in the room. Paula Thompson sat in the chair she had collapsed into upon hearing Steve's announcement. She was a close friend to both Debi and Steve, and in her eyes were all the things he was feeling: loss, shock, anger, and fear. She angrily dabbed at her face with a tissue from her purse.

"Well, that bastard actually did it. He actually killed her."

Bloomberg sat down in a chair opposite her. "I know."

"Have they arrested him yet?"

"I don't think so."

"Well why the hell not?" Paula slammed her fist down on the table and stood up, dislodging her lipstick from her forgotten handbag. "Why isn't he in custody? He said he was going to kill her, and he did. What's the problem?"

"I don't know." Bloomberg watched the tube of lipstick roll halfway across the table and come to a stop. Debi didn't wear lipstick. Debi didn't wear makeup at all, except maybe a little bit of that stuff women put on their eyelashes to make them darker. But Debi didn't use anything else. She didn't need to. She had flawless skin, bright eyes, and an openhearted smile with perfect, white teeth. She was always beautiful, and Steve had told her so many times.

"My God, Steve, you've got to get out of here."

Paula's voice brought him out of his musings. He looked at her wearily. "I'm probably safer here than anywhere else. I've already told security to watch out for him."

"Did you call the police? Did you tell them her husband has already hit her before?"

"I tried. But, you know, I'm not totally in the clear, either. I mean, to them."

Paula stopped pacing. "You mean they think you could have done this?"

Steve wanted out of this conversation. He wanted out of this reality. "Listen, I was at home alone last night. They've already asked me. I was the 'other man.' Hell, she even left him for awhile and then moved back into that damn house. And not long ago. So what are they supposed to think?"

Paula sat down heavily and began crying again. "Why did she go back? She had already left. She knew he was violent; he was threatening her. Why didn't she listen to us?"

"Because of her daughter."

Steve and Debi had spoken just two days ago about their relationship. In Steve's car on their way back from a conference, Steve told Debi he was impatient for her to divorce Harold and move in with him, this time for good. But Debi had told him to be patient.

Steve argued that she was in danger, but Debi insisted she wasn't afraid of Harold. He was angry, yes. And yes, he did say he would kill her if she tried to get custody of Jessica. But Debi maintained that was just his anger talking; he wouldn't do anything to hurt her. Besides, after Debi had told him about Steve, Harold had started sleeping with one of his coworkers. "I think she's been calling the house, too, and hanging up," Debi said. "Maybe she thinks we're fighting over Harold. I gave up that fight a long time ago."

Even though Debi reassured Steve that she loved him, she insisted it wasn't the right time to move out of her home. She and Harold needed to sell their house. And Debi was determined to come to an amicable agreement with her husband about what was best for Jessica. Harold loved their little daughter, and Jessica loved her daddy. Debi didn't want to take that away from him.

"I hear what you're saying, but I still worry about you," Steve had said, holding her hand as he drove. "And I hate to think of you in that house with him."

Debi smiled and patted his hand. "We hardly speak to each other. If I'm home, he usually spends the night out. Even when I'm not there, he sleeps on the couch. There's nothing for you to worry about. He's my past, and you're my future."

He grunted in a somewhat mollified manner.

"Besides," Debi said, smiling at having broken through his sullenness, "my mom says you sound like a pretty nice man. And she's a tough sell when it comes to me."

He smiled and squeezed her knee. "It's my Missouri charm. Women can't help themselves."

"Oh, puh-leez." Debi laughed, as he knew she would. He loved that sound.

Why hadn't they recognized their compatibility the first time they met in 1982? They had both attended a regional meeting, but they were in other relationships. The next year, Debi married Harold Whitlock.

Two years later, Steve had been assigned to the Merced store as its manager. His twenty years with the corporation had landed him exactly where he wanted to be. He enjoyed Merced. It was a small town with a comfortable atmosphere, and it was growing. He quickly became involved in local politics and city planning. When Debi Whitlock transferred to the regional office in Hayward, they began a close friendship. Her marriage was falling apart, he was alone, and the two recognized in each other a pairing of experience and aspirations. They brought out the best in each other. And they fell in love.

Debi finally decided to tell her husband their marriage was over. That had been two months ago. Steve believed the conversation became very confrontational, and while Debi didn't talk much about it, she had moved out of the house for a couple of weeks right after that. Then just as suddenly, she went back. She said she needed to stay at the house, at least several nights each week, because of her daughter. Steve had the feeling that Debi wasn't telling him everything, but he trusted her intentions. Harold Whitlock was the last roadblock to their future together. Steve tried to be patient.

Since that time, Steve knew Debi had struggled in her dealings with her husband. They had supposedly agreed to be civil while they sold the house and came to a rudimentary custody agreement. But Harold had again become uncooperative and surly. Other times he begged her not to leave, to give their marriage another try. When she refused, he called her horrible names and threatened to kill her. Steve believed Harold had even hit Debi, perhaps more than once. He was obviously out of control, and now he had made good on his threat to kill her.

And if he had killed Debi, why not kill her lover?

Steve was terrified.

While Steve Bloomberg looked over his shoulder and jumped at the smallest sound, Harold Whitlock sat in the downtown police station.

He had gone willingly with the two officers, riding in their unmarked car without restraint of any kind. They first took him to Doctors Medical Center, where they vacuumed his clothing with a special attachment that fed into a sanitized bag catching any debris. They watched as he was stripped and inspected for any scratches or cut marks that might lead to his arrest for murder. An ID technician drew blood from his arm and combed carefully through his hair.

"You said you didn't touch the body?"

"I touched her arm, I think."

"But there was no blood?"

"No. Not there."

The ID tech carefully clipped some of Harold's hair and put it in a small plastic bag. Then she held it in front of him. "Do you see that?" she asked, as he looked at the small tangle of hair. "It's blood."

Harold Whitlock said nothing.

A police officer was examining Harold's watch and rings on a silver tray nearby. "That's interesting," he said, "because I've got blood over here, too."

"Where?" asked Harold.

The officer held the ring gingerly between gloved fingers. Because the black stone in the ring's center was raised, there was a hollow space between the underside of the stone and the wearer's finger. It was into this hollow that the officer directed Harold's attention. "Does that look like blood to you? Because it does to me."

"I don't know," Harold said. "I don't think I touched any blood. And I know I didn't kill her."

The officer carefully dropped the ring into another plastic bag. "Then maybe you can tell us why there's all this blood on you, Mr. Whitlock. You obviously just showered, but somehow there's still some blood here. You want to tell us why?"

"I told you, I don't know." Harold crossed his arms, making the paper hospital gown crinkle. He shivered. "Can I get dressed yet?"

The police department was located in Modesto's historic district, although the phrase was decidedly more charming than the fact. The police car made its way down Tully Road and past the campus of Modesto Junior College, where Harold had taken classes years ago but dropped out after a few semesters. Gradually, fast-food restaurants and apartment complexes gave way to the sort of tired, utilitarian structures that make up a downtown in which the members of the Historical Society have yet to fully mobilize.

Tully Road fed into Ninth Street near the old Southern Pacific Railroad tracks. Modesto had been founded in 1870 as a stop for the line, its streets laid in a predetermined grid running A to O to the north and First to Nineteenth to the east. At the time, many of the forty-niners who had come searching for gold had found it in the form of wheat, and California's Central Valley profited from the steady export of grains to the East, where fertile valleys had become scarred battlefields.

At upper Ninth Street, the tracks for the Union Pacific split off to the north. A few blocks east lay the tracks for the Atchison, Topeka & Santa Fe line. In 1988, those abandoned tracks and the McHenry Mansion to the east were two of the few remaining memorials to Modesto's past. Time, fire, and wrecking balls had steadily destroyed the old hotels, the opium-filled Chinatown district, the saloons with their boardwalks jutting out over dusty roads that turned to muck in the rainy season. On the other hand, the vigilantes of Modesto's past were also gone, replaced by a police department headquartered on Tenth Street. Had those gunslingers still ruled the town, Harold Whitlock may not have lived out the night.

Harold sat alone in an interview room within the Modesto Police Department. Detectives had listened to variations on the same theme for hours: "*There's no way I could have killed my wife because at the time I was sleeping with my girlfriend.*" Some of the partygoers as well as the girlfriend, Heather Barnett, had been contacted and had verified the story, although there was almost an hour of Harold Whitlock's time unaccounted for between the two locations. Heather would come in later to give a blood sample and fingerprints. And Whitlock had directed detectives to someone he claimed was his wife's lover, a manager at the Sears store in Merced. He was at the top of the interview list.

Harold had continued to espouse his innocence. What about the fact that he had tried to arrive—OK, sneak—home before Debi woke up that morning? Surely he wouldn't have done that if he had known she was already dead. Or what about his wife's missing purse and car keys? Obviously the killer had taken those, which was proof of a robbery.

"But they didn't take her ring, Mr. Whitlock. What kind of burglar would kill a woman and then not take her diamond ring?"

"I don't know," Harold wailed, burying his face in his hands again. "Look, I know what you think, and you're wrong. You're wasting your time with me. Her boyfriend killed her. Steve somebody."

"Mr. Whitlock, our detectives are in the process of contacting him now. But what makes you so positive he killed Debi?"

"I know this sounds preposterous, but . . . but we had just decided to give our marriage another try."

The detective raised his eyebrow skeptically.

Harold continued. "Yes, OK, I screwed up last night. But I swear, Debi had just broken up with this guy. She moved back into our house just a couple of weeks ago. Maybe a month. And there have been these phone calls. The guy calls and then hangs up. At all hours."

"He identified himself on the phone?"

Harold shook his head in exasperation. "No, but of course it was him! He wanted her back, and she had told him we were going to work it out. Who else would call and not say anything? I bet he was watching the house. And last night, when I was gone, he came in, right? You guys keep saying she knew the guy. Well, of course she did! And he probably begged her to come back to him, and she must have said no, and he killed her out of jealousy."

The detective was jotting down information, then looked up and studied Harold Whitlock. He let the silence build.

Harold threw his hands up into the air. "Yes, OK, I went to my girlfriend's house last night, and I shouldn't have. I made a bad decision. Debi and I were supposed to be giving it another try, and I didn't follow through. But I didn't kill her! I loved her, whether you believe it or not. I wouldn't kill her."

The detective continued to stare silently. Suddenly a knowing smile came over Whitlock's face. He stopped shaking, and instead spoke in a very even tone. "You're not going to catch me at anything, because I didn't do anything. I've answered your questions as honestly as I can. And now I am finished. I'm not under arrest, right? So I'm leaving." And he stood up.

The detective jumped to his feet. What had just happened? How could this man change gears so suddenly? "Um, OK, I'll just have to check with my supervisor." He fought to regain the upper hand. "I agree that you've been very cooperative. You have to understand, Mr. Whitlock, that this is a very awkward situation. A horrible situation. And we're all doing our best here."

"I understand," said Whitlock in the same dead calm. "You go talk to whomever you need to. But in three minutes, I'm getting up and walking out of here. I'm exhausted, and you're wasting your time and mine."

The interviewer left the room and consulted with the DA's office. Even with all evidence pointing toward the widower, the case was not yet solid enough to arrest Harold Whitlock. That would have to wait until the blood and print matches came back later in the day or tomorrow at the latest. For the time being, Harold Whitlock was indeed free to go.

It was afternoon by the time Harold arrived at the Kramers' house. When he walked into the kitchen, Jessica saw him and ran to him calling, "Daddy! Daddy!" Her insecurity had been growing throughout the day, and her questions about her father and mother had been sidestepped. At this point even a three-year-old could detect something was wrong. "Where's Mommy?" she asked. "Why did you go away?"

Harold Whitlock scooped up his daughter and buried his face in her hair. Bob and Doris silently left, closing the door behind them.

I had been hiding out in my aunts' guest room for much of the afternoon, ever since getting off the phone with the detectives. A few people had called me in Savannah, but Mom and her sisters had done a good job of running interference. When Mom came in carrying the phone, I looked up blearily. She put her hand across the mouthpiece of the phone and mouthed the words *Your father*. I nodded. Of course I'd talk to him.

"Well, Rocky, I'm not sure what to say. I didn't mean to get into an argument. I guess you better talk to Angela."

She handed me the phone and whispered, "He hung up on me just a minute ago."

Great. Now they were arguing. "Why?" I whispered back.

"I guess I said the wrong thing." She shrugged. "You know your father. Do you want me to stay?"

"No, I'm OK." She left as I raised the phone to my ear. "Hey, Dad."

"Hi. Rough day, huh?"

"Yeah. You, too?"

He gave a derisive laugh. "Yeah. Me, too. Listen, the detectives told me some things that they claim came from you, and I . . . Well, did Debi tell you I was asleep in the bedroom?"

"Yes. The detectives said it wasn't you."

"It wasn't me."

"Well. That's . . . awkward."

"*Awkward, awkward.*" He was sizing up the sound of it. "A truer word has not been said. Do you mind if I use it?"

"Sure, go ahead." Why did we always fall into patter?

"Honey, the police said you actually heard someone in the back bedroom."

"I did."

"Tell me what happened."

I told him about standing in Jessie's dark room and trying to find her by the sound of her breathing, and how there were two sets of breath.

"Dad, who was it?"

"I wish to hell I knew. Obviously it was someone she didn't want you to know about."

"Her boyfriend? I thought you guys were getting back to-gether."

He sighed. "I thought so, too. We had lunch together Thursday." He paused. "I don't know who it was. The cops are questioning that guy she had been seeing, but they don't think it was him. You haven't thought of anyone who was mad at Debi, have you?"

"No. Not that I know of. Are you sure it wasn't an accident?" God, I wanted it to have been an accident.

"Not a chance."

I balanced his reticence to talk against all of the questions going through my head. "Can I ask you something?"

"Take a number."

"Where did you find her?"

"In the hallway."

"When you came in from work?"

"Something like that." It was a bizarre way to answer. What did it mean? He must have heard the question in my silence. "I was out at Ortega's, and when I came home, I found her."

During the next two days, my parents discussed the funeral and decided against me attending it. In my shock from Debi's death, it hadn't occurred to me that I might be in any danger. But my father and mother discussed the breather in the bedroom and worried between themselves that he might have seen me or might think I could identify him.

"I know Debi would be pleased that you want to come," Dad said, placating me, "but your mother is worried, and I don't think it's a good idea, either. Things are . . . really not good out here right now."

I had mixed feelings about the funeral. I had never found emotional solace at these events. On the other hand, missing Debi's funeral meant her sudden and inexplicable loss would remain almost unreal. Without the opportunity to put my hand on the cold, smooth lid of her closed coffin, it would take years for me to fully accept the reality of her death.

How could she be gone? After all, I still had her suitcase.

The Modesto Police Department did not arrest Harold Whitlock the next day. Or the day after that. Whitlock's prints were not on the murder weapon, and they were not a match to those on the wall, or Debi's heel, or pressed into Debi's blood on her nightstand. They did not belong to Whitlock's lover, Heather Barnett. Nor did they match those of Debi's self-confessed lover, Steve Bloomberg. Although he had no verifiable alibi, Bloomberg had given a very convincing interview, and his genuine terror of Harold Whitlock further convinced investigators that he had no involvement in Debi's murder.

Police continued to look for a match to the prints at the scene. The lead theory now was that Whitlock had hired the perpetrator. How else to explain all the extenuating circumstances, or the survival of Harold's young daughter?

On the night after Debi's murder, Harold Whitlock sat on a beige lawn chair on Bob Kramer's patio. Bob was next to him, barbecuing hot dogs and corn that nobody but Jessie would eat. Jerry Ortega sat on Harold's left.

The three friends had been through a lot together, but nothing like this. Bob and Jerry had tried to give Harold his space. Now, it seemed, he was ready to talk.

"So," he began, staring out at the Kramers' pool, "it should come as a surprise to no one when I say that the police think I did this."

Bob was silent. He had been at the house that morning and seen how everybody watched his friend. Jerry had missed that. "What do you mean?" Jerry asked, baffled. "You can't be serious."

Harold continued to gaze at the pool. "I read a lot, Jerry, and when women are murdered, it's usually the husband or boyfriend. That's just the way it is."

"What about, you know, the other guy?" Nobody wanted to say Bloomberg's name.

"Apparently he checked out. It's not as if the police are taking me into their confidence, but I assume they've cleared him. He hasn't been arrested, has he?"

"That doesn't mean anything," Jerry scoffed.

Harold sighed. "It means they don't have enough evidence to arrest him, just like they don't have enough evidence to arrest me."

"Who are these people who think you did this?" Jerry's eyes narrowed. "Let me talk to them. I'll straighten them out."

Harold cut him off. "They're going to be contacting you soon anyway," he said wearily. "That's what I need to talk to you about."

Bob stopped in the middle of turning foil-wrapped corn. Jerry sat back in his chair.

Harold continued. "The detectives—Fred and Bill, Ollie and Stan, whatever their names are—they're going to be calling to interview you real soon. And I want you both to know that I've been absolutely honest with them. They know about Heather. They know about the separation. So I don't want you guys doing anything . . ."

"Stupid?" Bob ventured.

Harold smiled. "Yeah. Stupid works." Harold looked from one to the other. "I need to ask you something that might be difficult. When they start asking you questions, be absolutely honest. Tell them the truth. Don't worry if it makes me look bad. It couldn't get much worse."

Jerry leaned forward, still struggling. "You cannot be serious, saying they think you did this thing. Anybody who knows you—"

"They don't know me. And even if they did, they might still think I killed her. Something like 98 percent of all murders are traced to the significant other."

Bob dropped his barbecue tongs and swore. "How could I have forgotten about Deputy Dickhead? That evil son of a bitch came back and killed her!"

That was their code name for Debi's first husband, Chuck Peters. A sheriff's deputy in the Bay Area, Peters had turned violent shortly after his marriage to Debi. And when she transferred to the Sears store in the nearby city of Modesto, she found a much-needed protector in a large, teddy bear of a guy named Bob Kramer. Bob took Debi under his wing when he saw her bruised face. His sound advice, and the way he confronted Peters when Debi's husband stormed into the store looking for trouble, had cemented their close friendship. Bob was Debi's big brother, protecting her from the bully; and Debi was Bob's Little Red, who felt blessed and protected by his friendship. With Bob and Doris's support, Debi had divorced Deputy Peters; shortly thereafter, Bob introduced her to his buddy, Howie, who had just divorced his wife. Harold and Debi had married in 1983.

Peters had known Debi's fear of having anyone touch her throat, and he had preyed upon that, throttling her until she almost lost consciousness. He also knew her fear of knives. And now someone who had a grudge against Debi had gained admittance to the Whitlocks' house and slashed Debi's throat with incredible violence.

Harold seemed to consider. He remembered Debi telling him

that Peters had once held her down on a bed for hours, his deputy's pistol cocked to her temple. "You know, someone at the Merced store told me a few months ago that they thought Debi had been talking to Dickhead again. I'd forgotten that until just now."

Bob swore loudly and began expounding on his suspicions about Peters, but Harold put up his hand. "I already told the police about him. They're checking into it."

"Why bother? He killed her!"

There was a knock on the kitchen window overlooking the patio. Bob caught sight of Doris's worried face. She frowned slightly and shook her head a fraction of an inch. Her look said that Jessica had heard her Uncle Bob shouting. Bob composed himself; Jessie was all he had left of Debi, and he would sooner cut off his hand than to cause his little goddaughter any more grief than she was already facing. Sure enough, Jessie came out of the sliding glass door, running to see what was the matter. Bob saw her and took a quick swipe at his tears. "I'm sorry, honey," he said, stooping to retrieve his tongs. "I dropped my hot dog grabbers. Did I scare you?"

Jessie nodded silently and climbed into her father's lap. He wrapped his arm around her. "It's OK, Jess. We're all upset that somebody hurt your mommy, that's all."

"Me, too," said the little girl, leaning into him.

Bob turned away, his shoulders shaking. Jerry patted the big man's back. "Out of the way, gringo. Let the expert show you how to do it." He turned and smiled at Jessica. "You watch this, Jessie. This is gonna be the best darn hot dog you ever had." He flourished the tongs dramatically, and the girl smiled.

While detectives conducted interviews and tried to connect the evidence in Debi's case, Debi's family and friends gathered to mourn her loss. Debi had wanted to be cremated, so after the autopsy Harold had given the directive to the funeral home handling Debi's service. According to several family members, Debi's father, Martin Garrett, had demanded to see Debi's body prior to cremation, but Harold had refused. "Martin, no one should have that image of Debi—of what happened to her. I'm sorry, but the answer is no."

Garrett flew into a rage. Why would Harold deny a father's wish to tell his daughter good-bye—to kiss her one last time? But Harold was unrelenting and later told his friends that the confrontation escalated until Martin finally accused Harold of Debi's murder.

The funeral was packed with Debi's friends and coworkers, with the press staked out a discreet distance away. Afterward, many people adjourned to the home of Raymond Leonard, a long-time friend of the Whitlocks; Ray worked at the Modesto store, but he and Debi were to make final arrangements for his transfer to Merced on the day she was killed. Ray and his wife, Rachel, owned a ranch on the outskirts of Merced, and they welcomed the large crowd into their home to tell stories, share hugs, and reminisce about Debi's life.

Ostensibly, that was the reason for the gathering, but images of this assembly would be played over and over again in the minds of those in attendance. Several detectives were present, both in and out of uniform, knowing that violent killers often take great pleasure in covertly witnessing the funerals of their victims. Their presence reassured some and disquieted others, who were aware that their attendance meant they still had no suspect in custody.

Steve Bloomberg was still jittery. He had spoken to Jacque by phone and felt she wanted him there, that she recognized him as someone who had genuinely loved Debi and shared the family's pain of a thwarted future. A group of Bloomberg's friends stayed close to him, openly glaring at Whitlock lest he suddenly lunge murderously at Debi's lover. For his part, Bloomberg watched the man closely and saw in him no sign of remorse. Frankly, the man looked completely unaffected.

Several of Harold's friends noticed Debi's father glaring continually at Whitlock and mumbling to those around him. Jerry and Bob, flanking their friend like mismatched hired guns, glared back unabashedly.

"That man is loaded, and the safety is off," said Jerry angrily, turning toward Bob and lowering his voice so Howie could not hear. "I see it at the bar all the time—people ready to be stupid and just waiting for the smallest excuse."

Bob nodded. "I keep waiting for him to head this way."

"Good," said Jerry, "because I've had enough of his evil eye. How dare he come in here accusing my friend of this?"

Harold had finished thanking the funeral director and turned to join the conversation. "You've got to remember this man just lost his daughter. He's angry, and he's hurting—"

"Yeah, but so are you," Bob said, his big hand coming to rest on his friend's shoulder.

"And he's being a jackass," Jerry added pointedly.

Harold shook his head. "He just lost his daughter. How would you handle it if one of your boys got killed?"

"I don't know, but not like this. It's just—"

"That's right, you don't know," Harold cut in. "I'm telling you: the man is hurting. Leave him alone. I don't matter to him. Why should I? He just lost his daughter."

Bob put his arm around Howie. "OK. OK."

Jerry glowered. "All right. Only because you asked. You know I'd do anything for you."

Bob tried to smile as he addressed Harold. "Only you don't

have to be so damn nice all the time. It's a little irritating, you know? Me and the Mexican here, we're ready to rumble."

Harold smiled wanly at his friends. Around the room, Harold Whitlock's smile was noted, judged, and recorded for future reference.

Bob sensed it. "Jesus Christ," he swore under his breath. Then he turned away and started to cry.

FIVE

Mother and Daughter

Jacque had waited several days after Debi's murder before flying out to California. The tragedy was still something that had only been reported by phone, but as soon as she arrived in California, Debi's death would become irrevocably real.

"Of course I want to be with Karen and Jessica," Jacque told her husband, speaking of her surviving daughter and Debi's motherless child, "but I don't want to bury my daughter. I can't do this."

But Jacque knew she had to go to the funeral. During the long flight across the country, Jacque was able to keep her fear of flying in check. Her claustrophobia still terrified her, but she thought about Debi. What terror had her child experienced in her last moments of life? Jacque tried to block the question, but it dogged her, nipping at her, tearing at her mind. Jacque knew Debi had died protecting her own daughter: she hadn't cried out because she hadn't wanted to wake her little girl. She hadn't wanted the killer to know Jessie was in the next room. No matter how frightened Debi was in those last moments, Jacque knew she had died a hero. In light of what Debi had suffered, Jacque could damn well make it through this flight.

Karen and her husband Cliff met Jacque and Dennis at the airport, and the women hugged and cried on one another. The no-longer-sister and the no-longer-mother-of-two. They had lost Debi, and now they were separated irrevocably from their former selves. It was like some devastating form of reincarnation.

Karen had made most of the arrangements for the memorial service and those attending were asked to wear blue, Debi's favorite color. Jacque didn't have a blue dress, so she and Karen went shopping the day before the memorial. Alone in the dressing room, Jacque hardly glanced in the mirror. What was the perfect dress to wear when burying your murdered daughter? There was none.

Inside the dressing room, a memory leapt out at Jacque. A couple of years ago she and Debi, both avid bargain hunters, had been shopping the sales rack in an upscale boutique. The shop exuded quiet self-importance. At least it did until Debi suddenly laughed.

It must first be explained that Debi's laughter was comprised of sudden expostulation with subtle nuances of gasping squawk. There in the boutique, Jacque halfheartedly shushed her daughter but smiled in spite of herself. Soon women all over the store were looking in their direction.

"Oh, honestly," Jacque said with exasperation, which only made her daughter laugh harder.

A woman across the room gave Jacque a covert grin, then turned her head to hide her own chuckle. Another shopper saw her and giggled. Soon the room was full of women's laughter. Debi's laugh was so contagious that people couldn't help themselves. Jacque had seen it a hundred times throughout Debi's life, and she smiled fondly at her daughter that day as the shoppers began to talk among themselves, their facade of pretentiousness put aside.

The memory raced away from her, stealing the smile from Jacque's face. She glanced at her reflection in the dressing room mirror. The dress was navy blue and slightly uncomfortable. Good enough. She had to get out of here.

Although Jacque hadn't spoken to him directly, she had heard through Karen that Howie had been questioned for hours by the Modesto police on the morning after the murder. In fact, Jacque had tried to reach him and couldn't. Eventually the police released him, and yet she heard they had questioned him several more times over the next few days. If he was not a suspect, why did they keep talking to him?

Jacque knew about Debi's affair. While Debi never discussed her romantic life with anyone, she and Steve Bloomberg had met Jacque's husband for lunch near the San Francisco airport when Dennis had a long layover. It was obvious that Debi and Steve were romantically involved, but Jacque respected Debi's privacy. When Debi wanted to talk about it, Jacque would listen. She did not know that Debi had asked for a divorce or that Howie had also begun having an affair. She certainly didn't know that Howie had spent the night of Debi's murder with his mistress.

Now Jacque could never ask her older daughter the questions she needed answered: Did Howie know about Debi's affair? And had that revelation incited him to kill Debi?

Jacque's mind was reeling from the double blow of grief and uncertainty when she saw Howie later that night. He had brought Jessie to Karen's house to spend the night with her gran, Aunt Karen, and Cousin Megan. Resilient as all children, Jessica ran inside excitedly as soon as her father parked in the driveway.

Jacque took the opportunity to walk outside where Howie was unloading Jessica's duffel bag from the truck.

"You didn't have to kill her," Jacque said carefully.

The man spun around, and Jacque watched for any reaction. He just looked at her.

"I said, you didn't have to kill her, even if you were having problems. I mean, there is such a thing as divorce."

Howie held Jessie's duffel bag limply at his side. "I didn't kill her, Jacque."

"Some people think you did."

He looked away from her then. What was he thinking?

"Karen said Debi had been thinking a lot about death lately," Jacque continued. "She had just talked to Karen and her father about her will. That was two weeks ago. How did my daughter know she was going to die?"

He looked back at her then, his expression haggard and exhausted. "I did not kill your daughter. I promise you that, Jacque. On my soul. She was Jessie's mother. We had our problems, but I would never do that."

Jacque studied him, then reached a decision. "I believe you," she said, and she meant it. She never questioned him again.

Jacque knew that her ex-husband would probably chide her for being naive. She had heard that Martin fully believed Howie was involved in Debi's death, and once he had decided, there was no changing his mind. He had always been like that: stubborn, opinionated, and fiercely protective of those he loved.

Jacque had been more child than woman when she met Martin Garrett in England in the early 1950s. Jacque's parents, both in the theater, had wanted a more stable career for their daughter.

They encouraged her to lie about her age on her nursing school application in order to be enrolled early. Jacque was accepted as a student nurse at Haymaid's Hospital at Bishop-Stortfort when she was barely in her teens.

Many of her sister nurses were "going steady" with Yanks, and Jacque met enlisted man Martin Garrett through mutual friends. Within five months of meeting him, Jacque accepted Martin's proposal. They married and moved into a small trailer in what Jacque euphemistically called a "little village" but was actually closer to a dumpy trailer park.

Deborah Anne Garrett was born on April 16, 1956, and came into the world squalling. She was a very colicky baby, and Jacque spent hours walking with her, rocking her, and trying to quell her cries. Eventually, Debi outgrew her fussiness. When her personality started to emerge late in her first year, Debi was already exhibiting the determination, stubbornness, and mischief that would mark the rest of her life.

For Debi's first birthday, Jacque baked her daughter a cake fit for a princess: an old-fashioned lady cake with a doll's upper torso sticking out of a cake shaped and decorated as the doll's dress. "Isn't it pretty, angel?" Jacque asked her little daughter. Debi had been toddling over to the table all morning to look at it. "Pretty dolly," Jacque cooed, "just like my pretty Debi."

Jacque strung a few streamers in the kitchen for the small party. When she turned around, Jacque gasped and then laughed. "Well, it *was* a pretty cake." Debi was now covered with icing and clutching the cake-crusted doll.

Jacque became pregnant again while Debi was still a baby. Jacque and Martin explained to their little girl that she was going to be a big sister, and Debi was very excited. As Jacque's pregnancy progressed, Debi would toddle over to her mother, give her growing belly an affectionate pat, and announce, "My baby!"

And when baby Karen arrived on June 20, 1957, Debi was absolutely thrilled.

Only a year later, Martin Garrett announced to his wife that he had been transferred to a naval base in Maine.

"You mean America?" Jacque swallowed hard. She didn't want to leave her home. England was all she'd ever known, and her daughters were too young to move. Marrying an American and raising her girls was all the adventure Jacque wanted at this stage of her life. Besides, she was just now old enough to sit for her nursing license. She had planned to go back to work soon.

On the other hand, America was supposed to be a land of opportunity and luxury, and Jacque was not immune to the opulence portrayed in movies coming out of Hollywood.

In 1959, the Garretts took a miserable transatlantic flight that instilled in Jacque a lifelong fear of flying. Maine was a lush, cold wilderness, and Jacque felt isolated and homesick. She stayed largely to herself, watching her beautiful young daughters play.

Debi and Karen were inseparable as they grew, and people often mistook them for twins. Debi had inherited her mother's small frame, while Karen had the larger build of her father's family. The sisters spent their days in carefree frivolity, playing cowboys and Indians, running through the small house and shrieking with delight. During the beautiful northern summers, Debi and Karen would take their dolls outside and have elaborate tea parties, sometimes playing with the other children on the navy base.

The girls were still in elementary school when Martin received orders to Key West, Florida. Jacque loved the warm salt air, palm trees, and sandy beaches. She sat for her nursing license and soon found a position as a vocational nurse for a kindly orthopedic surgeon. There were many benefits to Jacque's job. She made numerous friends and loved helping patients. The Garretts' finances also improved, and Jacque and Martin surprised their daughters with matching twin beds. Debi and Karen were thrilled with their frilly bedspreads and shams, but when Jacque peeked in on them later that night, she saw both girls snuggled in sleep in the same bed, as they always had been. Standing there in the dark doorway, Jacque smiled. Her girls were two parts of a whole. She had been twice blessed.

In 1965, the family was living in Riverhead on Long Island, when Martin received orders to Vietnam. Debi was nine and Karen seven when their father shipped out. Martin's absence fostered in Jacque the independence she had begun to experience in Florida. She got her driver's license and took over the household finances. Eventually she became comfortable making all the household decisions.

Martin spent two of the next three years in Vietnam. When he returned from his second tour of duty, he asked Jacque, "If you could live anywhere, where would it be?"

Jacque had wanted to return to England for so long that her answer startled her as much as it did her husband. Without hesitation Jacque announced, "California!"

Martin transferred to Merced, California, and the view from the airport surprised Jacque. Where were the beaches? Where were the movie stars? Instead, Merced was a flat, dusty, agricultural town that could have been anywhere. It certainly didn't have the glamour Jacque always associated with the state. But what Jacque discovered was a quiet, neighborly way of life that she quickly came to love.

Debi and Karen were now teenagers and excited to begin high school. They settled easily into the population of Merced High, where Debi's gregarious nature netted her friends immediately. Full of can-do attitude, Debi ran for class president and came only a few votes shy of winning. She also developed a love of woodworking, spending hours in shop class amid the wood chips and sawdust. It amused Jacque that her daughter was the only girl to join the Woodworking Club. Debi was comfortable in any group, and the Garrett home became the official after school hangout for Debi and Karen's eclectic collection of friends. Jacque didn't mind in the least and it gave Martin the chance to tell some of the boys they needed haircuts.

Debi and Karen were also very involved in the youth group at the local Catholic church. One year the girls collected clothing and books from area businesses and civic groups to deliver to a Mexican orphanage. The mission trip nurtured in the sisters a compassion that would always mark their characters.

Merced High had a work-study program, and during her senior year Debi decided to combine that opportunity with her love of fashion. Soon she was working weekends in the clothing department at Merced's Sears store. She earned school credit, made her own spending money, and best yet, discovered a real aptitude for the retail business. By the time she graduated, Debi had decided to work at Sears full time, where she soon became the youngest department manager the store had ever employed.

After graduating in 1973, Debi fell in love with a young law enforcement officer named Chuck Peters. Once known as a bit of a ruffian, Peters seemed to mellow under Debi's calming influence. Jacque watched proudly as her older daughter, already a successful businesswoman, walked down the aisle carrying a bouquet of white flowers wrapped in a blue ribbon. Karen, also in blue, stood beside her big sister.

Near the end of 1977, Jacque received an emotional double punch that left her reeling. First, she learned that her father had passed away in England several weeks before. Her mother had not wanted Jacque to face the expensive and frightful trip to attend her father's funeral. Then, in 1978, Martin asked for a divorce. Jacque was devastated.

Now young adults with husbands and lives of their own, Debi and Karen took turns as caregivers for the woman who had always cared for them. They frequently came by to take her out to lunch. When it seemed their mother might boycott the holidays, Karen and Debi decorated the house and fixed the family meal. When Debi's own marriage ended in divorce in 1981, mother and daughter grew even closer.

There were triumphs during this time as well. Jacque watched proudly as her daughter's career at Sears soared. Debi joined the American Business Women's Association and won Woman of the Year from the local chapter. And she married Howie Whitlock in 1983.

Jacque, too, had remarried, and she and Dennis moved to Mississippi when he received his last transfer before retiring from the Air Force. Still, mother and daughter remained close. Just a few weeks ago, Debi had called to tell her mom that she had been put on track to become the region's first female store manager. "Everything is going your way," Jacque told her daughter over the phone. "I'm just so proud of you, sweetheart."

That was the last conversation Jacque ever had with Debi. And today, Jacque had buried her oldest daughter.

On some level Jacque was aware of the tension at Raymond Leonard's house. She realized that people were covertly, or sometimes openly, studying Howie, but Jacque was too shrouded in her own grief to pay much attention. Surrounded by Debi's friends and family, Jacque caught herself scanning the crowd for Debi. It was unthinkable that her daughter was not here.

Finally Jacque and her husband returned to Karen's house, bringing Jessica with them. The mood was somber, and everyone's eyes were still rimmed with red.

Jacque went immediately to the guest bedroom, where she sat

down on the bed and stared at nothing. A short time later, Karen knocked softly on the door.

"Can I come in, Mom?"

"Of course." Jacque was exhausted.

Karen came in and sat on the bed beside her mother.

"Howie looked devastated at the funeral today. Did you see how everybody was treating him?" Jacque dabbed at her eyes. "I think Jessie is the only thing keeping him going. Debi always said he loved her to bits. I know he'll be a good father to her."

Karen did not reply. She had something else on her mind.

"Mom, I know you love Megan and Jessie."

"Of course I do!" Whenever Jacque saw her granddaughters together, she couldn't help but to see little versions of her own daughters playing hide and seek and having tea parties.

"Well, I want you to know that it's OK if you love Jessica more."

Jacque turned to her daughter. "What?"

"Well, maybe not *love* her more. But I don't want you to feel bad if you feel . . . you know, a stronger bond with Jessie than you do with Megan."

Jacque started to protest, but Karen stopped her. "You've lost Debi. In a way, Jessie is all you have left of her. And I want you to know I understand that."

Jacque wanted to deny it, but she couldn't. It was true. She loved both of these little girls dearly, but Jessica would never be just Jessica anymore. She would also be a version of Debi. Not a substitute, but a living reminder of the daughter that had been stolen from Jacque.

"I feel it, too," Karen said, her eyes welling. "I've not only lost my sister, I've lost my best friend."

At the end of the week, Howie returned for Jessica. He didn't say much to Jacque, just a quiet "Thank you." Jacque knew what he meant. He was grateful that she believed in his innocence. Howie also feared that Debi's family might try to take Jessie away from him, and he credited Jacque that they had not decided to pursue that option.

Jacque hugged her granddaughter for a long time, not sure what to say. She watched her former son-in-law load the girl and her duffel bag in his truck. Then he climbed behind the driver's seat and stared through the windshield at her. Jacque watched him point to himself, then cross his arms in front of his chest, and finally point at Jacque. *I love you.* Jacque smiled sadly and watched him drive away.

The following day, Jacque and Dennis returned to Minnesota. Jacque called the police every day for updates. The Victim/Witness Coordinators in the District Attorney's Office assured her the detectives were doing everything possible. She didn't know what that meant exactly, but she heard the sincerity in their voices, and she did not push them further. It seemed impossible that someone could kill Debi and get away with it. There was a killer out there. Surely the police would discover that person's identity at any moment.

But no word came.

Two weeks after returning to Minnesota, Jacque's hope was draining away. "Why aren't they calling us?" she asked her husband. "How can they not know who killed my daughter?"

Dennis watched helplessly as his wife seemed to fade away before his eyes. "You've got to eat," he pleaded.

Jacque pushed away her untouched dinner plate. "Debi isn't eating."

Dennis was afraid to resume his work schedule, which would leave Jacque alone in the house. He urged her to seek medical treatment, but Jacque knew she didn't need a doctor. She needed to know who killed her daughter, and why. Eventually, Jacque retreated to her room and rarely moved from her bed.

Finally one day Dennis came into their bedroom with a grocery bag. "Guess what I found?" he said with all the enthusiasm he could muster.

Jacque didn't bother to reply. She rarely spoke anymore.

Dennis reached into the bag and pulled out a small container. "It's that yogurt you love. I had a hard time finding it, but at the fourth store, there it was." He set down the spoon on the bedside table and opened the container.

Silent tears trickled down Jacque's cheek. Dennis wiped them away with a tissue. "Come on, sweetheart," he said, and he gently lifted her into a sitting position. Her head swam. "Please just eat a bite of this, OK? Please?"

Hearing his love and fear for her, Jacque forced herself to open her mouth. The yogurt tasted terrible, but she looked at her husband's tentative smile and made herself swallow first one bite, then a second. And suddenly it was the best thing she had ever tasted. Terribly weakened, she allowed Dennis to feed her the entire container. Then he put the empty container away and wrapped her in his arms. She had never felt so loved.

"I think I could eat a bit more," she said softly, and Dennis almost dropped her in his excitement to open another container.

Dennis's devotion had rekindled Jacque's spirit. Thinking clearly for the first time in weeks, Jacque considered her daughter's case. She knew beyond a doubt that whoever had killed Debi had confided his deed to someone. Now Jacque had to find that someone.

What would entice someone to speak? The *Modesto Bee* agreed to offer a one thousand dollar reward for information leading to an arrest. Jacque and Dennis offered another four thousand, and a final thousand came through private donors.

Unsure how to proceed, Jacque channeled her grief and anger

onto paper. She took up her pen and wrote a letter to her daughter's killer. She had to reach him or those who knew his identity. Then she called the *Modesto Bee*.

Nine weeks after Debi Whitlock fought a losing battle against her assailant, Modesto's daily paper featured a front-page article about Jacque. The headline proclaimed, "Mother of Slain Woman Seeks Solace in Letter to Killer." It recounted the facts of the murder, mentioned the $6,000 reward for information leading to conviction of the killer, and also gave the phone number for a tip line at the newspaper. At the bottom of the article, Jacque's letter was printed in eye-catching italics.

> *You. Her Killer. Wherever you are, you not only took my daughter's life, you saddened the lives of all she left behind.*
>
> *Our lives will never be the same. There is a loneliness that time cannot replace. Wherever you are, you'll never know any peace until you either turn yourself in, or someone who knows you has the courage and decency to phone the secret witness hotline and tell them about you. Only then will my nightmare be over and I can lay Debi to rest.*

The article ended by restating the hotline number.

The *Merced Sun-Star* picked up the story as well, and soon people all around the Modesto area were reading Jacque's plea for information. In the middle of her pain, Jacque said a quick prayer of thanks for this one small victory. She had taken the first step. Now that she was in motion, she would not rest until her daughter's killer was behind bars.

SIX

Father and Daughter

A week after Debi's murder, I flew back to California as planned. During my spring break in Savannah, my parents had broached the subject repeatedly, but I remained adamant: Modesto was my home, and I only had ten weeks until graduation. As long as I continued to stay with my maternal grandmother, none of us felt I was in any danger. In the end I was allowed to return.

Debi's death was something I still could not comprehend, but for the first time in months I felt a glimmer of hope about my relationship with my father. I prayed that somehow this tragedy would close the lid on the past and bring us into the kind of close father-daughter relationship I'd always wanted.

Also, there was Jessica to consider. My baby sister had just lost her mother. I couldn't let her lose me, too. Yes, I had moved out of Dad's house a few weeks ago, but now my father and baby sister needed me, and I was on my way to them. I may as well have been wearing a cape and matching tights.

My telephone conversations with my father since Debi's death had reminded me so much of the intense late-night talks we had shared when Debi moved out. She had left me a girlfriend's phone number and said I could reach her there in case of an emergency, but my father was convinced she had moved in with Steve Bloomberg. Dad was hurting and needed someone to talk to, and I could still remember how grateful I felt when he turned to me.

It was late that night, and I'd already brushed Jessie's teeth, changed her into her pj's, and tucked her into bed. My father arrived home shortly thereafter, and I looked up from the kitchen table where I had my precalculus book spread out in front of me.

"Hi," I said. "There's leftover soup in the fridge."

"Thanks," he replied. "I've given up food for the new year."

"Bummer of a resolution."

"It's not so bad. I just pretend to eat a couple of times each day." He mimed taking a bite of something, then smiled appreciatively at the imaginary people around him, saying "Mmmmmmm!" loudly. I laughed and he turned back to me. "I'm looking pretty svelte, don't you think?"

I stopped laughing. Debi had moved out only two days ago, and I didn't think my father had eaten at all during that time. "You didn't have much weight to lose, Dad."

"You know what Fat Charlie the Archangel said when he filed for divorce?" My dad knitted his brows, recollecting the Paul Simon lyrics. "There goes another year of my life. And then there's all that weight to be lost."

"You know what Campbell's says?" I shot back. "Soup is good food."

He smiled appreciatively. "Touché!"

My dad pulled a bottle of Zinfandel out of the refrigerator and poured it into two wineglasses. He walked them over to the table, sat down, and put a glass in front of me. Seeing my startled expression, he explained, "It's Zinfandel. It's the baby food of wines."

I didn't answer him. I hadn't been as shocked about the wine as I was the overture to an actual conversation. Usually when my father and I talked, it was the equivalent of fencing with Nerf foam swords. Now he was seated across from me, clearing his throat for what appeared to be an actual, frank conversation. I could count on one hand the number of times this had happened during my seventeen years.

"So, I have a question for you, because I'm really trying to wrap my head around this whole thing."

I understood "this whole thing" to mean his faltering marriage.

"What I don't understand, among many things," he continued in an earnest, self-deprecating manner, "is this idea of me not giving her what she wants."

I felt something was required of me. "OK."

"So what is it, exactly, that she wants?" He looked at me with frank interest, as if the fact that Debi and I both had ovaries somehow gave me insight into her needs. I took a sip of wine to stall for time. It was cold and sweet and tasted like it should come in a small waxed cardboard box with a short straw shrink-wrapped to the side.

"I don't know, Dad," I said carefully. "Has she, um, told you anything specific that she needs? I mean, that you're not giving her?"

"Not in so many words."

"But you have some idea?" I was afraid our new friendship would crumble if he felt like I was prying. "You don't have to tell me, but have you actually asked her, 'What is it that you need that I'm not giving you?'"

"She said she didn't know."

"OK. Did you ask her to think about it and get back to you?"

He looked at me incredulously. "What? You think she really doesn't know?"

"It is possible," I conceded.

"I thought she was just trying to back out."

"Well, speaking personally, I might have assumptions about what I really want, but then when somebody volunteers to actually try to give me whatever I choose . . ." I shrugged. "I might reevaluate, you know, if I think I actually have a shot at getting whatever it is."

He thought that over for a minute. "Give me an example."

I had the feeling I should have spent the last hour prepping for this conversation. "OK. Jessie wants a pony, right?"

"Right."

"Does she really want a pony?"

"Yes. I believe her exact words are, 'I want a pony.'"

"No. She only thinks she wants a pony. But if she were a little bit older, and you said, 'I'm going to give you what you really want,' then she might start thinking of the reality of a pony. She might start thinking of the responsibility it entails. Or she might say to herself, 'I'd rather have something else, like a—'"

"Wait, wait." Dad held up a hand. "Am I the pony? Because lately I've gotten the impression that I'm the manure."

"What I'm saying," I said, struggling to maintain my line of thought, "is that Debi might need some time, now that she knows you're willing to work with her, to figure out what she wants you both to work on."

"If anything," he added.

"If anything."

He drummed his fingers on my forgotten homework. "You know, that makes a lot of sense."

"Well, that's just a guess, Dad. I don't really know—"

"No, no. I'm replaying our conversation, and I think that's exactly what Debi was trying to say." He scrutinized me. "Have you talked to Debi about any of this?"

"No."

"Well, maybe you should." He sipped his wine. "So what about you?"

I raised an eyebrow. "What about me?"

"You. Romance. You got it all figured out?"

I laughed. "Hardly. I'm seventeen. I only know how to fake wisdom."

He grinned and shook his head. "Now you're avoiding the question."

"OK, fine. What do you want to know?"

"Well, do you think you're in love?"

I thought about my boyfriend, a sweet, goofy honor roll student with a growing penchant for playing his guitar on San Francisco street corners. "You know, I'm in first love. That's different, isn't it?"

"Don't ask me. I don't do so well with any of it, in case you hadn't noticed."

"OK. Well, let me put it this way. Sometimes I think I want a pony. And then I realize that I have absolutely no idea how to care for a pony. And it's too much responsibility. And I have nowhere to keep it . . ." I smiled at him. "You can interrupt this analogy whenever you want."

"I sort of wanted to see how far you'd take it."

"I think I'm done now."

My father rose from the table and took our wineglasses to the sink. "You know, your mom did a very good job raising you. You're levelheaded. You make good decisions. I credit your mother with that."

"She's a great mom." What else could I say? After my father had left, my mother raised me, solely supported me, put herself through school, and earned her CPA license. She had indeed done a very good job.

Over the course of the next two weeks, my father would come in from work or Ortega's late and pour two glasses of wine. We discussed pop culture, Reaganomics, and literature. Mostly, though, we discussed Dad and Debi's marriage. Debi hadn't yet made up her mind, and my father was growing weary of waiting to see if she saw something of value in him.

The first few days Debi was gone were, oddly enough, the best I had ever experienced with my father. I regretted his troubles, but I was grateful that he was turning to me when he needed a friend. Soon, however, my father's arrival home grew later and our talks less frequent. I stopped waiting up for him, although I would sometimes hear him arrive in the dark hours before dawn.

One morning I woke up to find my father's bedroom door closed and a woman's purse on top of the microwave oven. It was glossy black vinyl, and a set of keys with a glittery red heart fob sat beside it. The pair became a regular sight in the mornings; however, I felt that I was not allowed to ask about them. Instead, I would dress myself and Jessie and leave the house as quickly as possible, feeling like an intruder in my father's home.

Finally, one Saturday morning before I could effect a quick exit, Heather Barnett walked out of the bedroom. The first thing I noticed was that she was young. Eighteen? Nineteen? I could have passed her in the hallway at high school and never looked twice. She had on a bright red sweater and black jeans. Sparkling red earrings peeked out of her unruly short black hair. She approached me shyly.

"Um, I'm Heather?" she said, as if uncertain. "I work with your father?"

I decided not to point out that she obviously did more than that with my father. Instead, I gestured toward the microwave. "So you go with the purse?"

"What?" She looked genuinely puzzled.

"Nothing. I'm Angela." I extended my hand. What else could I do?

My hand coming toward her made her start with surprise. "Jeepers!"

Now it was my turn to start; I'd never before met anyone who used the word *jeepers*.

Suddenly my father was behind me, chuckling. "We stand on formality in this house." He smiled laconically and gestured toward my still-outstretched hand. "Later we'll be quizzing you on dessert spoon etiquette."

"What?" Heather asked him. Then she smiled at her tall, graying lover with his too-bushy mustache and matching eyebrows in a way that said, *I'm so incredibly lucky.*

I dropped my untouched hand and settled for, "It's nice to meet you."

"Same here," she said with genuine warmth. Maybe she was in her early twenties. She was still facing my father. "See you later?" she said, her voice full of meaning. I cringed. Then she picked up her purse and headed out the door.

My father cleared his throat uncomfortably.

"The owner of the purse presents herself at last," I said.

He had a goofy, aww-shucks expression and glanced downward toward his feet. "She's just . . . She . . ."

"Listen, I'm not going to tell you anything. You know the spiel. You can look it up yourself. It's under *R* for *rebound*."

My father laughed in spite of himself. "Under *R* for *rebound*? Where do you get this stuff?"

"Mom says it's genetic. And she's not happy when she says it, either."

He shook his head at the injustice of it all and began making himself a Bloody Mary. "Why do I always get in trouble?"

I forced a smile, but my mind was struggling to fit Heather

into the ever-changing dynamics of this family. My father sensed my discomfort.

"Listen, I'm not saying I want a divorce. Heather has just been a good friend at work during all of this, and now . . . Well, I won't pretend I know what I'm doing." He put the tomato juice and Tabasco sauce back in the refrigerator and pulled out a stalk of celery. "You pay your coin and get on the ride, and who knows what happens from there?" He washed the celery in the sink, then stirred his drink with it.

It sounded like a pretty irresponsible philosophy to me. "I just think that if the name of the ride is posted in big letters, and it's called something like the Huge Mistake, then maybe you should hold onto your token and look for another ride."

He furrowed his brows and nodded seriously. "I hear what you're saying." He took a sip of his drink and smacked his lips. "But I've got to do what I've got to do."

"Yes, you do," I replied carefully.

"And I have to live with the consequences."

I stopped myself from saying that his consequences affected all of us. Instead, there was an uncomfortable silence. I watched him return the vodka bottle.

"Hey, it's the breakfast of champions," he replied, catching my expression. "You're the one always saying I should eat more." He gave me a mischievous smile and took a big bite of celery.

"Sort of a breakfast salad in a glass?"

"Smirnoff's Zingy Breakfast Shake, now available at these fine retailers!" He drained the glass and rinsed it in the sink, munching on the celery. I got out the Raisin Bran and poured it into two bowls, one for me and one for Jessie. She'd be up any minute.

"Well, I gotta take the car in to the shop." Dad grabbed his keys from the hook beside the kitchen door. "I'll see you later."

"Will you be home for lunch?"

"No. Debi's coming to spend the day with Jessie. I'll probably eat at Ortega's. Come by if you want."

"OK," I said, knowing I wouldn't. If I wasn't taking care of Jessie today, I'd probably get together with some friends.

That was the last serious conversation we had about his life or his decisions until after Debi's death. Within two weeks my relationship with my father would utterly collapse, and I would move out of his house.

My exit left Dad in a bind regarding Jessie. I had been her primary caretaker since Debi moved out, particularly since he took up with Heather. Within two days of my leaving, Debi moved back in. She called me at my grandmother's house several times to alternately urge and cajole me into patching things up with my father, but I knew she didn't understand the extent of the damage done to our relationship, and I didn't bother to explain it.

I had no idea what was happening with my father's relationships, but a month later, Debi asked me to babysit. "Your father and I are trying to work things out, and it would help if we could go out to a nice dinner and discuss some things." I missed Jessie terribly and gladly agreed.

That night, after putting my sister to bed, there was a knock at the door. I opened it to see Heather's smiling face.

"Hi!" she chirped. "Is your dad here?"

"No," I said in confusion. "He's out with Debi." I regretted it as soon as I'd said it.

Heather's expression crumpled. "With Debi? Why? I thought that was over."

I wished I hadn't answered the door. Now I felt obligated to be truthful. "Well, Debi told me that they were having a 'date night.'"

"Is she back?" Heather asked, clearly fearing the answer.

"She moved back in a few weeks ago. I figured you would know that."

Heather started crying then. Real sobs. "No. No, I didn't—" Her breath was coming in gasps. "He didn't—didn't tell—"

"Do you want to come in?"

"Please." She walked into the house and sat down on a step leading down into the sunken den. She started pawing through her purse for a tissue. Her efforts dislodged an opened package of red licorice and several braided ropes landed on the brick steps. I got a tissue from a box in the living room, thought better of it, and picked up the entire box. I placed it within her reach on the stairs and sat down on the couch opposite her. She was still crying, angrily picking up licorice and cramming it back inside her black bag.

"Do you think it's true?" She looked up at me through wide watery eyes. "Do you think they're really trying to make it work?"

"I don't know."

Heather's sobs had ceased, and she looked around her like a lost child. "I love Harold, you know? I really do." I could tell by the misery in her voice that she was telling the truth. "She had her chance, and she gave him up. It's not fair." Her lip started to tremble again. "I can't believe he'd go back to her! She really hurt him!"

"I'm sorry," I said, not knowing what else to say.

"Don't tell him I was here, OK? Please? I don't want her to know."

"Sure." There was no point in telling her that my father had stopped talking to me altogether several weeks ago. If Heather didn't know about Debi, maybe she didn't know I had moved out, either.

Debi came back later that night without my father. She looked exhausted.

"How did it go?" I asked conversationally.

She smiled in a way that didn't touch her eyes. "It's hard to tell with your father." Debi sounded just like my mother in one of her more diplomatic moods.

"Jessie's been asleep for a couple of hours. I gave her a bath."

"Thanks." Debi's eyes softened at the thought of her daughter. "She misses you so much."

"I can't be here."

"You could try."

"I did."

"I'm still trying."

"And look how well it's going." Immediately I felt like a schmuck. "I'm sorry. It's late. Thank you for the time with Jessie."

Debi looked at me levelly. "You will always be a part of her life, Angela. No matter what. She's your sister."

I didn't talk to Debi again until the night of her death. Earlier that day I had called my father to arrange to borrow a suitcase for my spring break trip to Savannah. Our conversation was stilted and uncomfortable, and I put off going to his house until late. I also dragged my best friend Kelli along.

When Kelli and I finally did arrive, I was wildly relieved at Debi's mention that my father had already gone to bed. When I went back to kiss Jessie and heard his slumbering breath in the master bedroom, it had been music to my ears. Only later did I learn that the person I heard had not been my father. And Debi was killed later that night, in that bedroom.

Flying back to Modesto in the wake of Debi's murder, my mind bounced from memory to memory. But primarily I thought of my father, and I wondered if we could return to the friendship we had begun to develop after Debi had moved out.

Once I arrived in the San Francisco airport, I scanned the crowd, not seeing him. Then I did a double take. There he was. His hair was completely white, and he had lost a dramatic amount of weight. The look was Very Old Scarecrow. I made my way toward him and hugged him, and my hope for any intimacy crumbled in his stiff response. There was no emotion in him at all.

"How's Jessie?" I asked, desperate to draw him out.

"Fine, I think." Even his voice was different: sort of gravelly and hollow.

"I've really missed her. I can't wait to see her. She's with Bob and Doris, I guess?"

"Yeah. We're still staying with them."

We lapsed into an uncomfortable silence I had experienced often during our time together. How many times as a child had I waved good-bye to Mom and climbed into his car with my overnight bag, scrambling to say the right thing that might initiate his thaw? Eventually I had learned to just sit quietly in the passenger seat and wait. Top 40 songs would come and go on the radio, struggling against the silence, until eventually my father would begin to hum quietly. Soon we would both be singing along. Casey Kasem was our family counselor, and Bonnie Tyler's popular ballad, "Total Eclipse of the Heart," carried our relationship through the early eighties.

Out in the airport parking lot, my father silently turned the ignition in a car I'd never seen before. The radio was on again, but it couldn't break through my father's silence. I didn't know what the rules were this time. Was I allowed to talk about Debi? Would he invite me to stay with him at the Kramers' house?

While I nervously picked at my sweater, I cast my eyes around the car. A hairbrush with a red plastic handle. A pack of chewing gum.

"Whose car?" I asked.

"A friend's."

A gnawing suspicion entered my mind. This was Heather Barnett's car. Heather, the girlfriend he'd picked up as soon as Debi told him about her affair. The supposed ex-girlfriend. *Jeepers.*

I turned my thoughts back to Jessie. Surely Dad would need me to help take care of her. He could go back to spending inordinate amounts of time away from the house, and Jessie and I would be fine. In fact, it would be better that way.

When we got to Bob and Doris's house, I practically ran inside. However, I drew up short when I saw Heather in the kitchen. She was holding Jessie on her hip in a very practiced way and smiling at me shyly.

"Sissy!" Jessie exclaimed, but she made no move to get down from Heather's arms.

I walked over and tousled her hair. "Hi, sweetheart! I sure did miss you. Are you OK?"

"My mommy is an angel now," she said matter-of-factly.

"Hi," Heather said softly, meaning it for me but looking instead at my sister. She bounced Jessie up and down a few times.

I turned toward my father, hoping to read something in his eyes. But he ignored us all—me, Heather, Jessie—and grabbed a beer from the refrigerator. He took a swallow and set it on the counter. Heather held onto Jessie with one arm and put a hand protectively on my father's back while her eyes assessed every inch of his face. How was he doing? What did he need? How could she make this moment better for him? I saw a tough determination in her that I had not seen before. Heather had already decided to fill every void in these two lives.

Bob lumbered into the kitchen, his build filling the doorway. "That's right, Jess. Mommy is an angel, and she will always look out for you." He hugged me, a hug full of warmth and friendliness. He had been crying all week, I could tell. He cleared his throat. "How was your flight, kiddo?"

I made a perfunctory response. Some people play their cards close to their chest, but Bob good-naturedly laid his hand faceup on the table. Who cared about winning? Bob was in the game for the laughs. But there was no laughter now. He looked hurt and mystified. He had loved Debi, and he also loved my father. I hoped to get some clue from him as to how to play this particular situation, but it was clear that he didn't know any better than I did.

Not sure what was expected of me, I took Jessie outside to play, but she went back inside to be close to our father. I noticed she wouldn't let him out of her sight for very long.

Bob found me alone by the pool. He sat down in the lawn chair next to me. "Your dad's going through a hell of a time right now. A hell of a time."

"I know."

"Howie's gotta do things his way, you know? We gotta let him do his thing."

If Bob was telling me to lower my expectations of my father, there was no need. Those expectations had bottomed out as soon as I tried to hug him in the airport.

I had lost my father before: to alcoholism, to divorce, to long periods of absence when his guilt about leaving my mother kept him from even trying to contact me. And most recently I had lost him to his betrayal of our friendship. I had mourned him more times than I could remember, but this time there was collateral damage. Jessie was his child, not mine. Losing him this time meant losing her.

I started to cry then, and Bob, misunderstanding it, patted my knee reassuringly. "Your dad's the smartest man I ever met. He'll get through this." Bob told me I was welcome to stay, but I declined. Instead, I called Kelli to come pick me up, and her folks invited me to stay at their house until my grandmother returned from Savannah in a few days.

Before leaving the Kramers' house, I asked my father if I could see him and Jessie later that week. Without looking at me he answered, "Why don't you call me at work and we'll arrange for Jessie to spend some time with you?"

Heather stood beside him, her hand still resting purposefully on his arm. Looking at the two of them, I felt both hurt and relieved, as if I'd been snubbed an invitation to the worst party of the year.

The following day I stopped by my grandmother's house to pick up the mail. I also scooped up the newspapers on the porch and headed inside. My father had mentioned that the paper used a picture of me. I thought he meant a family photo, but I was wrong. Opening the *Modesto Bee* from the previous Saturday, I read the front page headline. "Woman Slain in North Modesto Home." Under it was my picture. Just me.

The article mentioned Debi's name several times. Anybody who knew me and actually read the article would realize that something was amiss. Besides the difference in name, I was unmarried, so it would have been impossible for my husband to have found me.

I continued to read the story. *Modesto Bee* reporter Michael Winters had covered the basics, some of which I had never heard before. For example, he mentioned my father arrived home from a bachelor party at 5:40 in the morning. That gave me pause. Hadn't the party been at Ortega's? The bar would have closed well before that time. The story also mentioned that although they had questioned my father downtown, "Police had found no grounds to hold Harold C. Whitlock, 39, as a suspect in his wife's slaying."

The neighbors, however, seemed to feel differently. Somebody named Gayle Stiffler said that Dad and Debi were "definitely not your average married couple. You never saw them together, they never worked in the yard, never had any visitors." I didn't know who Gayle Stiffler was, but she obviously didn't know much about Dad and Debi. They had company constantly. In fact, besides the numerous people who felt comfortable walking into the house at any time, the Kramers, the Ortegas, and the Whitlocks all had their electronic garage door openers set to the same frequency. Living with Dad and Debi had been like living in a slow-paced cocktail party.

Another neighbor, Jerry Jones, said he'd seen my father arrive home from work Thursday night looking "angry."

I put down the paper in disgust. Now that Debi had been murdered, all of our lives had become public domain, where truth is determined by consensus. And so far the consensus stood thus: a day after his estranged wife's brutal murder, Harold Whitlock had already been taken away in a squad car, spent hours in police custody, and been denounced by neighbors as a friendless, angry, yard-work-loathing man.

I was starting to understand what my father was facing, but I didn't realize how much it would affect me as well.

SEVEN

The Making of a Murder Suspect

Debi's father continued to proclaim his former son-in-law's guilt to the authorities. Investigators listened to Martin Garrett's theory that Harold Whitlock had denied him access to Debi's body and then destroyed unknown evidence through cremation, and they assured Garrett that Dr. Ernoehazy's autopsy would have revealed any evidence against Debi's husband.

After the autopsy, Debi had been dressed in a Christmas outfit from Jacque: a plaid jacket and skirt with a black turtleneck covering the wounds on her neck. Her hands were wrapped carefully around a bouquet of her favorite flowers, daffodils. Each member of the family had asked the funeral home to tuck something in the casket: Jacque had included a favorite flower brooch, a token of their shared love of costume jewelry. Harold enclosed a sealed letter. And then Debi was cremated.

Detectives understood Garrett's concern. While police had kept under wraps the fact that Whitlock had been with his girl-friend that night, the family discovered other reasons to doubt

Whitlock's innocence. Debi's sister found divorce papers in Debi's desk drawer at work shortly after the murder. And both she and Garrett claimed Debi had discussed her will and funeral wishes with them during the last few weeks.

Police continued to look for other suspects, but they also talked to many of Harold and Debi's friends and coworkers, piecing together what they felt was a fairly accurate version of Debi and Harold's relationship.

Harold Whitlock was in his early thirties when he met Debi at work. Both recently divorced, they were set up by Bob Kramer and hit it off immediately. She was pretty, fun, and outgoing. He was handsome, smart, and amusing. Professionally, they shared the same goals: it was a good-natured race up the corporate ladder of Sears. Personally, they both enjoyed taking weekend trips and hosting backyard barbecues for friends. They seemed like the perfect couple, and no one was surprised when they moved in together after dating only a short time. Romantic involvement between employees was frowned upon by store management, and their quiet wedding in June of 1983 was the worst-kept secret of the year.

According to friends, the carefree attitude Debi and Harold shared changed soon after the wedding. Some said Debi focused only on her career. Others defended her, saying she was still a fun and devoted wife, although she was increasingly concerned about retirement plans and financial security. "She was always taking one step and looking toward the next one, and she thought Howie should do the same," said one coworker. "But he's not like that." Debi's goal-setting made her incredibly valuable at work, but some said it rankled her husband. He wanted a Neverland companion, not a routine full of responsibilities. He wasn't even forty yet. He had time to worry about the future later.

Debi hoped to have a child, and she told her friends that Howie loved children and was excited about the possibility of having another. When she got pregnant a few months after their wedding, husband and wife seemed to enjoy watching Debi's belly get disproportionately large on her small frame. She gave birth to their daughter just before Thanksgiving in 1984, and she and Harold both appeared to be devoted parents.

The changes that had begun in Debi before the pregnancy only increased once she became a mother. She took over the bill paying and created a family budget. She cut off her long, lustrous curls and got a more professional haircut to match her rapid promotions at Sears, promotions that her husband was not receiving. Their parties were curtailed because Debi wanted to spend her evenings with her daughter and weekends with her sister watching their girls play together.

It seemed to those closest to the couple that Harold was caught between the life that was good for him and the life that he wanted. His baby daughter was wonderful, and his wife was starting to make good money and was on the track to managing her own store in the foreseeable future. Harold bought himself a sports car, a top-notch stereo system for the house, a new grill. But he became increasingly unhappy, spending more time at Ortega's Cantina. What's worse, Harold had gotten into several rows with his supervisors at work, finally delivering a series of scathing insults and resigning on the spot.

At first, Debi had hoped that her husband would rally now that he was out of his stressful work environment, but he seemed in no hurry to find another job. Months went by, and Debi wondered aloud if he was even trying. Meanwhile, Harold's restlessness, spending sprees, and increased drinking took a toll on the marriage. Debi, a natural problem solver, was progressively more frustrated with her husband's brooding silence. She tried to allow him room to pull himself around, but it wasn't working, and they were growing further apart.

Although Debi didn't talk about her marriage problems with her family, Jacque eventually learned the particulars. "Debi had to spend most of her retirement savings just to support the family," Jacque told detectives. "Howie refused to do his share. It wasn't fair."

Eventually, Howie took a sales job with Best Products. Debi told her friends that his mood had improved, and he had started to exhibit some of his former playfulness. He was also on a mission to prove himself at his new job. The couple seemed happier than they had been in months.

Harold Whitlock was always at the center of the in crowd at work. Customers loved him and requested him specifically, and he always went out of his way for them as well as those who worked under him. In short, Harold was a good friend, an amiable co-worker, and a supportive supervisor; however, he could be what one former manager called "a know-it-all pain in the backside."

When the detectives made their way around to the Cantina to interview Jerry Ortega, he tried his best to offer them a litmus test for all of the incoming information. "Listen, I know you guys are hearing a lot of crap right now out of some of the people Howie's worked with, but here's what you need to do." He leaned forward earnestly and put his hands on the corner table where they sat. "I can give you a list of everybody who used to go fishing with us. It was a big group. We'd go down to Monterey every year, and last year there were so many of us we had to charter two boats. And me and Howie and Bob Kramer, we were the ones who did the inviting. Now, that caused problems because, you know, there were some people who weren't invited, and they were jealous." Jerry gestured at the detective's notebook. "So when you flip through there, and you look at who is saying bad stuff about Howie, or about his marriage or whatever, then I'll bet you a hundred dollars it's not the people who were on the fishing trip—and those were the people who knew Howie and Debi best."

The detectives exchanged glances. "What about the fact that several people we've interviewed say they heard Harold Whitlock say he was going to kill Debi?"

Jerry Ortega looked shocked. "I don't know about that. People might say stuff when they're angry, you know? I might get mad at my boys and say, 'If you don't straighten up, I'm gonna give you something to cry about!' But I don't mean it. Not really. Howie loved Debi. I know that, and I'm telling you that. He would never hurt her. He would never hurt anybody physically. He doesn't need to. His mouth is his weapon. I've seen him cut people down, and it's faster and harder than a one-two punch."

"So, you'd say he's probably made some enemies?"

"Could be," Ortega said evasively. "What I'm saying is that the bad stuff is coming from the people who were on the outside looking in—the people who were so jealous that they couldn't stand it. And now they are happy. But it's an evil kind of happy. They are so happy to have you listening to them as they talk a bunch of junk."

Partially to humor him, detectives took the list of names of those people who went fishing and checked it against their information. Sure enough, most of the damning information about Harold Whitlock did not come from people on the boat trips.

But some of it did.

Some of those very people were the ones who heard Harold Whitlock say, "I'll kill her if she tries to take Jessie in a divorce," or sometimes, "I'll kill her." And while those same people said they'd never known Harold Whitlock to be violent, many agreed that he had undergone a noticeable personality change in the months before Debi's murder: he was irritable, brooding, and drinking more than ever. Frankly, said some of her friends in management at Sears, Harold Whitlock had recently become a professional liability for a woman experiencing so much success.

Debi's romantic life seemed to support the information coming in. When investigators compared Harold, the husband on his way out, to Steve Bloomberg, the boyfriend on his way in, the differences were stark. Bloomberg was a successful businessman and active in local politics in nearby Merced. He was serious, respectful, and respected. He had nurtured and encouraged Debi's professional aspirations and had, as a career executive at Sears, tried to bring her to the attention of regional management. It was in part due to Bloomberg's support that Debi was appointed assistant store manager just five weeks before her death. Detectives did not wonder that the woman supposedly destined to be the youngest female manager in the district would choose Steve Bloomberg over Harold Whitlock.

Yet Debi had moved back in with Harold Whitlock shortly before her death. What did that mean to the case?

The two men in Debi's life told different stories. Bloomberg said Debi had planned to divorce Harold to be with him, and that she had only moved back into the house she shared with her husband in order to tie up loose ends. Meanwhile, Harold claimed Debi had ended her affair and decided to work on their marriage. Detectives had verified that Harold and Debi had met for an amicable lunch on the very day she was murdered, and that the couple had been seen together socially on several occasions during the last two weeks.

It was impossible that Harold Whitlock and Steve Bloomberg were both telling the truth. Bloomberg passed his polygraph test with flying colors. Harold, on the other hand, had ambiguous results on the test even when he was stating things that were absolutely true, such as his name and date of birth.

What if both men were telling the truth as they believed it?

Was it possible that Debi had been stringing them both along? And if she had, was it also possible that she was involved with someone else—a third person who decided he had had enough, and who had killed her in a fit of jealousy?

Neither Debi's friends nor coworkers had seen her with anyone else, and they scoffed at the very idea. Debi was a woman who had loved her husband and who had tried to make their marriage work. As Harold had pulled away from her, she fell in love with an honorable man who was good to her and for her. Even Harold defended his wife, insisting that Debi was not the type to have casual affairs. "She told me she loved him, and I know the situation caused her a lot of pain," he said, obviously uncomfortable. "I can tell you there was no one else. That just wouldn't be like Debi."

If there was a third figure operating independently, it was likely that the man had become infatuated with Debi without her fully realizing it. Detectives combed the establishments Debi had frequented, especially those she had visited on her last day: the video store, the dry cleaner, the small bistro where she and Harold had eaten lunch. But they could find nothing.

Then who was breathing in the master bedroom on the night Debi was killed? If it wasn't Harold Whitlock, and it wasn't Steve Bloomberg, who was it?

A hired killer?

As soon as the blood tests from the few foreign drops at the scene had ruled out Harold Whitlock, the next most likely scenario was that he had hired someone to kill his wife. If this were true, was money his motive? The couple was financially strapped due to Harold's spending habits and long break in employment; however, shortly after the funeral, Harold had contacted a real estate agent and told her he was expecting a large sum of life insurance money from Debi's policy. The agent showed him some nicer homes currently on the market, but before a deal could be brokered, Harold had called to say he wouldn't be receiving any insurance money at all. Shortly before her death, Debi had let the policy lapse. Harold Whitlock was entirely broke.

Debi's family saw a dark significance in the fact that Debi had let her insurance policy lapse. Debi was a planner and saver, and they insisted she would never leave her daughter without assistance in case of her injury or death. "That just wasn't like Debi at all," her sister Karen said.

The lapsed coverage seemed highly suspicious, falling as it did so shortly before her unexplained murder. Had she suspected that her husband might kill her for the payoff? Had she been fearful of the temptation the money might exert on a man who had already threatened to kill her?

And what about Debi's boyfriend's assertion that Harold Whitlock had hit Debi? This could not be verified by another source, but it was well-known that Debi had been married to an abusive man previously.

Harold's friends pointed to Debi's ex-husband, Chuck Peters, as a primary suspect. Several friends and Sears employees could remember Debi's bruises from her first marriage, but those who knew Peters swore that he had changed. Furthermore, he had a solid alibi for the night of her murder.

Unlike Harold Whitlock.

Police officers, like social workers, know that women who are victims of abuse often emerge from one volatile situation only to enter another one just like it. It takes a total recalibration of the woman's concept of "normal relationship" in order to get her to break that cycle. Debi Whitlock had had the good fortune to meet Bob and Doris Kramer when she was at her lowest point in her first marriage, and they had supported her through her divorce. It seemed unlikely that they would exert so much effort to get Debi away from one abuser only to introduce her to another. And the Kramers, who saw the Whitlocks almost every day, would certainly know if Harold Whitlock was physically abusive. However, in spite of their hopes to find other viable suspects, the police kept coming back to the man with motive for Debi to die and Jessica to live, and the opportunity to make certain those things occurred. As they workshopped the case, detectives scrutinized the evidence and threw out possible, unexplored angles, but several felt they were wasting their time. Even if Harold Whitlock didn't wield the knife, it was ridiculous to think he was not involved.

Looking up at the dry erase board with the facts of the Whitlock case scrawled across its cool white surface, one detective threw up his hands in frustration. "How many times are we going to go over this? The husband hired someone to kill her. We all know it. Now it's just a question of finding the trail. That's our job now."

EIGHT

A Daughter's Retreat

Beyer High was a large public school, and I had always been just another face in the crowd. Now as I made my way toward my first class after spring break, I knew that had changed. Students I did not recognize seemed to nudge each other and whisper as I walked by. When I entered my classroom, I looked around at people I considered friends and saw them studiously avoiding me. No one spoke to me. No one.

I kept my head down as I walked toward my second class, wishing I could disappear entirely. Suddenly a woman screamed. I jumped and dropped my bag.

Everybody in the hallway stopped and turned. I saw my previous year's English teacher, Joan Laun, coming toward me with arms outstretched. She enveloped me in a hug. "Angela! Oh thank God! I thought you were dead!" She clung to me for several seconds, then pulled back, wiping away tears. "Your picture! I saw your picture in the paper. On television. Everywhere!"

The other students cut a wide berth around us. "It was a mistake," I mumbled.

"A mistake?"

"Somebody grabbed the wrong picture, I guess."

Anger shone in her eyes. "Those bastards. I've cried for a week."

I was so touched by her words that I hardly knew what to say. I adored Mrs. Laun. She was a terrific teacher, invigorating and excited about her subject matter, and we had bonded over our mutual passion for John Steinbeck.

"I'm fine, Mrs. Laun. The victim was my stepmother."

She shifted gears again. "Oh, Angela. Your stepmother? I'm so sorry. Is there anything I can do?"

"I don't think so."

She smiled. "People have probably been accosting you all morning. Or is it just me?"

I looked around. The hallway was empty. "Actually, nobody has even talked to me."

She patted me affectionately on the arm. "Give them some time. They're only teenagers."

"But I am, too."

She gave me a pitying look and squeezed my hand. "Not anymore. You just grew up. And I'm sorry it happened like this."

Mrs. Laun was right. Throughout the next several days, numerous students came up to me to express their condolences. But I was still the campus oddity.

It was unbearable.

I started cutting classes, driving my grandmother's car into the California foothills, taking some comfort in the brief greening of the landscape before summer's drought turned the vegetation into dry golden fodder for uncontrollable wildfires.

I needed to retrieve some clothes and my tennis racket from my father's house. I was nervous about visiting the house for the first time since the murder and asked Kelli to come along.

She pulled her red Nissan into the empty driveway. I didn't have a key, but I knew I could get in. Kelli stayed in the car while I walked down the side alley and entered the backyard through the gate. I crossed the yard and walked toward the covered patio. It looked exactly the same. There was the redwood picnic table and benches, the grill, and Jessie's baby pool. But something about the pool wasn't right. It was made of bright pink plastic, but that didn't explain why the water was so red. I stepped closer. The murky liquid inside emitted a strange, unpleasant smell.

I sucked in my breath. Oh my God. It was blood. There was bloody water in my sister's pool. Down in the murky depths I could make out a few dead flies.

Who would put blood in Jessie's pool? Was it a vicious prank? Or had the cleaning service, for some reason, emptied their Shop-Vacs—

I couldn't even consider such a horrible option. No, it was an evil, malicious prank. That had to be it. Somebody read the address in the newspaper. Then they got some blood from a butcher shop or somewhere, and they came into our backyard and poured it into the pool. Someone had meant to hurt my father, but I wasn't going to let that happen.

Fighting revulsion and holding my breath, I tugged the pool across the patio to a planter filled with juniper. Then I dumped the contents into the planter, pulled the hose over, and rinsed out the pool. There. No trace at all.

I dried my hands on my jeans and walked to the sliding glass door leading into the living room. Before the murder it was almost always unlocked, but now it was shut and locked securely.

No problem. The kitchen window was high and narrow, but if I stood on a patio chair, my legs were long enough that I could climb through. The lock on this window was very temperamental, and it took only a few seconds to jimmy it open.

I clambered into the kitchen and shut the window, this time making sure that the lock was fully engaged. As I turned around, my eyes went automatically to the kitchen counter. The knife block was gone.

Drawn by morbid fascination, I walked slowly forward. Someone had stood right here, looked at our knife block, and selected one of the largest to kill Debi.

I jumped as Kelli beeped her car horn. I went to the door leading to the garage and pressed the automatic opener for the large exterior door. As it opened I waved to Kelli. She rolled down her window.

"You OK?"

"Yeah, It took a while to get the kitchen window open."

She shrugged. "They always used to leave the sliding door open. I guess that's changed now."

"I guess so. I'll be out in a second."

Kelli nodded and flipped on the car radio while I headed back inside and down the hall toward my old room. Then I stopped. Debi was supposedly killed right here. I put my hand to the wall, trying to sense that I could still connect to her, that she wasn't entirely gone. I knelt down and touched the dark shag carpeting. Was this where Dad found her? Was some part of her still here?

"I'm so sorry," I whispered.

Suddenly every hair on my body stood on end. Forgetting my clothes, I jumped up and sprinted to the garage. I grabbed my racket, hit the button to close the door, and ran to Kelli's car.

The next week I was sitting in precalculus when a student

walked in and took a note to the teacher's desk. He read the note silently and glanced up at me. "Angela Whitlock, you're needed in the principal's office."

Was this because I'd been cutting so much class? Probably. Ignoring the stares around me, I gathered up my things, shoved them into my book bag, and followed the student out of the classroom. I cut left and entered the school's central corridor. The main office was through a set of heavy wooden doors. I pushed them aside and stood in a small room that was crowded with middle-aged men in suits.

"Angela?"

The principal was a nice enough guy. As editor of the past two yearbooks, I'd met him a few times. He faced me now. "There are a couple of police detectives in my office. They need to talk to you . . ." His voice trailed off.

Chest tight with fear, I walked resolutely into the room.

The principal's office was surprisingly homey. Wooden bookshelves lined one wall. A floor lamp and a few upholstered chairs clustered around the large dark brown desk of wood laminate. Two middle-aged men in crisp shirts and suit jackets faced me. They introduced themselves as detectives, but I was too distraught to register names.

"Have a seat," said the stockier of the two.

I didn't. "Is my sister OK? My father?"

The men registered shocked expressions. "Why? Is there a reason they wouldn't be?"

Good Lord, how dense were these guys? "Well, someone just got murdered in their house."

The thin guy flicked a smile. "Oh. No, they're fine."

The big guy still looked suspiciously at me. "Do you have reason to believe that some harm will come to your father or sister?"

I took a seat, hugging my book bag to stop my shaking. "Well, whoever killed Debi is still out there somewhere. What if they were really after my dad that night?"

"We considered that," said thin guy, leaning back in his chair, "but the evidence indicates your stepmother was the true target."

Big guy sat on the edge of the desk, pulling a notebook out of his inside breast pocket. He looked like he might have played football in high school. "We came here today to ask you a few questions pertaining to our investigation. Specifically, we're interested in something your sister said."

"Jessie?"

"Yes. According to Jessie, she saw you slap Debi."

I blinked. "What?"

"Jessie told one of our investigators that she saw you slap her mother." He made a show of flipping through his notebook. " 'Angela hit my mommy,' is what she said. We'd like to know about that."

I sat, stunned. They thought I had killed Debi. That's why they were here. I glanced at thin guy, but he and the other one were wearing matching expressions of guarded interest.

"That's not true. That never happened." I tried to force my voice to be calm. This was too important to fall to pieces.

"Are you saying you never hit Debi in front of your sister?"

"I am saying I never hit Debi. I never even raised my voice to her." It was true, but I could tell the detectives didn't believe me. What teenager doesn't argue with the adults in the house?

Thin guy cut in. "Could Jessie have been confused? Maybe Debi hit you?"

"Debi and I never fought. Not with words, not with our hands. We wouldn't hit each other."

"Huh. You think maybe your father hit Debi?" That from the big guy. He was actually trying to say it nonchalantly, as if he'd just thought of it.

"No. My father's not like that."

They seemed skeptical.

"Look, he fought more with my mom, and he never hit her, either."

I thought back to the times I had seen my dad the angriest. During my parents' separation and even after the divorce, my father would often drive over to our house late at night and sit in his car by the curb. He would stay there for hours, the orange tip of his cigarette the only indication of movement within the car's dark interior. He sat there thinking, smoking, drinking. If he drank up enough resolve, he might come up the concrete walkway he had poured years ago and knock on the door. He might even stay and shout while my mother's voice softly pleaded with him to leave. But he never hit her.

The detective cleared his throat meaningfully to bring me back to the conversation. "So you believe your father wouldn't harm Debi?"

I glared at the big guy. "My father didn't hurt Debi. Ever."

Suddenly, something that had been bothering me about Jessie's statement came together.

"I don't know who told you that my sister said I hit Debi, but they're lying."

"Oh?" big guy said skeptically. "What makes you think that?"

"I don't think it. I *know*. You said she called me Angela?"

"Yes."

"Jessie never calls me Angela. I'm always Sissy."

"Well, if she was talking to someone else—"

"No. I'm telling you that she always, *always* refers to me as Sissy." Even if they didn't believe me, I felt inordinately better. I knew now that Jessie had never said that. But who would lie about me?

"OK. Let's change gears a little bit. Why did Debi ask you to move out?"

I had been expecting the topic, but not the wording. "Debi never asked me to move out. In fact, she—" I cut off the words. Debi had wanted me to come back. She had proposed that, after her divorce from my father, I would stay in the house and care for Jessica during the week while Debi stayed in Merced. She was lined up to transfer to that store soon, and she could arrange her schedule so that she would be home most weekends and several nights during the week. None of this, however, was the detective's business. Furthermore, I was convinced it had nothing to do with Debi's death.

Big guy prompted me. "In fact she—?"

"In fact, I didn't actually move out. I have always stayed with my grandmother sometimes and my dad and Debi at other times. I've still got some clothes and stuff over there."

"Then can you explain why your fingerprints were all over the kitchen window, showing you had come in through there recently?"

Holy crap. They really did think I had killed her. "I didn't break in! I live there. I needed my tennis racket, I didn't have my keys, and so I went around back. The sliding glass door is usually unlocked, but that day it wasn't. So I went through the kitchen window, got my racket, and left."

"Through the window?"

"No. Through the garage. I used the automatic opener from inside and ran out underneath as it closed."

Thin guy looked at his partner. "That is the same answer we just got from Kelli Clark."

They had already talked to Kelli, already knew the truth. Were they trying to trick me? Or scare me?

Big guy flicked an annoyed look at his partner. Maybe I wasn't supposed to know they'd talked to Kelli. "You say the sliding glass door was always unlocked at your father's house?"

"Yes, almost always. Except that day. I guess because Dad's not living there right now."

"Someone else said that door was always locked."

"They're wrong. I forget my house keys a lot, but it's never a problem because nobody locks the back door."

He scratched his chin. "Your prints were on the front bedroom window as well."

"That's my room."

"Your father said you used to sneak out at night through that window, and that's why you had to move out."

Another lie. Did Dad really say it?

"That's not true! I went out that window once. I got angry at my father, and I climbed out the window and walked to a friend's house. Typical teenage stuff. It was one time. You can check with my friend—or the family."

"We'll do that." Big guy stood. "We're done for now. I'm going to leave you my card so you can reach us if you have anything further to add. Or if you want to change anything you've said today."

Fighting back tears, I stood up and slung my backpack over my shoulder. I marched by the startled figure of the guidance counselor outside the door and kept walking down the hall and into the sunshine outside, stopping just long enough to throw the detective's business card into a trash can. I kept walking through the quiet campus, taking the route to my grandmother's house. Was it possible my father had told the detectives he made me move out? Had he painted me as some kind of teenage delinquent? And if so, why?

I tried to puzzle through the implications of the situation. The paper claimed the police didn't suspect him, although given my conversation with them today, I wondered if that was true. If they did suspect him, maybe they thought I had moved out shortly before the murder because . . . because I feared my father? Because I thought he might do something violent? If that was their reasoning, then of course my father would want to make it look like I hadn't moved out voluntarily.

I arrived at my grandmother's house, slammed my pack onto the floor, and headed toward the phone. The operator at Best Products put me through to my father.

"Harold Whitlock."

"Hi, it's me." My voice was shaking so much I could hardly talk. "Some detectives showed up at school today."

He sounded wary. "Yeah? They're like a couple of bad pennies, aren't they?"

"They asked about Jessie."

"Oh. They asked if you'd hit Debi." It wasn't a question.

"You knew about that?"

"Yeah. They asked me about it, and I told them they were full of it."

"Same here. Then they asked if maybe Debi had hit me. Can you believe it? Or if you had hit Debi."

"They asked that?" His voice was suddenly hushed. Some employee or customer must have come near him.

"Yes, they asked that. Of course they did!"

"What—what did you say?"

"What do you think? I told them no, of course. I know you never hit her. Don't worry about it. They're just scrambling."

"Well, they wouldn't be the only people to think the worst," he said. "If thoughts were daggers, I'd have been dead as soon as this happened."

The sorrow in his voice deflated my anger. I had considered asking him if he had really told the police I used to sneak out all the time, but now I decided against it. "It was in the paper that you were at that bachelor party, so I don't understand why anyone is giving you a hard time."

"Thank you. It means a lot to hear you say that." He cleared his throat. "But don't worry about it. I won't be around long. I'm expecting Debi's dad to kill me anytime."

"What?"

"Martin. He thinks I did this."

"No way!"

"Yep. Apparently he's got reward posters up and everything. Bring him my head in a bag, and you get a Ricky Skaggs album and a coupon for 25 percent off the all-you-can-eat buffet at the Pig Palace."

He was obviously joking, so I laughed. "Listen, I've got to grab some lunch. I love you. I'll pick up Jess this afternoon and bring her by the Kramers before dinner." Ever since our falling-out three months ago, whenever I told my father I loved him, I always said it in a rush, sandwiched between other thoughts. He often ignored it, but not today.

"I love you, too, honey. Bye."

I put down the receiver, my mind restless. I had no intention of going back to the silent spotlight at school. By now it would be common knowledge that the detectives had shown up. I cranked up the radio to drown out the whispered speculations I imagined circulating through the hallways: "I heard some police officers questioned Angela Whitlock this morning. They probably came to tell her they had arrested her dad."

I was starting to question my return to Modesto. Sure, I had only a month left of class before graduating from high school, but the situation was taking a huge toll on me. Being the stepdaughter of Modesto's most famous murder victim was an uncomfortable role, particularly for a shy teenager who was working through the emotional impact of that murder, as well as several other recent events.

I first met Jack Kaleb at the beginning of my junior year of high school. We had friends in common, and we dated a few times. It was nothing serious, and we soon drifted into other relationships, although we continued to cross paths amicably.

One day in the winter of my senior year, Jack told me he had written a play. I was surprised. Jack had never shown much interest in creative writing. He claimed he was "too shy" to tell anybody else about the play. "It's probably crap, but I wish you would take a look at it." Since I had some errands to run after school near his house, I agreed to stop by later.

In retrospect, there were so many reasons to suspect something was amiss. Take, for example, that Jack swore me to secrecy about our meeting because he supposedly didn't want his friends to know about his foray into creative writing. Or that he was obviously nervous when he answered his door later that afternoon. Or that his father was standing in the entryway, suitcase in hand, complaining because he was already supposed to have left for an overnight business trip.

Minutes after Mr. Kaleb left, Jack had me pinned to the living room floor, one hand frantically pushing up my skirt as his torso pushed painfully into mine. I lay there frozen in shock and confusion, my body betraying none of the panic flooding my mind. How had this happened? How could I have been so stupid? And why in God's name wasn't Jack's father coming back through the door, saying he had forgotten something?

My mind was screaming at me to do something, anything, but it seemed completely divorced from my body.

Suddenly I remembered my mother telling me about a time she

found herself in a similar situation. *I was so scared, but you know what I did? He was trying to shove his tongue into my mouth, so I finally let him. And then I bit down—hard. He jumped off of me, cussing, bleeding. But I got away!*

I heard her in my addled mind, and my body finally started to respond. Jack could easily overpower me, but if he thought, even briefly, that I was amenable to this, maybe I could get away. I closed my eyes and kissed him.

There was a pause in his frantic activity. I opened one eye to see him looking at me in startled surprise. Then he smiled. He returned my kiss, grunting with pleasure as I braced both hands behind me against the floor and rolled us over together. As soon as his weight was off of me, I jumped up and ran toward the door.

By the time I got to my father's house, my face was tear-streaked, and I was shaking uncontrollably. I walked directly to my room and sat silently on my bed, staring at the rust-colored carpet and trying to pull myself together.

There was a knock at the door. My father opened it and peeked in. "You had a call from—What's going on?"

I looked at my father, standing in the doorway and looking at me with genuine concern. We had grown so close during the last few weeks of late night conversations. I had listened to his confusion and heartbreak, and we now had a shared understanding, a support network that, right now, I needed desperately. I needed a friend as well as a parent: someone who would listen, who would be outraged for my sake, who would hug and comfort me, and who would know what to do.

And so, with complete confidence in our relationship, I told my father everything. I cried as I recounted how I had let myself be duped, and how afraid I had been during the attack. And even though I had gotten away, I still felt hurt and betrayed.

I talked until I was done, hiccupping with tears, and the room lapsed into silence. My shaking had subsided to the occasional tremor. I wiped my eyes on the back of my hand and studied the carpet, suddenly embarrassed by my outburst. Why wasn't he saying anything?

"You know,"—my father's voice from above me sounded almost conversational—"in one way I'd like to get your great granddaddy's shotgun out of the closet and go over to Jack's house right now and take care of this. But at the same time . . . Well, look at how you're dressed."

Surely I had misheard him. I looked up at my father to see him leaning against my doorway, studying me with detached disregard as he might a display case at his store. Then I looked down at my clothes. I was wearing a dark plaid skirt that came to my knees, hose that now showed several runs, and low-rising boots. I had on a nondescript black shirt with a modest neckline, and a warm, somewhat bulky blazer. There was nothing risqué about my clothing.

"Wh—what?" I asked, my voice small in the enormity of what my father seemed to be saying.

"Look at what you're wearing." He shrugged. "What did you expect?"

At that moment, the fragile relationship I had so recently established with my father shattered, its shards cutting deeply into me.

I moved out, and we had not spoken more than a dozen words from that time until the day he called me in Savannah to tell me Debi had been murdered.

Years later I would realize that my father's harsh words on the night Jack assaulted me may have had more to do with Debi than me. After all, the clothing I was wearing—the clothing he denounced—belonged to Debi, the woman who had just moved out and was seeing another man.

During my time in my father's house, I wore Debi's clothes so regularly that she took to calling some of her outfits "ours."

"Good morning!" she would call out, strolling into my room even before the alarm clock sounded. "Have you seen our green blazer? Do you have our black knit skirt?" Debi laughed when she said it, pushing around the clothes in my closet. "I don't know why you don't wear some of your own stuff."

"I like yours," I would say, yawning and rubbing sleep from my eyes.

"Yes, but you're a teenager. Why don't you wear the clothes I buy you out of the juniors' department?"

"Because they make me look like I'm trying out for MTV."

In fact, the very first time I met Debi's mom, Jacque and Dennis had come into town for a visit. It was a school morning, and I was wearing one of my favorite outfits, my green plaid skirt with a white button-down shirt and "our" black suit jacket. After our introductions Jacque looked me up and down and said with evident commiseration, "I had to attend a Catholic school, too."

I was bewildered, and the fact that Debi was laughing loudly only confused me more.

"No, Mom," Debi said. "Angela actually *chooses* to dress that way."

Jacque looked to me for confirmation. "You do? You mean, that's not a school uniform?"

"No!" I said indignantly, sending Debi into more peals of laughter. "I like this outfit!"

Jacque shook her head gravely and turned on her daughter. "You have to do something about this," she declared, as if I was covered in grime and her daughter had the only soap in town. "You work in fashion, for God's sake! Can't you help her?"

Debi sobered somewhat, defending herself but still snickering. "I buy her other clothing. Popular clothing! She won't touch it!"

By this time I was smiling in spite of myself. "Some people would think this is a perfectly fine outfit."

"No, dear." Jacque turned back to me. "It took me years to get *away* from that outfit!"

When Debi moved out, she left behind a few of my favorite items of her wardrobe. The fact that I continued to wear them may have upset my father. Did he view it as a form of betrayal? I'll never know. At the time, it didn't even cross my mind.

But talking to my father on the phone directly after Debi's murder, he had sounded so alone and grief stricken that I had returned to California, harboring fantasies of a father-daughter reconciliation. That hadn't happened. Instead he had all but disappeared, never initiating contact, and distancing himself whenever I called.

School wasn't going much better. The gossip mill that had generated numerous mistellings of my encounter with Jack Kaleb six weeks earlier only gained momentum in the wake of Debi's murder. Many of my friendships had fallen away, and those that hadn't, I abandoned out of a misguided sense of self-preservation. In a world where friends make schemes of sexual assault, where fathers absolve their daughter's attacker, and where people murder and get away with it . . . well, in that world, nobody can be trusted.

My emotions careened violently from one to another as unsteadily as if I were standing on an active fault line. Growing up in earthquake country, I had learned that if I were in motion, I wouldn't feel the shaking underneath me. Now that my life was in turmoil, I could only feel stable if I were walking or driving out through the foothills. I almost never went to class anymore.

Two weeks after the murder, my friend and classmate Jim tracked me down. Jim's aunt had died under suspicious circumstances years earlier, and although the case was eventually ruled an accident, Jim understood more than others the tumultuous daze in which I dwelled. So it was Jim who stepped into my chaos one day and suggested with a kind smile that we "go play tennis like normal people."

After the game, Jim drove me back to my grandmother's house. I put my racket away and rummaged around in the refrigerator looking for something sugar-laden. From the kitchen, I could hear him flipping through my collection of vinyl records by my grandmother's turntable in the living room.

"Oh my gosh, you have the worst taste in music!" he called out, laughing.

I opened a lone can of Cherry Coke and divided it between two ice-filled tumblers. "What's so bad about it?"

"Barbra Streisand? Are you kidding? Tell me this is your grandmother's!"

"Don't knock Barbra!" I came into the room, handed him his glass, and took the album from his hand. "Sit!" I commanded, sliding the album from its cover.

He stared at me incredulously. "You've got to be kidding."

"Nope. You've got to hear her cover of 'There's a Place for Us.' That's from *West Side Story*, by the way."

"It's from a musical? This just keeps getting worse."

"Hush! This moment calls for reverential silence." I smiled at his discomfort, centering the album over the player's silver spindle. "Would Oreos make this better for you?"

"Do you have anything crunchier? If I chew loud enough maybe I won't hear the music . . ."

I shot him a withering glance and headed back to the pantry as Barbra began to voice the fervent hope of West Side's Maria and Tony that "Someday, somewhere, we'll find a new way of living."

I had finally located the cookies in the back of the pantry and was putting them on a plate when the doorbell rang.

"Hey, Jim?" I called over Streisand's insistence that there was both a place *and* a time for us. "Could you get that?"

"Sure." I heard his footsteps on the tile in the entryway.

Picking up the plate of cookies I headed out of the kitchen and through the living room. I was nearing the front entryway when I heard the sound of a scuffle.

"Jim?"

"Ooof." The noise sounded unmistakably as if Jim had just been punched in the stomach. I rounded the corner just as my grandmother's door slammed shut.

Panic gripped me in a tight fist. What should I do? I set the plate of cookies on a small table but misjudged its marble edge. The plate toppled onto the tile, breaking into large pieces and sending cookies skidding across the floor. I ran to the door and peeked through the keyhole, but its distorted view showed me nothing but a small shadow moving in the sunlit yard. I opened the door a fraction of an inch. The stoop was bare. I looked toward the street in time to see Jim's father slam the back door to his own car, with Jim bent over in the back seat holding his midriff. Jim's father didn't look toward the house at all. He climbed quickly into the driver's seat, slammed his door, and drove away.

I stood on the porch, stunned, not sure what to do.

What the devil was going on in the world?

A couple of hours later, Jim's sister knocked on the door.

"Tasha! Where's Jim?"

She looked at me without expression. "I'm not supposed to talk to you. I just need to get my brother's tennis racket, and I think he left a jacket over here."

The racket and gray Members Only windbreaker were by the door, and I handed them to her. "I don't understand." I wanted to ask if her father hit Jim, or any of the family. I felt concern for all of them, but wasn't sure what to say.

"Jim knows what he did," she answered cryptically. "He understands what happened."

The look in her eyes made me start. "It was me? He wasn't supposed to be around me?"

"That's between him and my father," she said matter-of-factly, but I knew I was right. She turned and left without another word. I looked toward the darkening street and saw the family car. Was that their father behind the wheel? Tasha got into Jim's Jeep, and the two cars drove away.

The following Monday, Jim would not meet my eyes. We usually sat next to each other in U.S. Government, but that day he went to a desk at the far side of the room. Again, I didn't know the right course of action. Had his father threatened to hurt him again if Jim was seen talking to me? I didn't want to do anything to jeopardize my friend, so I chose to approach a mutual acquaintance. Putting on as much of a breezy voice as I could, I ventured, "Hey, what's up with Jim today?"

His friend looked knowingly at me. "You don't have to do that. I know what's going on. Tasha told me. Their folks just don't—there's just some question as to what's going on with your family. Or with you, I guess."

I could feel my face flush. "What do you mean, some question?" I heard the quavering challenge in my voice. "What exactly is the question?"

"Don't ask me," he said, backing down. "That's just what Jim's sister said. And I got the idea that it would go bad for Jim if, you know . . . if he was friends with you."

Now I knew that the adults in the community were judging not only my father, but me. Was Jim's father worried for his son's safety? Was he concerned that I or my father, having murdered Debi, might target Jim next?

During the next week, someone left a threatening message

on my grandmother's answering machine. The police wrote it off as a prank until two days later, when someone tried to break into my grandmother's house shortly before I arrived home from school.

That night I moved in with Kelli, with the intent of finishing out the school year there. Meanwhile, Dad told me the detectives had notified the school that I may be in some danger, and that I shouldn't be alarmed if I saw men standing around near my class-rooms. Additionally, my maternal grandfather claimed he had "made arrangements" for some private security at the school. I never mentioned this to anyone else, but now I was even more paranoid.

As I walked to U.S. Government class one day the following week, I saw an older gentleman standing near a cluster of young palm trees outside the building. Our eyes met briefly. He nodded almost imperceptibly, and I looked away, tears coming into my eyes. I walked into the classroom, pulled out my books, and kept my eyes cast downward as a few teardrops splashed onto my note-book. Damn it, was I sentenced to suffer crying jags for the rest of my life?

I wiped the drops away angrily, stood up, and abruptly left the class. Once outside, I looked toward the palm trees where I'd seen the man a few moments ago. The area was empty. I continued around the building and came to a rest away from prying eyes. I buried my face in my hands and let my tears come freely.

Soon I felt a gentle hand on my shoulder. I turned to see Jim standing behind me, his eyes full of sadness and compassion.

But wait! What was he doing? He wasn't supposed to be near me. What if word got back to his father? I knew what it was like to feel threatened. I couldn't stand to endanger one of my few re-maining friends.

"No! Get away from me!"

Jim reared back as if I'd slapped him, his face red. He hurriedly walked away from me.

We never spoke again.

Kelli's folks had been very clear about what they expected from me while I stayed with them. I was to attend class regularly and keep up with my homework. I was to call if I was going to be late in any way, and I absolutely could not be out after 10 o'clock at night. "These are the same rules we use for Kelli," her dad explained, "and you've become like a second daughter to us, Ang."

Their rules seemed reasonable, and they were established out of love. I knew that. But no amount of lovingly laid-down parameters was going to curtail my obsessive need to walk. Instead, I would wait until Kelli and her parents had fallen asleep and then, very quietly, open the guest room window and drop into the planter outside. The night air in late April was cool while the pavement retained heat from the afternoon sun. I wandered the residential streets, letting the restlessness of my mind come out through the motion of my feet. Had the killer seen me that night at Dad and Debi's house? Is that who had been breathing in the bedroom? Had he tracked me to my grandmother's house? Did he leave the phone message? Did he try to break in? Did he know where I was right now?

I was tired of being afraid. On these lonely midnight walks, I dared him to find me. If he was going to come get me, damn it, come on. Here I am, my nightgown tucked into a pair of jeans, my sneakers drumming steadily against the pale sidewalk. Was I truly safe? Or was I only experiencing a moment of grace until a knife came out of the darkness?

If I timed it right, I would outwalk my restlessness and have just enough energy left to pull myself back in through the window. Then, as I lay on the bed staring through the glass at the early morning sky, perhaps sleep would find me.

But one night as I turned my tired feet up the walkway to the Clark house, Kelli was there. I saw her sitting pale and shaken on the front porch step.

"Ang?" She jumped up and came toward me, her voice high and anxious. "Where were you? I knocked on the door to your room, and you didn't answer, so I came in. Where did you go?"

"Nowhere. Just walking. I have to walk a lot. At night." It sounded so stupid.

"You walk a lot at night." She said it like she was chewing on something bitter. "Do you know how upset my parents would be?"

I couldn't even look at her. "I'll stop."

"No, you won't. I know you." There was no point in arguing; she did know me. "So what you'll do is, you'll come get me, and we'll both go."

"No way! I don't want to put you in danger."

"You don't make the rules."

"Oh, and you do?"

"Yes I do, unless you want me to tell Mom to put a lock on your window." It was the kind of line that should have been followed by a smile, but it wasn't. The silence stretched out between us and was finally broken when she sniffed.

Oh, crap. She had been out here crying.

"I'm sorry," I said, and I meant it.

"Fine," she said, dropping her arms. "Let's go."

"Yeah, but—" She stomped past me toward the lamplit sidewalk. "But I've already walked." I broke into a trot to catch up with her. "Besides, you're in your robe."

She stopped and looked at me, flabbergasted. "We're two teenage girls walking around the streets in the middle of the night, the guy who killed Debi is still out there and might be after you, and you're worried because I'm in my robe?" Her voice was inching into the higher registers. Her folks might wake up at any minute.

"No, that's fine," I said quickly. "It's just hard to climb through the window in a robe."

"Silly me," she said, dramatically smacking her hand against her forehead. "I used the front door." The pale light gleamed on the edge of her house key, which she tucked back into her robe pocket. "Now," she said with evident self-satisfaction, "why don't you show me our route?"

It didn't take long for Kelli's folks to catch on to our late night excursions, and we both got chewed out. What were we doing, endangering ourselves like that? Hadn't Debi's murder taught us that there were real dangers in the world? Kelli and I hung our heads and apologized, but I couldn't make her parents understand that my restlessness came from the realization that the world was fraught with real dangers.

With my midnight wandering curtailed, I felt claustrophobic, suffocated by my fear and disappointment and disbelief in any underlying goodness in the world. I called Mom and tearfully told her I was ready to come home. The following day an educational counselor pulled together six weeks of curricula for me to finish long-distance in order to graduate. I left the campus without a look back.

That afternoon I drove my grandmother's car to Best Products. An employee led me into the back offices to where my father was working.

Dad looked so much older now, stooped and emaciated, his white hair unkempt. Eyes followed me with undisguised interest as I walked toward him, but my father seemed oblivious to the tension crackling around him.

"Hi," I said, coming up to his desk.

He looked up. "Hello. What brings you here?"

I looked for somewhere to sit but didn't see another chair nearby. Then I surveyed the room. Two guys standing by a snack machine had their heads together, one of them staring at me, trying to size up the situation.

"Can't a girl come by and see her dad?" I asked loudly of my father, shooting a glare toward the guys against the far wall. Jerks. Weren't they supposed to be working?

My father followed my glare "Don't worry about it," he said softly. "I'm not exactly low profile these days."

Several people in the room drifted out the door and back toward the sales floor, and the guys in the corner had the decency to get engrossed in their own conversation. My father stood and walked toward a raised worktable in the opposite direction, and I followed. Binders of computer-generated data littered the table's surface, and he silently shuffled through them.

"Dad, I'm moving back to Virginia."

"I see." He glanced up. "When are you leaving?"

"Tomorrow."

His face clouded over, and he looked away from me. "That's sudden."

"I guess." I watched his hands reach toward another stack of papers. "I can't do this anymore."

"Yeah, well, life gets hard sometimes."

"I know," I whispered, suddenly ashamed.

"Then you should also know that you can't run away from your problems." He picked up a notebook and turned his back on me, retracing his footsteps to his desk. I had been dismissed.

We were the only people in the room now, and yet we were more alone than if we had each been by ourselves.

"Well, I just wanted to tell you good-bye. And ask if I could see Jessie tonight."

"Do what you want."

"Then I'll pick her up this afternoon and bring her back to Bob and Doris's tonight, OK?"

He made no reply.

That afternoon I took Jessie to the mall for our favorite treat: vanilla yogurt with M&Ms sprinkled across the top. We went to a park to play, but Jessie was not the same sprightly little girl I'd taken to parks so many times before; she was more quiet now, and her laughter had lost some of its joy. Later, as we sat in the theater and my sister watched Disney's animated film, *The Fox and the Hound,* I tried to memorize every bit of her: her curls, her eyes, her smile, her little feet tapping against the big theater chair.

When I took her to Bob and Doris's house that night, my father was not there. I knew why. There would be no good-bye.

NINE

Mother's Crusade

Jacque's open letter to her daughter's killer, published in several Central Valley newspapers, hadn't produced any reliable leads for the police. Still, Jacque felt she was finally doing something productive. The *Modesto Bee* continued to post notice of the $6,000 reward. Surely that amount of money would get someone's attention.

Yet Debi had been dead for more than a month. What were the chances of finding her killer now?

Jacque's calls to the Modesto Police Department were usually routed to a public information officer. This family liaison would promise Jacque that the detectives were doing everything they could. "It's early in the investigation. Don't give up hope."

On those occasions when she *did* reach Detectives Vaughn or Grogan, Jacque pled for answers.

"What leads do you have? I need to know you're making progress."

"We're following up on our initial investigation, and we're

looking for further information. But the truth is, there's no word out on the streets."

"Then listen harder!"

Jacque knew someone out there had the answers she needed. Maybe they were afraid to come forward. Or perhaps they were too busy with their own lives to recall a whispered conversation they overheard weeks ago. Jacque had to keep Debi's death in the spotlight. But what could one mother do?

From her home in Minnesota, Jacque surveyed her resources. She and Dennis had spent most all of their savings to build their new home. She had no connections to law enforcement personnel or politicians. What she did have was time. Jacque had retired from over twenty years in the nursing profession and now worked weekends at a local department store. During the rest of the week, she was free to work on Debi's case.

So how do you solve a crime?

Jacque familiarized herself with the vast array of televised crime shows and talk shows spotlighting survivors of violent crime. She began watching these shows religiously, looking for ideas that had helped other families. Parents, siblings, and children would tell their stories of horror and loss, while pictures on the screen showed smiles from happier times. The host—Phil Donahue or Geraldo, someone like that—would always say the same thing: "So, you still have no idea who killed your sister." (It was always said as a statement, not a question.)

The family member in the interview chair would nod from behind a moist tissue.

"But surely the police must suspect somebody?"

This is where the shows would get interesting. Sometimes the family would say that yes, there was a suspect, but they weren't allowed to know who it was. At other times the family would complain that law enforcement had dodged that question altogether, instead reassuring the family that they would be the first to know if there was an arrest.

That made sense to Jacque. She had learned that most murders were committed by someone who knew the victim. In fact, it seemed like random crime against adults was virtually unheard of. A stranger might abduct a child, but by and large, adult crimes resulted from relationships gone bad. So if the perpetrator was someone who knew the victim or a member of the family, then investigators would need to keep all evidence to themselves. They couldn't risk tipping off the murderer.

It seemed to Jacque that the most important thing happening on these daytime talk shows was the solicitation for information. Sally Jesse Raphael would turn to the camera and say, "The Smith family needs your help. If you have any information about what happened to Linda, please call the number on your screen." The toll-free number would appear periodically throughout the show.

Prime-time shows about true crime were similar to their daytime counterparts. However, in addition to interviewing victims' families and friends, shows like *America's Most Wanted* would also interview the investigators involved in the cases. This was particularly helpful to Jacque, as she imagined these other investigations as a blueprint for what must be happening in Debi's case. In her living room, Jacque listened as detectives discussed gathering evidence from the scene and trying to extrapolate possible crime scenarios.

Jacque applied this information to what she knew of Debi's murder. There was no forced entry into the house, which meant that someone had used a key or been allowed into the home by Debi. Jacque had been told there was no sign of a struggle, which further convinced the authorities that Debi knew her assailant. Nothing was missing from the house except Debi's purse and car keys. Two days after the murder, a neighbor had spotted Debi's butterfly key ring in his side yard; the purse, however, had not been recovered. Had the killer been looking for something he knew was in the handbag?

What was in Debi's handbag?

Howie had mentioned the checkbook and credit cards, but police had been watching these accounts, and they showed no activity. That seemed to indicate that there was something else in Debi's purse that the killer may have been after.

Jacque imagined all kinds of scenarios: her daughter had witnessed a crime and jotted down some notes about it to share with the police later. Or some man obsessed with Debi had written her a love letter and given it to her; he had stalked her and killed her, taking the purse and the evidence it contained. These ideas seemed far-fetched at best, but what else did Jacque have to go on?

Jacque learned that another important element of nighttime crime shows was reenactment, in which actors who looked like the people involved would go right to the crime scene and do the same things that led up to the crime. Here was the exact house, or parking lot, or discount store where the crime occurred. Here was a sketch of the perpetrator, or maybe only a description of clothing and mannerisms. Suddenly the whole nation was on a unified manhunt for a tall Caucasian woman named Cindy who had frizzy dye-damaged hair, weighed 140 pounds, and drove a white Toyota Camry with the vanity plate GRLPWR. Or people who ate at the IHOP in Franklin, Tennessee, on the night of September 18 were suddenly trying to recall if they had seen a short Latino guy with sideburns and a zippered fleece jacket.

As she watched the tip line's 800 number light up her television screen, Jacque knew that people watching this same show were reaching for the phone. They were supplying these families with the information they needed to solve the case of their loved one. And they were doing it right now.

This is what I need, thought Jacque. *I need to tell Debi's story to the nation and ask them for help.*

Jacque started keeping a pen and paper on the living room coffee table to jot down ideas and information. Names of producers were listed in the closing credits for these shows. Could she call them directly? Sometimes daytime talk shows actually solicited calls. "Is your child's father denying his paternity?" Well, no, but Jacque still needed to get her daughter's story on the show, and she wrote down the number anyway.

Her first call was to *Unsolved Mysteries.* The operator took her information and told her that a producer would call her back. Producers decided which of the hundreds of cases brought to their attention would be profiled. Jacque sat by the phone for hours, afraid to leave the house, waiting for calls that never came. In the meantime, she began calling other shows.

While her days were full of frenetic energy, Jacque's nights were pure torture. Dennis had resumed his regular flight schedule, and his overnight trips left Jacque alone in the house. The first night he was away, Jacque lay sleepless in the bed. She had stayed up watching BBC America as a diversion, but with the lights off and the house silent, Jacque's thoughts turned toward her daughter's last minutes of life.

Suddenly Jacque heard a noise in the house. Now sitting upright with her senses kicked into overdrive, she strained to hear other sounds. Had she locked all the doors? Of course she had. They had been locked day and night since Debi's murder.

Mackie, her miniature schnauzer, was resting on a pillow by the bed, and although she was eyeing Jacque curiously, the dog was otherwise unperturbed. Certainly she would have sounded a warning if somebody were near the house. It was probably fine. Jacque was just being jittery.

She rolled over and tried to go back to sleep, but now she really was awake, and she needed to use the restroom. Jacque swung her feet to the floor and put on her slippers, reaching for her robe at the foot of the bed. She was still tying the sash around her waist when she reached the bedroom door. She opened it and froze.

The man in the hallway was all dark and shadowy menace. He raised his arm and came at her, and she saw the dull glimmer of the knife in his upstretched hand. Stifling a scream and clutching her throat, Jacque stumbled backward, almost losing her footing.

The man vanished.

Even though she knew he wasn't there, that he had never been there, Jacque slammed the bedroom door and locked it. Then she sat on her bed, pulled Mackie into her lap, and cried until dawn. Her darling, beautiful daughter—how could someone have killed her?

The shadow man became a regular part of Jacque's nighttime terrors, and although she didn't tell anyone about him, her friends noticed the deterioration in Jacque. Cathy Wood started spending the night at Jacque's whenever Dennis was away, but the fear that sudden catastrophe would strike her family or friends left Jacque in severe emotional distress. Finally she made an appointment with a grief counselor, a soft-spoken middle-aged woman who listened as Jacque cried and told her story. Over the next few months, these sessions became a safe place for Jacque to cry piteously or scream at the cruelty of the world—to let go of everything she kept bottled up. As Jacque shared her feelings, the woman responded with both sympathy and honesty. "I can teach you ways to cope with this pain, Jacque, but I can't take it away. It will never go away."

While that might seem a hopeless pronouncement, Jacque recognized the truth of the woman's statement and appreciated her candor. Years later Jacque would tell other grieving mothers the same thing: "Nothing will ever take your pain away. No matter how long ago your child died, it's like it just happened. It always just happened. But you can survive with that pain."

Jacque's best reprieve came from working at the department store on the weekends, where she could experience an anonymous normalcy. She didn't have to be the mother whose daughter was murdered; instead, she was the friendly woman who offered shoppers a little spritz of perfume. Jacque listened as customers and employees discussed grandchildren's exploits or the latest rumors coming out of Hollywood. These moments were reminders that life was still happening all around her, even if she no longer felt a part of it.

Months dragged by with no break in Debi's case. Jacque continued to call television shows every day, and by now she was developing relationships with the voices on the other end of the phone. She made notes of the information she learned—who was a parent, who had pets. The next time she called, Jacque made sure to incorporate that information into the conversation. "Oh, Wanda, hi. It's Jacque MacDonald again. How's your son's cold this week?" The technique didn't make the show's producers return her calls, but Jacque was being remembered by *somebody* there. Maybe one day that would give her an advantage.

Jacque knew she was competing with hundreds of other grieving parents, just as she knew that only her determination would put Debi's story on the TV screen of that one person who could solve the case. Her fight on Debi's behalf was the most important thing she had ever done. She was going to get her daughter on these shows. Period.

She made her calls and shared some rare smiles with the women at work, but inside Jacque was miserable. The first holiday season without Debi was horrible, and Jacque again slipped into depression. Dennis sat across from his wife at the kitchen table and watched her distractedly shoving food around her plate with a fork. Finally he cleared his throat. "I think we should move back to California."

Jacque looked up at him. "You mean, sell the house?"

"Why not?"

"Because it's what we both wanted." She bit her lip. What she wasn't saying was that they would lose a lot of money on the property if they sold now.

Dennis seemed to read her thoughts. "What's money?" he said with a tender smile. "Family is the important thing. You need to be with Karen. And Jessica needs her gran."

Tears swelled in Jacque's eyes, and she thanked God once again for the man sitting across the table from her. They were finally living the life they had envisioned, but now Dennis was willing to let it go. He was offering her everything he had hoped for, just as easily as he had offered her a cold glass of orange juice on the hot summer day they met.

In February of 1989, almost one year after Debi's death, Jacque and Dennis sold the house of their dreams and moved into a modest duplex that Karen had secured for them. It was small but clean, located on University Avenue in Merced and only minutes from Karen's house.

The area had changed a lot in the time she'd been gone. When Jacque and Dennis had moved away in 1980, Merced was an unhurried place with country music drifting out of truck windows and open fields dotting the town. Now, nine years later, Jacque barely recognized the place. New shopping centers obscured or replaced old landmarks. The streets bustled with new cars, new people, and new housing developments. However, as she wandered through the Merced Mall one morning, she was thrilled to see a familiar sight: See's Candies. "Oh, thank God!" she said, and laughed at herself immediately. Other women popped antidepressants; Jacque ate truffles.

Karen was very happy to have her mother home, and she frequently picked up Jessie and brought her, along with her daughter Megan, to visit their gran. At lunchtime Jacque would often meet Karen at a restaurant near Karen's work, where the women would recount their memories of Debi.

"Do you remember when Debi and I were studying for first communion? She would *not* stop talking. The sisters were at their wits end."

Jacque laughed. "I remember. She was always saying whatever was on her mind—"

"—and it didn't matter if you were wearing a habit or not, she was still going to say it!" Karen laughed.

"Hi, I hate to interrupt you ladies—" It was the waitress, a pen poised over her order pad expectantly.

"Oh, that's OK," Jacque answered with a smile. "We were just talking about my other daughter. She was murdered last year."

"Mom!" Karen murmured.

"What?" Jacque turned to the startled waitress and gestured toward her daughter. "She hates it when I tell people about her sister."

"I'm so sorry," the waitress said, at a complete loss.

"Well, her name was Debi Whitlock, and she lived in Modesto. Somebody cut her throat while her daughter was asleep in the next room."

The waitress's eyes went wide. "Oh my gosh. I remember that case. That was horrible. It was her husband, right?"

"No, he was at a bachelor party and found her when he came home." This was the truth as Jacque knew it, both from the police and from her son-in-law. "They still don't know who killed her, so if you hear anything about it, please notify the police."

"Of course I will," the waitress said kindly.

After Jacque and Karen gave their order and the waitress walked away, Karen turned to her mother. "Mom! Do you have to tell everybody about it?"

"Yes! If we don't remember, how can we ask others to?"

Karen looked at her mother. She loved the woman dearly, but sometimes she wished they could be together without the cloud of Debi's murder hanging quite so heavily over them. Instead, whenever Karen felt the sun shine in her mother's company, her mom launched into a rain dance.

Karen sighed. "So, have you had any luck with your phone calls?"

"No, not to television. But I think the *San Francisco Chronicle* is going to do the story for the first anniversary. And national magazines read big papers like that to see if there's anything they want to cover."

Jacque looked around at the other diners. "Don't you ever look at the people around you and wonder, Is *he* the one?"

It took Karen a moment to catch up with her mother's train of thought. Then she, too, looked around. "No. I guess I still believe it was someone she knew."

"Me, too. But what if it's somebody *we* wouldn't recognize? Think about how many people Debi must have known that we don't. Think of how often she might have come to this very restaurant. Think of how many people here she may have talked to."

"I try not to think about it too much, Mom," Karen said

pointedly. "I miss Debi so much that I would spend all my time crying. But I can't. I am a wife and a mother. I have people who need me."

Jacque hadn't heard her; she was still eyeing the other diners. "I wonder about people all the time. I pass by people in the mall or the grocery store, and I think, *Did you kill my daughter? Or do you know who did?*" Jacque ran her thumb across the condensation on the outside of her water glass. "I know it bothers you, but that's why I talk about her all the time and remind people about her. Someday, someone is going to get so tired of me that they give us the answers we need, just to shut me up."

Now that she had moved back to Merced, Jacque realized she was the public liaison for Debi's case. Somebody had to do the job, because she was convinced the answer was out there, in the public. And while she may be inexperienced at networking, Jacque was not without role models. In fact, she need look no farther than her father.

Robert O'Brien was the manager of a small theater troupe that performed in and around London. Her mother, Violet, was the company's lead actress, and her parents traveled from town to town. Her father fought successfully for theater space in a crowded market, primarily because he was brilliant at networking. Jacque often tagged along as he gained backstage access to almost every theater in London and its surrounding towns. She rubbed shoulders with some of Britain's most famous theatrical talents and was completely nonplussed. Didn't all fathers receive letters from Charlie Chaplin and Danny Kaye? Didn't every little girl drink soda at the notorious Windmill Club while her father talked business with the manager?

Robert and Violet O'Brien had succeeded at doing the one thing they most believed in. It took patience, determination, and a thick skin when it came to setbacks. But mostly it took networking. And while they had sheltered her from the crazy ups and downs of their own careers, they nonetheless gave their daughter an education she would one day need in order to win the biggest fight of her life: keeping her daughter's mysterious murder in the spotlight until the case was solved.

Considering her task with this renewed perspective, the answer became perfectly clear. First she needed a local ally.

Daryl Farnsworth had been a crime reporter for eight years with the area's largest daily newspaper, the *Modesto Bee.* Jacque had spoken to him on a couple of occasions, and she had a hunch that this man would become one of Debi's champions. When they talked the previous summer about Jacque's letter to Debi's killer, Jacque had sensed in Daryl a love of family and justice. Now, in a letter dated March 1989, Jacque pled her case:

Dear Mr. Farnsworth,

> *I hope you remember me, the mother of Debi Whitlock. You were kind enough to print my letter to her killer in the [Modesto Bee]. I believe it came out on Father's Day '88. It will be 1 yr on the 25th since we lost Deb. The worst [year] of our lives . . . No one thinks of the aftermath of murder on the remaining family members.*

> *Mr. F, recently our [Minnesota] news media did an [update] on unsolved murders. Would you consider doing such an article? Unless I can get some newspaper and media coverage, people [will] forget, and I don't want her murder to be unsolved . . .*

> *You know, there are so many programs about the penal system and rehabilitation of prisoners and commuting sen-*

tences. I ask you . . . who will commute ours? Who will give
us back the happiness that only Debi could give us? I can't
find an answer. Can you?

Jacque MacDonald

Her intuition paid off. Daryl Farnsworth wrote an article re-
prising several unsolved homicides in Modesto, including Debi's.
More importantly, he had a genuine sympathy for victims of violent crimes. He had worked crime for over a decade already, and
instead of becoming calloused to the heartbreak around him,
Daryl Farnsworth was both touched and inspired by the families
that tried to fight back. He became a friend and an advocate for
Jacque's efforts.

Jacque used Daryl's first article to contact larger papers, and
she soon found other journalists willing to recap the murder.
Now, as she made her phone calls to television shows, she mentioned the current news articles as proof that Debi's story was still
generating interest.

One day, as Jacque sat in front of her telephone calling her
same list of phone numbers, she got the break she'd been waiting
for. She had been given yet another phone number, supposedly
belonging to a woman connected with an evening crime show.
When Jacque told the woman her reason for calling, the other
woman seemed completely mystified. "I'm not sure what I can do
for you, Mrs. MacDonald. I'm sorry about your daughter, but I
don't have a say in who gets on any show."

The frustration in Jacque's voice was evident. "Listen, they
gave me your number. I've talked to about twenty people so far,
and nobody can help me." And then, to prove it, Jacque rattled off
a list of the names and dates of her phone calls.

The woman on the phone was silent for a moment. "They've really given you the runaround, haven't they?" She sounded genuinely compassionate.

"Please," said Jacque, her anger spent. "I don't know what else to do."

The woman seemed to consider. "I don't know what I can do, but let me see if I can help you. I have a friend who works over at the *Sally Jesse Raphael* show. I'll call her. And I promise, I really will call you back."

She didn't know it yet, but Jacque had finally found someone who kept her promise.

Jacque took a bouquet of daffodils to Debi's grave on the anniversary of the murder. She came here often to feel close to her daughter and to bolster her own resolve. Today she was pleased to see that several people had already visited, and she bent to rearrange the assorted bouquets and make room for her own. A small, handwritten note fell from a grouping of violets.

"You would still be alive today if you hadn't married him."

Jacque crumpled the unsigned note and put it in her pocket.

Once Jacque was promised a spot on a future national show, local news and crime shows were very accommodating about booking her as a guest. Debi's murder offered several morbidly tantalizing elements: a woman slain, a little girl sleeping undisturbed nearby, no sign of struggle, no suspects. This was the most baffling homicide to hit the Modesto area in a long time. Who cared whether Jacque MacDonald gave a decent interview or not?

People Are Talking was broadcast from KPIX on the corner of Battery and Vallejo Streets in San Francisco. Jacque would be allowed to speak only briefly from the audience. "You'll have less than a minute," an assistant told her. During the taping of the show Jacque stood up in the small, dark studio and quickly gave the facts of the case. The host asked a few follow-up questions and reiterated the family's request for information. There were no calls from the appearance, but it was a foot in a door Jacque was determined to bust open.

In the spring of 1989, Jacque boarded a plane to go film an episode of the *Sally Jesse Raphael* show. She had flown from Minnesota to California for Debi's funeral at a time when her shock and grief had combined to trump her claustrophobia. Now, however, Jacque was only too aware of her fear of flying. But she had to do this for Debi. There was no way around it. "I am going to get on that plane," Jacque told Dennis. "I'll wait until it's all over, and *then* I'll have a breakdown."

This became Jacque's mantra.

The limousine driver delivered her to the studio early the next morning, and she made her way to a waiting area called the Green Room. Today's show featured four parents, each of whom had lost a child to violent and unsolved crime. Some of the other parents were old pros at these television appearances. They introduced themselves and tried to abate Jacque's nervousness, but mostly they swapped stories of other shows. Jacque felt shy about interrupting, but the opportunity was too important. "Pardon me, but if you have any contacts at those shows, I wish you'd give me their names."

Of all the people she'd asked for assistance, other families of homicide victims were the most helpful and supportive. As parents around the room began jotting down names and looking up phone numbers in their address books, Jacque realized that she was now a member of a close-knit society. The cost of membership was devastating, but fealty within the group was incredible.

Jacque's tragedy was the most recent of all the guests', and she still carried a frightened disbelief in her eyes. Up on the stage among the other panelists, Jacque looked small and nervous. She spoke quietly as she told Debi's story and answered Raphael's follow-up questions.

"She was just found dead in the hallway in her sweats," Jacque whispered, willing it to be true. She smiled slightly as a memory came to her. "I used to tease her about that. I told her she should buy a pretty nightie."

Viewers could tell, watching this small bereaved mother, that the ghost of those conversations with her daughter cut through Jacque's nervousness and made the moment, and her purpose, suddenly real. She blinked back tears and straightened herself in the chair. Her gaze swept the audience and cameras. These would be the arenas in which she would conquer her own fears and stalk the shadow of her daughter's killer. With new resolve, Jacque looked pointedly at the host. "One day Jessie will come to me and say, 'Well, Gran, what did *you* do to find my mum's killer?'" Jacque had already determined her answer: everything she could.

Sally Jesse Raphael seemed to sense Jacque's increased resolve and, like any talk show host worth her salt, she prodded Jacque gently. Had the police offered any hope that the investigation was still productive?

Jacque had heard there was "some physical evidence" at the scene, but she was afraid to ask too many questions. "I feel in my heart Debi knew her assailant, and what if [the police] tell me something, and I say too much to the wrong person?"

When Raphael opened the show for audience participation, most of the questions were directed at the other guests. Eventually, a woman in a bright red skirt and jacket raised her hand. Sally walked toward her, and the woman addressed a question to

NO ROOM FOR DOUBT   157

Jacque. "How far away from home was your son-in-law's bachelor party? What are the chances that he could have gotten back to
the home while your daughter was sleeping? He could have gotten
into the home, out of the home, completely unnoticed!" The
woman's excitement was growing, and the folks around her nodded. "I would be keeping my eyes on him and the kind of life he's
leading afterward."

"No." Jacque shook her head emphatically. "The police did
interrogate him, because he told me how he felt being interro-
gated. He kept thinking, *I know they have to do this to me, but I
just found my wife dead*."

Feedback from this first show offered nothing to further the
case, but it did a world of good for Jacque. Now she knew it could
be done. More importantly, she realized that publicity begets publicity. Using her growing network of connections, she finally got a
call from the national crime show *Missing: Reward*. Immediately
after setting up an interview with one of the show's producers,
Jacque called Daryl at the *Modesto Bee* as well as an editor for
the *Merced Sun-Star*. Both newspapers featured stories about the
upcoming show and used their contacts with local television stations to get coverage for Jacque there as well. "Local Mother
Takes Story of Daughter's Murder to the Nation." Jacque was finally in motion.

Harold Whitlock agreed to be interviewed on the national evening crime show, *Missing: Reward*, and to allow the crew to
shoot a reenactment at the house. Throughout her years of searching, Howie would never refuse to help Jacque, even though it
meant putting himself in the spotlight again and again.

Jacque stayed at the house all day and watched the replay of events during Debi's last night alive. The actors bore a passing resemblance to Harold and Debi, and to see the woman playing her daughter attacked was almost more than she could stand.

Eventually the show would feature footage of interviews with a few police officers as well as Debi's widower, boss, sister, and mother. During Jacque's portions of the show, the close observer would notice her increasing comfort in front of the camera. She was beginning to demonstrate her potential as an impassioned, well-spoken mouthpiece for victims' families.

Merced Sun-Star reporter Rose Certini came to Jacque's house to watch filming for *Missing: Reward* and noted with surprise that Jacque was "a reluctant subject, even though she actively seeks shows to appear on."

Ms. Certini didn't know the half of it. Jacque would get physically ill after every interview, sometimes spending the entirety of the next week in bed. During these times, Jacque's friends would rally around her.

Two days after the *Missing: Reward* team left, Katrina Lundberg came to Jacque's house. Dennis was flying overseas, and Katrina found Jacque lying in the guest room, which looked like a shrine to Debi. Everything was blue: the walls, the curtains, the bedding. Angel figurines and family photographs cluttered the dresser and shelves. It was a room of comfort as well as incredible sadness, offering Jacque a host of memories she needed but almost couldn't bear.

"Jacque, you're not answering the phone," Katrina chided.

The grieving mother's voice was muffled under the blue comforter. "I can't."

Katrina patted her friend's shoulder. "Have you eaten today?"

Five minutes later, Katrina was back in the room bearing a

tray with the same meal Jacque had brought to invalids in Hay-maid's Hospital years ago: warm milk and bread. Katrina set the tray next to the bed. "Come on, Jac. You have to eat." She watched Jacque squirm into a sitting position. "By the way, there was a note taped to the milk."

Jacque smiled for the first time. "Dennis. He always leaves me little love notes around the house."

Katrina put the tray across Jacque's lap. "If you ever get tired of him, I'll take him."

Jacque chuckled. "Sorry, darling. I'm keeping him."

Tossing some stuffed bears out of a nearby chair, Katrina sat down and started flipping through Jacque's telephone log. "Look at these calls! You're getting to be a pro at this."

"I never wanted to be a pro at this. I'd much rather go back to my quiet life."

"But you're a fighter now, Jac," Katrina said, trying to rally her friend. "You can do this."

"I have to do this. Debi would do it for me."

Every year on the anniversary of Debi's death, Jacque would come up with a new idea to garner media attention for Debi's case. She called it her "jump start." Like a New Year's Day, Jacque's calendar now began on March 25. And every year, Daryl Farnsworth would write another article for the *Modesto Bee,* re-capping the murder: "Mother Slain while 3-Year-Old Sleeps Be-hind a Closed Door Only 4 Feet Away. No Suspects. Reward Available." Mike Delacruz often wrote a corresponding article in the *Merced Sun-Star.*

Jacque continued to cultivate relationships with people in tele-vision and print media. She found out about other Brits working in the media and called on them, realizing that in this industry, like the military bases she'd lived on a lifetime ago, the British kept up with one another. When a producer or assistant would comment on Jacque's accent, she would send them teas and dainty cups. If the producer was a parent or grandparent, Jacque sent them pictures of Debi holding her baby daughter in her arms. If the contact showed any spiritual leanings, Jacque sent lapel pins in the shape of angels.

"I'm not fighting fair, and I don't care," she told her daughter, Karen. "And I believe your sister is helping me. Debi wants justice, and she's going to help me get it."

Karen smiled sadly. "I hope you're right, Mom."

TEN

Trial by Reenactment

Debi's episode of *Missing: Reward* aired almost two years after her death. The residents of Modesto watched the show with great interest. There had been a lot of local news coverage immediately following the slaying, and even more speculation. Now it appeared an unbiased, reputable outside source had sifted through all the facts and assembled the truth. That's what the people of Modesto tuned in to see: the truth.

Few local residents had met Jacque MacDonald, but she was obviously a loving and devoted mother, and she spoke proudly on the television show of her daughter's many accomplishments. Even Debi's boss, Steve Bloomberg, talked about what a good person she was.

Those who loved Debi tried to express what it was like to live in the wake of an unsolved violent crime. "You think that when you wake up the next morning, it will just be a nightmare," Jacque said, dabbing her eyes. "But you wake up, and it's still there. And it's still a nightmare."

Harold Whitlock's interview was partly used as a voice-over during the show's reenactment of Debi's last night. He explained that he'd been at an all-night bachelor party and had come home at about 5:15 a.m. to find Debi dead. "I remember reaching out, touching her cheek, feeling how cold she was. I remember thinking that it wasn't really happening. It's like your mind goes numb. You deal with it from somewhere else."

Debi's widower seemed thoughtful but not distraught. Shouldn't he be shedding tears like Debi's mother and sister?

The reenactment showed an actor appraising with mild concern the body of his dead wife on the floor. Together, the staid reenactment and the matter-of-fact interview combined to form a composite of a man who did not feel his wife's loss deeply at all.

It was trial by reenactment.

Captain David J. Scott of the Modesto Police Department insisted no one had been cleared from the suspect list, adding, "It was a friend or someone she knew." He also said there was "no evidence of molestation or rape."

Any sparks of doubt about Debi's husband were fanned into flame during the next segment. Jacque shared how particularly horrible her daughter's death was because Debi had always hated anyone touching her throat. Eyes wide with terror, Jacque subconsciously touched her throat as she spoke, empathizing with her daughter. Then Harold Whitlock was back on the screen. "The only other phobia she had—things that she really hated or was afraid of—was knives. You know, she didn't like to cut vegetables for salad because she was afraid she'd cut herself." Then he chuckled. Sure, it was without humor, but it was a chuckle nonetheless. "And I can't—It's like a horrible, horrible joke, or some macabre sense of humor, that Destiny had, that this had to happen to her." Harold smiled bitterly.

Just like his wan smile to a friend at Debi's funeral, this particular moment, where it appeared Whitlock saw the joke in his wife's death when no one else did, was recorded and used against him time and again.

While actresses reenacted Debi's last night, Harold explained that his older daughter and a friend came to the house. "Angela, when she went back to kiss Jessica good night in her room, which is adjoining our room—she told me later that at that time she heard someone back there and didn't really think anything about that because [Debi had told her] I was back in the bed asleep. And it is certainly a point that bothers me. It bothers all of us."

Stacy Keach, the show's host, listed other bothersome factors: Debi's lapsed life insurance, her recent discussions with her father and sister (but not her husband) about her funeral arrangements, and her impending divorce from Harold Whitlock.

Viewers no doubt wondered if Debi believed her husband might kill her, at least in part for the insurance money. And if that was true, why didn't she tell her family? Jacque's answer to that question was on the screen seconds later: "Debi would never tell you anything about her personal life, so as far as we knew, everything was all right."

Although Harold Whitlock had an alibi for the time of the murder, Captain Scott reiterated that "*everyone* is a suspect yet. Ummmm, and I say that they may not individually be suspects, but there's a possibility that . . . people may have *hired* people to do this, and we have not discounted *anyone* at this point."

From my mother's house in Virginia I watched the show with morbid fascination. My father had told me that Jacque had lined up a crime show to profile Debi's case, and while he had refused to give them my contact information, he had agreed to cooperate with their efforts. Watching him on the screen now, I felt he had made a huge mistake. I knew my father had been truly devastated by Debi's death. Further, the way he was talking about it was perfectly normal for him. But that didn't come across in the show. Instead, he seemed detached and, God forbid, vaguely amused by the violence perpetrated against Debi.

I was not surprised about the divorce papers found in Debi's desk, but I was horrified that the information had been broadcast. After all, I believed it had nothing to do with Debi's murder. I had been in the house when Debi told my father she was through with the marriage, and if he was going to become violent, I knew it would have been that night.

It was early January 1988. Jessie and I were in the den watching *Lady and the Tramp* while Debi was in the back of the house picking out her clothes for the next day. Jessie and I had just finished dinner, and I was wondering if Debi would be getting her ready for bed of if I should.

My father came in, poked his head into the room to say hello, and headed back to the bedroom. I returned my attention to the movie.

Before long, I heard the sound of arguing in the master bedroom. Well, I wouldn't be taking Jessie back there right now. The argument escalated, and someone slammed the bedroom door closed. I glanced at my sister, hoping she would stay engrossed in the movie.

"Lady and the Tramp are sharing some spaghetti, aren't they?" I asked with enthusiasm.

"Den dey kiss!" Jessie giggled.

My father was yelling now, something I hadn't heard since his drunken nights in my mother's foyer. Jessie heard him and looked up at me.

"Oh, you're right!" I said, motioning toward the television. "Look! They're getting ready to kiss!"

Debi was saying something in a soothing voice, but it didn't defuse the situation. "Who's Steve?" my father shouted. "You're sleeping with him, aren't you? Tell me! Tell me!"

The bedroom door opened, and my father stomped through the den. He opened a cabinet, grabbed a stack of papers, and stomped out again.

"Daddy?" Jessie asked.

I put my arm around her and pulled her onto my lap.

"It'll be OK, honey," I said. "Sometimes grown-ups just—"

Another door slammed and locked. Debi's voice came from the hallway. "Harold? Open the door."

My father was in the front bathroom. "You lied to me!" he bellowed, his hurt and rage echoing off the tile. "Liar!"

Debi's voice was still calm. "Harold? Don't act like this. Open the door."

"How dare you tell me you love me! Liar! Do you tell *Steve* you love him?"

Jessie slipped her hand into mine. What was I supposed to do?

There was silence, then I heard Debi talking on the phone in the master bedroom. I couldn't hear what she was saying.

"Sissy?"

"Honey, it's time for us to go." I stood uncertainly. We could go to my grandmother's house. Should I take clothes for Jessie? That would mean walking to her room in the back of the house. I didn't want to go back there. Instead, I looked around for a piece of paper I could write a note on.

Carrying Jessie on my hip, I walked toward the kitchen, passing the entrance to the hallway en route. Debi was standing by the bathroom door, her ear pressed to the wood.

"Harold? It doesn't have to be like this. Can't we just talk?"

No answer.

She sniffed. Was she crying? "What are you doing in there? Open the door. Open the door right now!"

Oh my God. Was my father killing himself? Was he unconscious? I tried to think about what was in the front bathroom. My razor. A curling iron with a long electrical cord.

Debi must have been thinking along the same lines. Losing her composure, she pounded on the door. "Let me in! Harold? Let me in right now!"

"Go away!"

So he wasn't dead. I needed to get Jessie out of here. "Right," I said aloud. I sat her on the bar while I wrote a hasty note. "*Took JJ to Nana's*," I began, but my writing was so shaky that the words were practically illegible.

Suddenly Bob Kramer barged in through the kitchen door. "Where is he?"

I pointed.

"Bob?" Debi called from the hallway. "Get the girls out of here!"

He scooped my sister off the counter before I could protest, then looked at me. "You shouldn't be here," he said kindly. "Come on over to the house."

"I'm going to my grandmother's," I said. I needed to be somewhere comforting. And I needed my sister with me.

"OK," he said. He poked his head around the bar to look at Debi. "You gonna be OK? You want me to talk to him?"

"Just take JJ," she said. "I've got it under control."

The thing about Debi was that she did have it under control. Sure, her marriage was in the toilet, and her husband was behind a locked door doing God knows what, but Debi remained calm. Eventually he would come out, and they would talk, and the necessary plans would be made. Face the problem, find a solution. That was Debi.

I found out the next day that my father had burned their wedding pictures on the bathroom linoleum. He was mad and felt betrayed and disappointed, but he didn't resort to physical violence. He wasn't that kind of person.

After that night, my father began sleeping on the couch. Even on the nights Debi was away, he still would not sleep in the bed they had shared.

Then he took his girlfriend into that bed.

Then Debi came back.

Then she told me they were working things out.

Then she told me my father was home when he wasn't, but *someone really had been back there.*

Then she was murdered.

And now a television show was encouraging the nation to believe my father was her killer.

Kelli called me shortly after the show aired. As my best friend, she had known all about Dad and Debi's marriage problems, so she was not surprised by the news that Debi had gone so far as to prepare divorce papers. However, something else was bothering her. "It was weird to see us on television. Or some version of us."

I thought back to the show. During the reenactment, the actress playing Debi had opened the door to reveal two teenage girls. The one playing me had highly moussed hair, protruding front teeth, and white pants so tight she could hardly walk. The show's Kelli had oversized hair and breasts, and was inexplicably ensconced in bib overalls and a plaid flannel shirt.

"It was horrible," I agreed. "We looked like Lumberjack Barbie and the Bucktoothed Whore."

"No, no," Kelli said. "I mean, it was freaky to see them talking to her, in the same kitchen, saying the same words. It—it bothered me a lot, really. I try not to think about that night at all."

I, too, had been disturbed by the show. "I guess I was more bothered by the picture of Debi at the end."

The final shot of Debi, the one they showed while pleading for information and announcing the reward, showed Debi standing in the living room and smiling shyly toward the camera. It was a private moment. It was a smile for me.

An amateur photographer, I constantly walked through the house taking pictures. That day the late autumn sun was shining brightly through the sliding glass door in the den, and I was on the floor in front of my sister, trying to capture the way sunbeams played in her curls.

Debi walked into the room to put something away in a cabinet, then stopped to watch me. "Jeez. Take a few pictures, why don't you?"

I was embarrassed, but only for a second. Then I turned the camera on Debi, who was notoriously camera shy. She turned away from me, laughing, as I stood and walked toward her, clicking away. The camera caught her return smile, her lovely eyes twinkling and her face framed by the short hair she had favored since her pregnancy.

I had sent Jacque a copy of the picture shortly after Debi's murder, and now it was the official image of Debi used again and again on television, posters, and eventually billboards. Debi smiling at me, standing in front of the same door that her murderer would walk through five months later.

It occurred to me now that nothing about our lives was private anymore. It was all tagged as evidence and presented to the jury of public opinion, awaiting their judgment.

By the time *Missing: Reward* aired, Jerry Ortega had been living in the Whitlock house for several months. Debi's murder came at a particularly difficult time in Jerry's life. He and his wife were in the process of separating, and since Howie was staying with

Bob and Doris Kramer, he offered Jerry the use of the house. Jerry gratefully accepted.

A few months later, Howie and Jessica moved back in, and the three of them became housemates. It was a comfortable arrangement in uncomfortable times, and the men provided each other comfort and friendship at the lowest point in either of their lives.

Jerry often wouldn't arrive home until after he had closed the bar at 1 a.m., and more likely than not, he'd find Howie sitting in his chair in the living room with a novel. Jerry would go to sleep and wake up hours later to find his friend in the same position.

Jerry knew about the upcoming episode of *Missing: Reward*. The producers had filmed the interviews and reenactment inside the house, and Jerry made himself scarce. He saw the toll filming was taking on his friend and suggested that Howie change his mind. "This is obviously hell for you. Why don't you just back out?"

He just shook his head sadly. "I've got to do this for Debi's mom. And besides, what if it does some good? What if it actually makes a difference in the case?"

Jerry admired his friend's commitment to do whatever he could for Debi's mother, but he watched with anger as the situation turned against Howie. The show had been a fiasco, casting doubt on his friend and reaffirming local suspicion that Howie had been involved in Debi's death. They had stopped answering the phone and disconnected the answering machine due to all the hateful crank calls, and now they were waiting for the phone company to assign them an unlisted number.

Harold usually avoided going out in public except to Ortega's. Jerry had laid down the law with his staff: Howie was off limits. They could be nice to him, or they could stay the hell away from him. Ortega's had always been Howie's refuge, and damned if that was going to change now. Oh sure, one of the bartenders had come up to Jerry only that week, telling him to wake up and accept his friend's guilt. Jerry's hot temper burned white, and he suddenly found himself in a stillness like the eye of a storm. He looked levelly at the bartender. "Look, I've let you have your say, and I want to make one thing absolutely clear: I'm not going to fire you for this." The guy looked relieved as Jerry clapped a hand amicably on his shoulder. "But the next time you mess up, you're gone. It's going to happen. Break a dish, you're fired. Show up late, you're fired. Forget your uniform, you're fired. Understand?" Jerry gave the guy another quick pat and smiled as the guy struggled to make sense of the words. Then Jerry walked away, the waitstaff parting silently in front of him and avoiding his eyes.

But tonight Jerry wanted to try a new Italian café that had recently opened near the mall, and Howie had agreed. And almost as soon as they walked in, Jerry knew he had made a mistake. As he, Howie, and Jessie followed the hostess to their seats, the normal restaurant chatter turned to whispers.

"How's this?" the hostess asked, showing them to a centrally located table for four.

Jerry scanned the room and saw a booth to the side. "How about over there?"

"No, this is fine," Howie said, reaching toward a chair.

Jerry glanced around. "It's a little chilly here."

"It'll be chilly over there, too."

They all sat down, and Jerry turned to talk animatedly to Jessie about the kids' menu items, but his ears were buzzing with the whispers in the room. The waitress came, took their drink orders, and left.

"My friend," Jerry said quietly, "I am a fool."

"What's a fool?" Jessie asked, her little voice abnormally loud in the too-quiet of the restaurant.

Howie smiled at her. "It's the man who tells jokes for the king. Do you think Uncle Jerry could do that?"

She wrinkled her nose. "I guess so. He's funny."

"Hey," Jerry laughed. "I don't have to wear any tacky outfits, do I?"

Howie took a breath and began to speak, then shook his head. "Nah. Too easy." He gestured at Jerry's tropical shirt.

Jerry looked offended. "Hey, now, don't mess with the shirt." He turned to Jessie. "Don't you think this shirt is classy?"

"It's pretty," Jessie said, grinning. She knew they were playing a game.

"It *is* pretty," said her daddy. "And you should see the matching hat with the little bells on it."

Later that night, Jerry stayed close to Howie as his friend read a good night story to Jessie. The little girl slipped off her father's lap to play with her mother's Barbies and eventually left the room, unnoticed for the moment by the two men. Howie, his eyes intent on the page in front of him, continued to read with conviction, his voice changing for each character and the lines delivered with maximum drama. For a moment, Jerry felt like the story was more real than the nightmare in which they were all trapped.

Howie's voice had stopped. Jerry looked up suddenly. "What?"

"I said, at this point I'm only reading for your sake." Howie smiled, his chin resting against his hand.

"What? You got a problem with that?"

Howie chuckled. "Ortega, I'm sitting here reading *The Three Little Pigs* to a thirty-five-year-old Mexican guy. I feel like an idiot."

"Yeah, but I'm into it! Jessie don't know what she's missing! And besides, if you stop now, I'll never know if the wolf gets a BLT for lunch."

Howie snickered. He picked up the book, flipped a couple of pages, and cleared his throat. Then, in a voice of full-bodied urgency he said, "Just then, a messenger arrived with an urgent Candygram. It seems that the pigs' cousin, Porky, was being held under suspicion of taking indecent liberties with Mary's Little Lamb."

Jerry leaned back in his chair, clasping his hands behind his head and stretching his legs out in front of him. "Now we're cooking."

Howie laughed. A real laugh. Jerry held his serious expression as long as he could, and then he was laughing, too. Laughing like the old times, like Jerry and Howie had laughed hundreds of times before. And for a minute, the fantasy of a predetermined happy ending seemed almost within reach.

ELEVEN

Fresh Blood

Detective Bill Grogan had made a personal commitment to bring Debi's killer to justice, but it wasn't happening. Coworkers noted that he was dispirited and surly—and very honest about his frustration with the case. For a good cop with great luck, the blow of having the case unsolved for so long was unbearable. Worse yet were Jacque's weekly calls to the precinct. And if Jacque wasn't calling, it was some reporter Jacque had convinced to profile the case. They all asked the same question: why hadn't Debi Whitlock's killer been apprehended?

Grogan had agreed to cooperate as much as possible, but giving the same interview over and over again wasn't accomplishing anything. He needed a break in the case if it was going to move forward. Maybe all the media exposure would eventually net some answers. Or maybe each profile of the case would only continue to bring every nut out of the forest and into Bill Grogan's office.

Meanwhile, Detective Ray Taylor was no longer the new

rookie. An amiable family man with a neat appearance and a penchant for books, his coworkers had to admit he was a good and dedicated cop. But what made the homicide team groan was his unflagging enthusiasm. Here was a guy who logged a full day at the office, rode his bicycle home, took his daughters to karate, enjoyed dinner with his wife, and then somehow found the energy to spend a few hours furthering his education. He paid his own way to weekend seminars on witness interview techniques, weaponry, and the relatively new field of criminal profiling. Then he'd come in the next day and say something like, "Guess what I just learned? We should overhaul our methods immediately!"

To the long-timers on the force, Ray Taylor was a well-intentioned nightmare.

More than that, he was unquestionably good at what he did. As a certified blood spatter expert, Taylor could walk up to a detective's desk, look at a few pictures, and start spouting out impact and trajectory ratios for the scene. At a live scene, he would stand quietly tuning out conversations about possible scenarios, then clear his throat and say, "Here's what happened." And sure enough, the guy was almost always right. It could be pretty damn irritating.

One of the bees currently in Taylor's bonnet was the haphazard way in which crime scenes were managed. Rotating CSMs meant no uniformity in the department as far as the way scenes were processed and recorded. Each detective had his own way of doling out responsibility at the scene. No one person was in charge of, say, fingerprinting or collecting weapons. Sure, those things got done, but Taylor argued they could be done far more efficiently with what would eventually become known as a Crime Scene Investigation (CSI) Unit. In 1989, Taylor became the Modesto Police Department's one and only homicide crime scene manager. And soon, Debi Whitlock's murder would be the primary instigator for founding the department's CSI Unit.

This was the situation when, in October of 1989, Jacque went to the chief of police. Sitting across from him and feeling small but determined, she laid out her case. "I'm not saying Detective Grogan hasn't tried to find my daughter's killer, but the man doesn't speak!"

The chief didn't dare grin, but everyone knew Grogan was notoriously quiet.

"So I'm telling you right now, I want a woman on the case."

"Mrs. MacDonald, I don't have a female officer in homicide with the seniority to take over your daughter's case right now."

Jacque would not be deterred. "Then give the case to somebody else! Somebody who will talk with me! I've moved to California, I've wiped out my savings account, I've ruined my health, all to work on Debi's case—" Jacque saw the chief draw a breath to interrupt "—and I know I can't have access to all of your information. I'm not asking for that! But I need someone who will work with me. Somebody who can carry on a bloody conversation!" She caught her breath, regaining her composure. "I'm sorry, but if Detective Grogan was going to solve this, it would be solved. It's time for a change, for a lot of reasons. I'm begging you."

The chief was not an unsympathetic man. He tapped a pen on his blotter, studying the woman across from him. Jacque MacDonald was articulate, photogenic, and passionate, and the press had started to latch onto her. In her appearances on local television and radio shows, she had always been complimentary of the department.

"Mrs. MacDonald, I want you to know that I hear what you're saying. And I'm going to make every effort to fix this for you."

Jacque looked relieved. "Thank you. I'm not trying to be a bother."

"I know this is hard for you."

"It's hell. Just like it is for so many other people. And I know you're doing what you can. But I also know that the killer is out there. And this department is going to find him. You have to. That's all there is to it."

The chief didn't know if her words were more of an encouraging pat or an insistent shove, but his hand was already dialing the commander of Investigative Services before Jacque had time to reach the end of his hallway.

A voice rattled over his phone speaker. "This is Captain Scott."

"Dave," said the chief, "we're reassigning the Debi Whitlock case."

.His superior was one of the few people who was not irritated by Ray Taylor's vigorous campaign to improve the homicide unit. However, the way Taylor understood it, the gauntlet had been thrown down. The captain knew Taylor had been doing good work on recent crime scenes, but the Whitlock case was going to be a challenge on a different level, and the department would be watching him to see how far his skills could take him.

Detective Taylor thought in lists, and within minutes of receiving the Whitlock case he was already ticking off the obstacles:

1. The victim had been murdered over a year ago.
2. He would never see the crime scene—only the photos, the video, the notes.
3. People's memories had already changed.
4. There was a lot of suspicion in the community against the widower.

For that matter, there was a lot of suspicion in the department. Whenever detectives got together to talk about the case, either formally or informally, their conversation gravitated back to the husband who had initially lied about his whereabouts on the night his wife was killed. A narcotics officer on the scene that morning believed Harold should have been tested for drugs. "The guy just wasn't acting right. Not even for a guy in shock. He was definitely exhibiting signs of narcotics usage." The officer also believed that Whitlock's appearance looked "too neat" for him to have been wearing his clothes as long as he purported. Harold Whitlock looked as if he'd just finished showering and washing his hair. Harold's own girlfriend fueled their doubt: the pants Harold Whitlock was wearing at the scene were not the pants Heather Barnett recalled him wearing as he left her house.

There was a fifth item on Taylor's list of obstacles, and it certainly wasn't the least important. Taylor knew he had already stepped on toes. Last month when Dick Ridenour had told him to "get the hell out of my crime scene," Dick had only been half-joking. Now, for the first time in Taylor's memory, an active case had been taken away from the lead and given to another detective.

Grogan soon got word of the reassignment. Taylor knew not to let resentment build up in the unit, so shortly after leaving the captain's office, Taylor went to Grogan's desk. Some of the guys were milling around, sensing unease. Grogan made a show of shuffling papers as Taylor approached.

"Bill, this is pretty awkward for me. I didn't ask for this, and I didn't want it." He left out the part where he had decided, about three minutes ago, that he was really looking forward to taking a crack at the Whitlock case.

Taylor was to work the case as if it had just occurred, beginning with a reconstruction of the crime scene and making his own path from there. He spent the rest of the week pulling together evidence from the crime scene and isolating himself from the many opinions circulating around the unit. His calendar had been mostly cleared, and he had a week, maybe a bit more, to throw himself wholly into the strange circumstances surrounding Debi Whitlock's murder.

He was irritated to find the files a mess. The office had been moved in the last year, and he assumed some of the records had been lost during transport. Most of the initial interviews conducted by Grogan and his partner, Fred Vaughn, were missing from the files. Taylor pulled another box toward him, removed its cardboard top, and rifled through it. More omissions. There were no notes from interviews with Harold Whitlock. No notes from Debi's boyfriend or Harold's girlfriend. Nothing. He'd have to start from scratch.

Taylor turned his practiced eye toward the video that Technician Denise Ducot had taken at the scene. There was Debi Whitlock's body in the hallway, shot from various angles. The camera panned from her face, still partially covered by her bloodied shirt, her arms above her head. Taylor reached silently for the autopsy report while the camera panned down the victim's torso, and he mentally checked off details as they played across the screen. There was a small mark on her torso. He scanned through the patchy paperwork in the file and found no mention of it. The autopsy report did make note of a small laceration on her rib cage. Taylor could see that the wound hadn't bled. He made a note to check with the medical examiner about any other postmortem marks.

He noted the blood smear on Debi's foot and the clean white walls around her. She hadn't been killed anywhere near these pristine walls. The perpetrator had cut her in a different room, then dragged her into the hall by her feet.

He watched the rest of the video carefully, noting the blood evidence in the master bedroom and recognizing the feathery red marks on the doorjamb where Debi's bloodied hair had brushed as she was dragged by.

Where was Debi's clothing? Taylor walked to the evidence room and meandered through the labyrinthine shelves until he located Debi's file number on the outside of a box. Inside and duly tagged was the evidence bag containing the victim's clothes; the original seal from the scene had never been broken. He pulled latex gloves from a nearby container, slipped them over his hands, and carefully removed a woman's turquoise sweat suit. Laid out on a sterile examination table, the clothing clearly indicated that the victim had been attacked in a kneeling position: her blood had spilled down her shirt and onto her thighs, but not below.

Plugging this bit of evidence into what he'd already pieced together, he now knew that Debi Whitlock had been killed while she knelt on the floor between her side of the bed and her dresser, her attacker standing behind her. Space there was limited, and nothing in the room was upset. It was quite possible that she was asleep in her bed when the killer found her.

If he had only intended to defile her, why had the perpetrator taken her so far into the hallway? Had he first attempted to drag the body out of the house completely, then lost the strength to carry out the plan? Or had it been his intention to create a morbid display of her body—and the weapon—in the heart of the house?

As Detective Taylor replaced the clothing in the evidence box, he noticed a dark blue fiber on Debi's clothing. He very gently lifted it between his gloved finger and thumb and inserted it into a small, sterile evidence bag. He'd have to take this to the lab. He was fairly certain that the fiber did not come from the Whitlocks' home.

Laying the bag aside, Taylor rummaged through the rest of the box. One large carving knife was sealed and labeled. Where was the second knife?

He returned to the video, fast-forwarding until he saw the Whitlock kitchen. A few drops of blood on a mottled, brown and beige tile countertop. The block of knives with two slots empty, and yes, there it was: a smaller knife in the sink. It was smeared with red liquid, which had run off the blade and gathered into a small puddle in the aluminum sink. Why would the same person make one knife part of a gruesome death display, but place the other neatly in the sink? And what happened to the second knife?

Flipping through the incomplete paperwork in the file, he saw no record that it had been removed from the scene. He checked with some of the guys who had been at the house. No one recalled bagging it.

Ray Taylor had been a boy who loved to solve puzzles, and it was that love that eventually led him into police investigation. But the Whitlock case was quickly becoming the most frustrating puzzle he'd ever worked on. The more pieces he tried to fit together, the more he realized that there were very important pieces missing. Take, for example, Harold Whitlock's ring. What looked like blood had been found on the ring, and it had been taken from Harold's possession on the morning of the murder. Now Taylor found a note saying the ring had been returned to Whitlock just a few months ago. In all that time, no one tested the substance on the ring.

No second knife, no tests on the ring, no tests on the blood in Whitlock's hair (the amount collected the morning of the murder was insufficient for testing). To the highly organized Detective Taylor, the situation was interminably frustrating.

Taylor viewed the footage of the crime scene over and over again. He'd never been there, but he wanted his experience of the Whitlock house to be as real as possible. What's more, something was missing. He didn't know yet what it was, but it irritated him like the buzz of an unseen mosquito. How many times had he told his crime scene crew that "the hardest thing to see is what's not there"? The difference was that in those situations, he'd already spotted what was missing, and he was testing his team. Now he was the student. The question kept playing through his head, and he felt the frustration of being on the other side of it.

Debi Whitlock's wedding ring was still on her finger.

Her purse was missing, and they'd never found it. No one had ever attempted to use her credit cards.

All of her clothing was there. Even what had been removed was still at the scene, tossed into the doorway of the guest bathroom.

The guest bathroom.

Taylor sat up suddenly and hit the Rewind button on the remote control. The camera panned through the Whitlocks' guest bathroom to the left side of Debi Whitlock's feet. The room was painted blue. It had a tub with a small, opaque glass window inset in the wall. There was a single vanity and sink, also blue. The toilet was recessed beside a built-in medicine cabinet with a mirrored front. A large vanity mirror was opposite the door. Looking into it now, Taylor could see Officer Ducot, her camcorder obscuring half her face. The white trim of the bathroom door framed her, and beside her was an empty towel bar.

Where were the towels?

Taylor rifled through the file folders in front of him. He had seen a note about towels. His hands found the reports from the officers on scene, and there it was: Officer David Rhea had examined the exterior of Whitlock's truck and had noted through the window a pile of towels in the front passenger-side floorboard. There was nothing else in the file about them.

Taylor walked to Rhea's desk and showed him the report. "Do you by chance remember if those towels were ever collected?"

Rhea took the report and looked it over. Then he thought for a moment. "You know, I'd forgotten about the truck. The husband was really weird about it."

Taylor pulled out his notebook. "What do you mean?"

"Well, we're at the house that morning, right? And I'm outside pretty early into it, so I go over to see if the truck's warm. You know, standard procedure." Taylor nodded as his pen ran across the page. "Anyway, every time I got close to the truck, the guy starts—I don't know—crying and moaning. Being disruptive. The first time, I sort of went over to see if he had something to say, and he settled down. Then I went back to the truck, and again the guy starts carrying on."

"He asked you to move away from the truck?"

"No. It's like he would suddenly start falling to pieces. Except after a while, I wondered if he was faking it. So I looked through the windows and didn't see any blood or anything. Just a few papers and the towels on the floor. But I couldn't get in yet because we were still waiting for the search warrants."

Taylor stopped writing and looked up. "Right. So what about after the search warrants arrived?"

Rhea shrugged. "I was doing other duty at that point. I never got sent back to the truck. It was only something I did because we were outside waiting for the warrants and, you know, I was just looking around."

Now the towels, the truck, all evidence was long gone. Taylor barely hid his irritation as he tried to gather his thoughts. "Do you remember if anyone else saw Whitlock's 'disruptive behavior'?"

"Not really, it's been awhile. But—wait. I do remember the ambulance guy talking about it. I mean, he was waiting outside, too. The paramedic. And we kind of looked at each other a few times like, *Why is this guy going on like this?*"

Karen and her big sister, Debi,
on Long Island. *J. MacDonald*

Debi and Jacque at Debi's first communion.
J. MacDonald

Me and my father on Easter morning. I was six years old.
D. Whitlock

My father and Debi were married in a very private ceremony in their living room in June 1983. Debi wore blue—her favorite color.
K. Hazeltine

This is my favorite photo: Jacque and Dennis on their wedding day in 1981. Jacque always says she could never have accomplished so much for our family or others without Dennis's love and support.
J. MacDonald

Dad took this photo of me standing with Debi and Jessica in the front yard less than a year before Debi's death. Jessie's window is on the left; Dad and Debi's bedroom window on the right. *A. Dove*

I took this photo of Debi and Jessie (wearing one of Debi's baby dresses) on the back patio in the summer of 1987. Jacque sent this photo to many producers in her efforts to show the emotional impact of Debi's loss. "I didn't fight fair," Jacque says proudly. *A. Dove*

Jacque secured California's first billboard for a murder victim.
Courtesy of The Modesto Bee

One of Modesto's largest supermarkets agreed to put Debi's information on all of their grocery carts. Jacque used all of the money from her mother's estate on the project. "From mother to daughter, and then for another daughter," Jacque says. "It felt right." *J. MacDonald*

ABOVE: This alleyway, which runs parallel to Dad and Debi's house (visible on right), was the murderer's presumed escape route. RIGHT: Officer Ed Steele's respectful treatment of the informant helped solve Debi's case. *A. Dove*

Jacque and her longtime friend Conressman Dennis Cardoza have worked together for years to help bring justice to victims and their families. *A. Dove*

Merced Sheriff Mark Pazin is a frequent guest on *The Victim's Voice.* *J. MacDonald*

Scott Fizzell's residence in 1988.
A. Dove

This is the view Scott Fizzell would have had of our house had he stepped just a few yards off his regular route from his home to Grace Davis High School.
A. Dove

The mug shot of Scott Fizzell.
Courtesy of the Stanislaus County Sheriff's Department

Robin Adam became Jacque's friend and ally when he worked as an aide for Assemblyman, and then Congressman, Dennis Cardoza. Now with Assemblywoman Cathleen Galgiani, Robin is helping to draft a new version of Debi's Law, which Galgiani plans to take before the California Assembly in the near future. *A. Dove*

Jacque holds her National Crime Victim's Service Award. Also pictured (L to R): Dennis MacDonald, Office for Victims of Crime Chairman John Gillis, and Merced County District Attorney Larry Morse. *A. Dove*

I sent Jacque this photo I had taken of Debi shortly before her death, and it quickly became the official photo displayed on flyers, shopping carts, billboards, and bus signs. *A. Dove*

Back in his cubicle, Ray Taylor looked up the paramedic's name and gave him a call. Kevin Silva worked with a private ambulance company that contracted with the MPD, and he had been assigned to the call that morning. When Taylor described the call to Silva, he remembered it in vivid detail.

"I don't remember the crying as much as I remember how he treated his daughter," said Silva. "I had the little girl in the ambulance with me for a long time, checking her over and kind of waiting to see what was going to happen." Eventually, Whitlock came over and told the girl he had to go with some officers downtown, and that she should go with some family friends who had just arrived. "Even then," Silva said angrily, "he never touched her. Never said anything comforting to her, he was just matter-of-fact. And she said—I remember this—he was walking away, and she sort of called out, 'Where's Mommy?' The guy just kept walking."

Ray Taylor was determined to keep an open mind while looking for suspects in Debi's case. A researcher by nature, Taylor turned to the writings of Robert Ressler, the FBI's senior criminal profiler since the mid-1970s. It was Ressler who developed the idea for the National Center for the Analysis of Violent Crime (NCAVC), which oversaw all the criminal behavior studies at the Academy.

Ressler's primary contribution to criminal studies was the differentiation between organized and disorganized crime scenes. These categories, which help law enforcement look for personality types and traits of perpetrators based on crime scene data, had proven invaluable in solving even the most perplexing homicides. Taylor had long been interested in this science, and took the opportunity to apply Ressler's theories to Debi Whitlock's unsolved murder.

He started by listing those elements of Debi's murder indicating a disorganized killer, one who had not premeditated his attack:

1. Perpetrator apparently walked to scene—no tire marks.
2. Perpetrator improvised, using weapons at scene instead of bringing restraints/weapons.
3. Covering victim's face indicates obliteration of personality, possibly indicative that victim was simply a stand-in for someone else whom the killer fantasized was the victim.
4. The body was left at the scene of the crime, a possible indication that the killer did not possess the frame of mind to move the body or hide it.

If Debi was killed by a disorganized killer, that indicated the perpetrator was an introvert with a mental disorder of some kind, unable to express his anger. He was likely a social outcast, perhaps with some kind of disability or generally considered unattractive. He would be an underachiever who was unable to sustain long-term personal relationships. He would probably be considered quiet and shy, easily overlooked.

Taylor stopped writing and reached for his well-worn copy of Ressler's book, *Whoever Fights Monsters*. Flipping through the pages, Taylor found what he was looking for. "The disorganized killer may pick up a steak knife in the victim's home, plunge it into her chest, and leave it sticking there. Such a disorganized mind does not care about fingerprints or other evidence."

Reading further, Taylor noted the crime scene also seemed to contain numerous elements pointing toward an organized killer—one who planned to kill and carefully followed through with that plan. Reaching for a new sheet of paper, Taylor carefully wrote the words "Organized Elements" and began his list.

1. Phone calls indicate stalking.
2. Careful arrangement of body as display.
3. No sign of forced entry indicates that killer may have used a ruse to enter house.
4. Took keys (but dropped them?), unrecovered purse now a trophy of the kill—something tangible to help him "relive" the murder???
5. Use of control—forcing victim to be quiet? Forcing victim onto her knees in posture of supplication? Forcing victim to keep presence in house a secret when daughter came over for suitcase?

If Taylor was dealing with an organized killer, the situation was exceedingly more dangerous. Such a culprit would have stalked Debi beforehand, fantasizing about the kill to come and revisiting those fantasies later. The killer would be a popular person with an inflated sense of self-esteem, someone generally considered smart but who may also be confrontational, and may become aggressive very suddenly. He would enjoy keeping tabs on the investigation, relishing his power over first the victim and now the police. However, Ressler's research indicated that most premeditated murders leave the perpetrator feeling somewhat dissatisfied, and postkill fantasies become a training ground for how to make the next murder more rewarding.

During unit workshops for unsolved crimes Dick Ridenour, crime scene manager at the Whitlock house, had posited time and again that the placement of Debi's body indicated some form of "message" from the killer. "And what if that message isn't understood, or acknowledged, by the person it's intended for?" Ridenour would ask with obvious alarm. As hostage negotiator for the force, Ridenour often read crime as a form of communication. "If we don't understand Debi Whitlock's killer this time, he might say it with more force next time."

But two years later there still hadn't been a next time. If Debi's killer had killed only once, then chances were good that they were dealing with someone who was mentally unstable versus thoughtfully evil. The most likely scenario was that the killer knew Debi, had a grudge against her, and had something to gain from her death.

Taylor scheduled his first interview with Harold Whitlock within the week. He explained to the widower that he had taken over the case and would be conducting his own interviews and tests. "I know you've been very cooperative with the department, and obviously we're doing everything we can to solve your wife's case. So I have to ask you to be patient, even though you've been through a lot of this before."

"Of course. Whatever I can do to help."

Whitlock explained again how he had left the bachelor party at midnight and had gone to Heather's house. "I had to call a supervisor when I got there, so you can check the time through phone records, I guess."

Taylor tried not to look incredulous. "That was pretty late to call a supervisor, wasn't it?"

"Well, he was a supervisor in Fresno at the time," Whitlock corrected himself. "Al Bates. Before that we were department managers together at the Modesto store. And now he's back as the store manager. But at the time, that night, he was just a friend living in Bakersfield who knew company policy."

How convenient, thought Taylor. Only long-distance calls would register exact times on Heather Barnett's phone records.

And the husband of the victim was lucky enough to have made one at the time of his wife's mysterious murder.

"Why did you need to call him?" Taylor asked.

"A work matter. At the party that night, another department manager said some inappropriate things to another employee, and I needed to ask Al what I should do."

"So, what time did you arrive at Ms. Barnett's apartment?"

"I think it was close to midnight, maybe right after. I stopped at a stop sign for a few minutes. Just to think some things through. And then I went straight to Heather's."

Taylor went back through Whitlock arriving home and finding Debi. Whitlock was adamant that he didn't touch any blood on his wife, but only felt her leg to confirm his suspicion that she was dead. He still had no idea why blood would be in his hair or on his ring. "They gave that ring back to me a couple of months ago," Whitlock volunteered, "and I figured if anything had come of it, they would have talked to me. But they didn't say anything." Yes, there was still some kind of crusty red stuff under the stone, said Whitlock, and so he had the ring professionally cleaned. At his work.

Instead of declaring his doubts, Taylor thanked Whitlock for his assistance, asked him to submit to a new blood test and polygraph, and told him he was free to go. But Harold Whitlock's responses and demeanor seemed odd.

As Taylor contacted the other guests of the bachelor party, the story became more convoluted. Harold Whitlock had supposedly organized the party that very day, and coworkers now recalled that Harold had seemed "desperate" for people to attend. He could only pull together a handful of coworkers willing to show, and once they arrived at Ortega's, several attendees said he was anxious that no one leave. At 11 p.m., one of the guests told Harold he needed to get home because he worked early the next day, and Harold had cajoled and bullied him into staying for another fifteen minutes. When the last few guests got ready to leave at midnight, Harold urged them to stay and finally invited them to his home.

Taylor looked up from the pad where he was recording notes of his interview with Best Products employee Tim Green. "I'm sorry? Harold Whitlock invited you to his house?"

"Yeah, the three of us who were still there at the party. He said why didn't we come home with him. In fact, he was really insistent."

"What was your response?"

"Well, I knew his wife had to commute out of town sometimes, and I asked wasn't she and their little girl in bed already. And he said that was fine, his wife wouldn't care. And he told us just to follow him in our cars."

Harold's friend at the Cantina, Jerry Ortega, verified that as the party left, Harold mentioned they were all going to his house.

"Had he invited you to his house previously?" Taylor asked Green.

"No."

"And I take it you did not go that night, either?"

"No. Things got really weird." Green explained that the two other employees still present were male and female. While walking out to their cars, the male made a sexual advance toward the female, who turned him down and said she was going home. "That's when Harold started getting really mad. I mean, mad. The rest of us were fine. Sure, Mike said something out of line and was just being drunk and obnoxious, and Susan sort of blew him off, told him he was a jerk, and left it at that. So me and Mike are kind of laughing and I'm like, 'Man, you shouldn't have said that,' and then Harold starts yelling at us—especially Mike. Then he gets into his car and burns rubber out of the parking lot."

Taylor next interviewed Heather Barnett, who was now living with Harold in the house where Debi was killed. She verified that Harold had come to her house that evening, but she placed the time at almost an hour later than he did. "He told me he went to a park to think things over," she said. "He just sat in his car for awhile, then he came to my house."

"Had he made plans previously to come to your apartment?"

"No. I had gone to bed, but I wasn't exactly surprised, either. He sometimes came over late."

"Because you were involved sexually," Taylor prompted.

"Yes."

Heather went on to explain that when Harold came in, he was obviously upset about the people at the party because he kept pacing around and saying to himself, "How am I going to explain this? How am I going to explain this?"

"Explain what?"

"Well, whatever Mike had said to Susan, I guess. He didn't really say. But what else could it be?" She looked at him with blank, innocent eyes. Taylor could tell she wasn't acting.

"Well," Taylor replied, ticking off points as he tried to answer her question, "Harold Whitlock was sitting in his car at a park, you believe, to cool off and think about this sexual remark between two coworkers. Almost an hour later he's still highly agitated about it? And he's talking to himself, asking how he's going to explain something? And he hardly even speaks to you when he comes in, because he's still so upset about this comment between two coworkers?"

"I guess," she answered simply, her eyes full of nothing but blue sky.

After letting Heather know to expect a call for a polygraph and blood sample ("just to rule out everybody that we can"), he looked up Heather's old apartment at 1118 Virginia Avenue on a Modesto city map that was already marked with the Whitlock residence and Ortega's restaurant. In his own car Taylor clocked driving times.

From Ortega's to Heather's: twelve minutes

From Ortega's to the Whitlock house: four and a half minutes

From the Whitlock house to Heather's: ten minutes

And all of those times were in traffic that would not have existed at midnight. If Harold Whitlock left Ortega's when he said he did, and arrived at Heather's two minutes prior to making the long-distance phone call noted on her phone records, then he was below the radar for almost fifty minutes.

Taylor ran through what he knew of the scenario. At Heather's house, Harold is pacing and distracted. He calls Al Bates. He has sexual intercourse with his girlfriend. He leaves at 5 a.m., wearing jeans. He returns home, finds his wife, calls 911, hangs up, and when the first responders get there he has showered and has on light-colored pants. And blood in his hair. And maybe blood on his ring. And maybe he's on drugs. And he's not talking to his daughter. And he's highly anxious whenever the team goes near his truck, which has towels in the floorboard, which may be the missing towels from the front bathroom.

On the other hand, the blood at the scene belongs only to his wife and an unknown person.

The prints on the knife that was bagged belong to an unknown person.

The bloody thumbprint on the dresser belongs to an unknown person.

Taylor wanted to know more about Harold Whitlock's

long-distance, late night phone call, and that information needed to come from the party on the other end of the phone: Harold and Heather's boss, Al Bates.

Introducing himself as the new detective on the case, Taylor met with Bates to "verify certain information" Bates had no doubt given to Detectives Grogan and Vaughn shortly after the murder. Bates proved to be extremely talkative. He agreed that Harold had called him that night from Heather's, complaining that an assistant manager had made a sexual remark to an employee and wondering if he should refer the matter to the corporate office. They chatted for twenty minutes and hung up.

"Yes, I guess it was odd for Harold to call me so late. It was close to one o'clock in the morning, and the matter didn't seem all that important. But he and Heather had called me at home before, so I didn't think too much of it at the time."

Al Bates had been aware of the affair when he worked at Best Products in Modesto. He claimed that he and Harold had been casual friends and coworkers, sometimes meeting Bob Kramer for a drink at Ortega's after work. He also mentioned that he and Harold had once taken a road trip to Tahoe. They had seen each other occasionally during Al's one-year stint in Orange County before he transferred back to management in the Modesto store, shortly after Debi's murder. However, Bates said Harold had never spoken about Debi's murder, and Bates hadn't pressed him for details. "All he ever told me was that it was a really bad thing, what happened to Debi."

Bates had met Debi a few times and had even spent the night at Harold and Debi's house a few weeks before the murder. Again, Taylor wondered how casual the friendship was at the time. Was Bates distancing himself from a man he no longer trusted?

"How would you characterize Harold's behavior at work now?" Taylor asked.

"It's sad, really. He's upset. A lot of people around here believe he had something to do with it. Even people at work. So I'd say he's trying to get through, but it's just really hard."

"And what about Heather Barnett? What is she like at work?"

Bates looked at him quizzically. "Heather doesn't work there anymore." Then he grew noticeably uncomfortable. "She resigned. Like I said, the environment at work hasn't been very good for Harold or Heather."

"What do you mean?"

"Well, there were some questions about Harold being connected to some missing merchandise. That really upset Heather, and she left."

According to Bates, two months after Debi's murder, some anonymous tips had come into the loss prevention 800 number concerning missing inventory and cash in the jewelry department. "Based on the tips," Bates explained, "I went through the cash receipts drawer one day and happened to notice there were a lot of cash returns for big-ticket jewelry items. It looked suspicious, and Harold was standing there watching me, but we didn't talk about it until a week or so later." Shortly thereafter, an attorney forwarded a check to Bates, written out to the store, for $4,200. Harold simultaneously received an envelope that contained a large amount of jewelry that had previously been missing from inventory.

"And who were the envelopes from?" Taylor asked.

"There was no name on either of them."

So now there was money involved. Murder and money almost always went together, but it hadn't been a big part of this case. Until now.

Harold had admitted that he thought Debi's life insurance policy was in effect at the time of her murder. Ray Taylor pondered what it must have been like for Harold to realize he wouldn't have the means to bury his wife, much less move to another house. Surely it was difficult to live in the house where Debi was killed. If Harold had taken the jewelry, was it to scrape together a down payment for a new house? Or was it possible that Harold Whitlock owed someone a lot of money for doing a job? Say, someone who had no qualms about killing? Was Whitlock indebted to the murderer?

Taylor put in a request to all the Modesto and Merced area hotels and motels for listings of guests who stayed there during March of 1988. It would take him months, once the records arrived, to comb through all the names and compare them to police records of known and potential killers for hire.

Meanwhile, Taylor met with the other leading man in Debi Whitlock's life. According to Steve Bloomberg, the last time he saw Debi was at the Merced store sidewalk sale on the Monday before she was killed. Some of the managers had gone for drinks after work, and Debi had accompanied Bloomberg out for dinner and then back to his apartment for a romantic evening. Bloomberg had no alibi for the night of Debi's murder, and he was concerned about clearing his name. "I understand you're asking some people to take polygraphs, and I'm asking you to take mine," he said earnestly. "Let's do it right now. I don't want you to have any doubts."

"You sound pretty confident," Taylor said with a faint smile.

"Actually, I'm scared to death. I know how one word can trip you up on those things. But I also know I didn't kill Debi. I loved her."

Bloomberg still believed Harold Whitlock had killed his wife. Whitlock had threatened Debi's life at least once, he asserted, and Bloomberg also believed Harold had hit Debi. "He's never come after me, but that only makes him a coward on top of everything else." Bloomberg and Debi had planned a future together. Now, a year and a half later, Bloomberg said he wasn't seeing anyone else. "I just can't let go," he confided.

By the end of his second week on the case, Detective Taylor had called in Tom Keener from the California Bureau of Investigation. Keener administered the polygraphs, and while they were inadmissible in court, they did indicate that Steve Bloomberg and Heather Barnett had nothing to do with Debi's murder. Harold Whitlock's results were mixed.

Mixed, too, were the reports about Harold and Debi's marriage. Detective Taylor heard rumors that Harold and Debi had been swingers involved in a large spouse-swapping group that included Bob and Doris Kramer, Jerry Ortega and his former wife, Ray and Rachel Leonard, and a few other couples that were known to socialize with that core group. Further research revealed that this same large group of friends did get together at least once every year, but for nothing more scandalous than deep sea fishing.

However, all those people who frequented the Whitlock house verified that towels always hung in the guest bathroom. Always.

Taylor sat down and listed all of the people he could possibly think of with even a tenuous connection to Debi Whitlock. Based on that list, he ordered blood samples from over thirty different people and prints from even more.

Preliminary blood test results began coming in from the local lab, and Taylor had several moments where he felt he was close to making an arrest. Those samples that typed O+ would be sent on to the state lab for more thorough results, and among those people were Bob Kramer, Ray Leonard, and two of Jerry Ortega's brothers. Taylor questioned each of them again, this time more strenuously, but four to six months later the state tests ruled them out. They had the same blood type as the killer, but there was no genetic match.

As many times as Taylor followed one lead and then another, it seemed to him that all paths led back to Harold Whitlock. Eventually, Harold was terminated from his job at Best Products. Taylor once again called store manager Al Bates, to get a better understanding of what had happened.

"Really, the company is restructuring, and a lot of middle management has been let go," said Bates. "But it's true that Harold's productivity never really improved. I'd see him sitting at his desk, staring into space. It just had to end."

Now that his professional and personal relationship with Whitlock was over, Bates had some other thoughts on his mind. "Do you know he had me take Heather Barnett to Debi's funeral?" he asked somewhat indignantly. "I mean, the guy had me take his girlfriend to his wife's funeral! And lots of people knew about the affair. That was just odd. And I'll tell you something else," Bates continued. "After the funeral, he let his little girl go with Debi's parents, and then he and Heather came over to my house and just sat around making small talk, like it was just any other day."

Taylor agreed that this seemed out of character for a man whose wife—even an estranged wife—had been so brutally murdered.

"But then he turned around and started stalking that other girl at work! I didn't say anything to him at the time, because I knew he was going through a lot, but what kind of guy does that? And right after his wife was 'mysteriously murdered'? It makes you wonder, doesn't it?"

"I'm sorry?" asked Taylor. "What girl are we talking about?"

TWELVE

The Sting

Callie Smallwood had been working at Best Products since graduating from high school in 1986. When Debi Whitlock was murdered two years later, Callie was working in Cosmetics. Her department manager was Heather Barnett.

Callie knew assistant store manager Harold Whitlock somewhat. He was graying, friendly, married, and having an affair with her supervisor. Callie claimed Heather talked about the affair a lot. In detail. Callie chalked it up to Heather wanting a friend at work; after all, they were close to the same age.

When Harold's wife was murdered, it came as a terrible shock. Callie never suspected Harold, but vicious rumors began circulating through the store immediately. Heather had taken several days off to be with Harold just after the horrible event, and Callie called her at home to see how Harold Whitlock was holding up.

"He's a wreck," Heather replied. "Their marriage was over, but he still cared a lot about her. I'm trying to help out however I can."

The next few months at work were horrible. Many of the employees thought Harold had killed his wife, although Callie did not. She couldn't believe how some of her coworkers treated Harold, glaring at him and making snide comments. For his part, Harold was quiet and withdrawn. Heather, on the other hand, was openly hostile to anyone who doubted her boyfriend, not realizing she was feeding those doubts. Then one day in early summer, Heather called Callie at home to say she had resigned, claiming she was tired of the way she and Harold were being treated.

Within a month, Whitlock appointed Callie department manager of Small Appliances. Callie was thrilled with the increase in responsibility, and Whitlock seemed pleased with her work. He commended her performance and even talked to her a little about her life outside the store—her interests and hobbies. They weren't exactly friends, but they were amiable coworkers.

Callie's opinion of Harold Whitlock changed one night about six months after Debi's murder. The managers had gone to Ortega's for drinks after work, and Callie noticed that Harold was particularly quiet. She turned away from the happy chatter of the other managers and went to the bar to sit next to her boss. He was staring down into his drink and stirring it listlessly with a black straw.

"Hi. Can I sit down?"

Whitlock glanced up at her, and she thought his eyes looked close to tears. "Sure, if you dare." He nodded toward her empty glass. "You need another?"

"OK."

He motioned for the bartender, who brought Callie a new beer and took her old glass away. She took a swallow. "So, how are you holding up?"

"Oh, you know," Whitlock said into his drink. "Sometimes you're the hammer, sometimes you're the nail."

Callie was unsure what to say. "You've been through so much. I can't imagine."

A tear dripped down his cheek, and he ignored it. "It's been really difficult. It's been hell."

She reached over and put her hand on his arm. "I'm so sor—"

"Don't touch me!" he hissed, suddenly turning to face her. His face at that moment, in the dark, scared her.

"I—I'm sorry. I didn't mean—" She fumbled for her glass and headed back toward the others, who assumed she had only gone to the bar for another drink.

Whitlock rejoined the group shortly, and although she felt his eyes on her, Callie avoided his gaze. It was after midnight when she finally stood up to leave, saying good-bye to the group. Whitlock rose as well. "I should be getting home, too. I'll walk you out."

She looked around to say she would go with someone else, but no one else was ready to leave. Instead of making a scene, Callie let her manager walk next to her as they made their way up the ramp to the exit. Once outside, Callie said briskly, "Well, I'll see you later."

"Which car is yours?" Whitlock asked.

"I'm right over here," she said, indicating a compact car a few yards away.

"Well, I'll walk you over there, just to make sure you're safe."

Callie tried to smile. "I think I'll be fine." Still, he continued to walk with her. He waited while she unlocked her car, got in, and started the ignition. "OK. So I'll see you later," she repeated, and closed the car door. *I'm being silly,* she thought. *He only feels bad for snapping at me like that. He's trying to make amends.*

Callie pulled her car out of the space and circled the parking lot to the exit. She pulled out onto Sisk Road and noticed her gasoline light was on. She'd need to fill up before taking the highway home. She pulled into a Shell station a few blocks away, got out of the car, and went inside to prepay. When she came out, she noticed with a jolt that Harold Whitlock was sitting in his car next to hers.

"Hello again," she said. "You needed gas, too?"

"No. I'm just keeping an eye on you." He wasn't smiling.

She reached for the pump. "I'm fine. There's lots of lights here, and a few other people inside. You don't need to wait for me."

"I don't mind."

What was she supposed to do now? She began filling up her car silently, averting her eyes from Harold Whitlock. Why wouldn't he leave? She turned to face him and saw that he was still staring at her. She was intensely uncomfortable. "I'm fine, OK? I'm a big girl. I can take care of myself." She tried, and failed, to smile.

"It pays to be safe."

"I get gas by myself all the time, and I've never had a problem." Callie felt her heart thumping faster.

"Believe me, I know how things that seem safe sometimes aren't."

Callie felt relief when the automated gas nozzle cut off, indicating her tank was full. She returned the nozzle to its holder, replaced her gas cap, and got into her car. She locked her door, too. She no longer cared if she seemed rude, even if Whitlock was her supervisor.

She drove out of the parking lot and headed toward the on-ramp of Highway 99. With mounting panic, she watched in the rearview mirror as he followed her. She drove all the way to her exit and swore silently as he exited the highway. They wound through residential streets, Callie speeding now to get away from him, but he was right on her tail. She finally parked in front of her modest house. She jumped from the car, fumbling for her house key as she ran to the door. Behind her, she heard Whitlock's car pull up to the curb and stop. She rammed the key into the lock, turning her doorknob. "Open open open," she pled, and with a sigh of relief she was inside. She slammed the door closed, locking the knob and then the dead bolt. Then she backed away from the door.

She waited, expecting to hear his car drive away. Instead, there was only silence. Keeping her lights off, she crept to the window and peeked outside. His car was still there. In the gloom, she could just make out his silhouette.

He was just sitting there.

What should she do? Why wasn't he leaving? She thought briefly about calling the police, but at the same time, he wasn't exactly on her property.

On the other hand, what if he tried to come inside? What if she walked away from this window and he got out of his car and started looking for a way into the house? What if he went around to the back, by the patio door—the same way it was rumored someone came into his house and killed Debi Whitlock?

Callie knelt on the floor and watched Harold Whitlock's car through the window. Occasionally she saw the orange tip of his cigarette. He stayed there for an hour. Then she heard the engine start. The headlights came on, and the car pulled slowly away from the curb. Callie stayed at the window for a while longer, waiting for the car to come back, but it didn't.

The next day, Callie turned in her resignation to Al Bates.

"And you say this happened six months after Debi Whitlock's murder?" asked Ray Taylor.

"About then," Callie answered into the phone. She was now living out of town. "I know this happened a while ago, but believe me, I remember it."

"And can anyone verify this?"

"Well, like I said, I didn't call the police, but I told Mr. Bates about it when I quit. I guess you know that, since you called me."

Ray Taylor believed Callie's story. The girl's voice still shook when she talked about it. She must have been terrified that night.

What kind of man follows a girl home like that—especially a man who has been questioned repeatedly about his wife's mysterious murder?

It was a Friday night in the fall of 1990, and Nan Davidson walked into Denny's with the Modesto Hoedown square dancers. The group, mostly comprised of senior citizens, had just performed at Vintage Faire Mall. The women wore red and white checkered dresses lined in eyelet lace over big white petticoats, and the men wore white country-western shirts with ties of the same red and white fabric as their partners.

Nan chatted happily with her friends as she wove carefully through the restaurant, trying not to brush her petticoat into the other diners. Then she saw Harold Whitlock sitting by himself at a booth in the corner.

"I'll be right back," she told her friends and headed to his table.

"Rocky?"

Harold shifted his gaze from his coffee cup and looked up at this small woman in a dress that was practically as wide as it was tall.

"Aren't you supposed to say trick or treat?" he asked, his voice more full of exhaustion than humor.

Nan ignored her former son-in-law's joke. "Rocky, you look horrible!"

"Really? I was going for *atrocious.*"

"Can I sit down?"

"I don't know. It might tarnish my reputation."

Nan ignored that, too, and sat down.

"Thank you," he replied, in a rare moment of candor. "I don't get much company these days." He motioned a waiter over.

Nan ordered coffee and a piece of pie. The waiter commented on her accent, and she told him she was from Virginia. "He is, too," she motioned to her dining companion, "but he lost his accent years ago."

After the waiter left, Nan studied the man across from her. He needed a mama right now, and she'd been close to that while he was married to her daughter. She figured that was good enough in a pinch.

"Angela says she hasn't heard from you lately, and she's worried. I'm worried, too. How are you doing, Rocky?"

He appeared to think of a witty reply, but abandoned it. "I'm dying by degrees."

Nan reached for his hand, and he didn't take it away. "I'm so sorry all of this is happening. Surely they'll find the killer."

"Nan, they're not even looking anymore."

"Of course they are! Debi's mama isn't gonna rest until this is solved."

Nan removed her hand from his as the waiter returned to the table. He set down her coffee and pie, then turned toward Whitlock. "Refill?"

"Sure." He nodded toward his former mother-in-law. "It'd be rude to finish before my date does."

Nan took a bite of her pie. Apple. It wasn't warm enough. She chewed thoughtfully for a moment. "Debi's mom said on the TV that there was some other evidence in the house, like someone else's blood. You know anything about that?"

Whitlock met her eyes. They had always been honest with

each other, even during the demise of his marriage to her daughter. She was a part of his younger self, the high school kid who had won so many accolades in spite of the odds. And although they rarely saw each other, he always felt safe with her. "They hurt her real bad, Nan." His eyes dropped down to his coffee cup. "I saw it. I see it all the time. I can't believe how bad they hurt her."

"I heard that," Nan said softly. "Somebody in my bridge club has a nephew who works with the Modesto police."

"I would never have done that to her. Even if we were finished, she was still Jessie's mom."

Nan knew about Rocky's troubled past. She knew about his drinking, about his tendency to defeat himself before anyone else had the chance to. Now she sized up the man across from her. That high school valedictorian was still in there somewhere. She straightened herself in the booth.

"Rocky, you listen to me. I know it was horrible, but you can't think about that now. You've got a little girl who needs you. You come talk to me whenever you want, but you be strong for Jessie. You're all she's got now."

"I know it. She's all that keeps me going." Something else seemed to be bothering him, and Nan waited for him to speak. "I'm scared for her, Nan."

"For Jessie?"

"Yeah. What if . . . what if she didn't sleep through it? What if she really knows who did it?"

"You mean, what if she saw it happen?"

Harold raised his hand as if he might grasp the words out of the air. "Not exactly see it, but what if she knows who was there? What if he was there before she went to bed? What if that's who Angela heard in the back bedroom?"

Nan's eyes went wide.

"What if the person who killed Debi that night knows that Jessie can identify him? What if he comes back for her?"

Nan grabbed his hand. "No! Don't even say that, Rocky. She didn't see it. You asked her, right?"

"I ask her all the time. She's probably sick of hearing it. But that doesn't mean she doesn't know. Maybe she locked it away somewhere, and it will come back to her." He pressed his hands into his eyes. "I'm so afraid for her, Nan. I won't let her out of my sight. I stay up at night to keep guard. I make sure someone picks her up after school if I can't get her myself."

Nan knew who "someone" was. It was common knowledge that Rocky's girlfriend had moved into the house.

"Rocky, you listen to me. The Good Lord's looking out for that little girl. He protected her that night, and He's not going to let anything happen to her now. I know you're not a churchgoer, but you just trust me on this. That little girl is going to be OK. You don't have to be afraid for her."

Harold Whitlock wiped his eyes with a napkin and seemed to pull himself together.

"Jessie needs you to be strong for her. You think about that."

He nodded.

"Now," she said, changing the subject, "tell me how Jessie's doing. Angela used to bring her over a lot, but I haven't seen her in almost a year."

He sighed. "She's amazing. So strong. But this isn't easy for her." He leaned back and rubbed his eyes. "I've been thinking about moving back home—back to Virginia. I'd do it, too, but I don't want to take Jessie away from Debi's family."

"Then take her somewhere else."

"I've been thinking about Oregon, actually. I've got some good friends moving up that way. And it's close enough Jessie could still visit Debi's mom and sister pretty regularly."

They spent the rest of their visit nursing their coffee and talking about Jessie, and Harold promised to bring her by Nan's house the next week. Then they stood up and hugged through barely concealed tears.

Nan wiped her eyes. "Looks like my group's gonna leave me," she said, motioning to some men in bright western gear making their way toward the cash register.

"Well, I guess you better hop on the wagon train, ma'am," Harold said in a fake drawl, lifting an invisible hat from his brow.

Nan smiled. He really was the same boy underneath. She patted his arm and walked away, her skirt swishing seismically.

Lead Detective Ray Taylor had made further inquiries in light of his conversation with Callie Smallwood, the woman Harold Whitlock had followed home. Now he made a list of the elements of any crime, and how they applied to Harold Whitlock:

OPPORTUNITY

Whitlock was at a nearby bachelor party, then at his girlfriend's house, with up to an hour unaccounted for in between.

MOTIVES

1. Custody of younger daughter. Debi was divorcing him and would probably be awarded custody—Whitlock had even stated to several people that he would kill Debi before allowing that to happen.
2. Debi's life insurance money (he didn't know policy had lapsed). The Whitlocks were in debt, and while Debi's

promotional track indicated a series of pay increases, he would have no access to that money after the divorce.

3. Revenge. Debi had recently confessed to her husband that she was involved with another man.

Any one of these motives would be enough to drive some men to kill. Put it all together, and it was a very compelling case. Blood evidence at the house indicated that Harold did not actually wield the weapon, but he could have hired it done and even, perhaps, have participated. The second knife had never been fingerprinted. And why else was Debi's blood behind his ring and in his hair even though he continued to insist he'd never touched her blood?

Why would Harold's younger daughter be unharmed in the attack? For that matter, the older daughter may have heard the killer in the master bedroom, and yet she, too, was unharmed; the killer had waited until the teenagers left before killing Debi. So only the unfaithful wife, in the midst of filing for divorce, was killed. Harold's daughters were spared.

More to the point, there was no one else who stood to gain from Debi's murder.

What if Harold had hired someone to kill his wife, promising them part of the insurance money as a payoff? Was it coincidence that Harold was implicated in theft shortly after he found out there was no insurance money?

"Nothing is adding up," Taylor explained to his captain. "I doubt Harold Whitlock physically killed his wife, but I need to bring a lot of pressure on him. I need to bring him in."

The captain and district attorney discussed all the evidence, which was voluminous but inconclusive. There simply wasn't enough cause to arrest Harold Whitlock, but Taylor was right; they needed to turn up the heat. However, by this time Harold had moved to Miner's Cove, Oregon, with Heather and Jessie. If

Taylor couldn't arrest Harold Whitlock, he'd need the coopera-
tion of other detectives. And Jacque MacDonald.

Ray Taylor regularly discussed the case with Debi's mother,
being as forthright with her as possible while not divulging anything that might jeopardize the investigation. When Jacque got an
idea for further publicity for the case, she would call Taylor and
he, in turn, would encourage her to do anything she possibly
could to keep Debi's case in the mind of the public. Jacque was
determined to reach what she called "the one person who knows,"
and listening to her, Taylor believed Jacque might be able to pull
it off. In the meantime, he needed her help. He needed to intercept
Harold Whitlock on California soil.

When he called Jacque, she told him her former son-in-law
would be driving Jessica down to Merced for a visit this coming
summer, in just a couple of months. Taylor liked the timing, as it
allowed him to put the other pieces of his operation together. He
was already jotting down a time line when he realized Jacque had
stopped talking.

"I'm sorry?"

"I said, I finally got a spot for Debi on *America's Most
Wanted*."

Taylor was impressed, and he told her so. "That had to be a
real challenge."

"It was," Jacque agreed, "but there was a catch. And I need
your help."

Taylor assumed it was another interview, but Jacque's current
request was something entirely different. In order to land on this
highly competitive show, Jacque had hired a famous criminal psychic, Norene Renier, to do a reading for the cameras. The name
meant nothing to Taylor.

"So she'll need some items of Debi's, and the knife," Jacque
explained. "She also wants to talk to you about the case."

Ray Taylor was skeptical. He envisioned some crackpot in too much jewelry whispering that the killer had recently gone on a journey and had something to do with the letter *M*: vague, so-called clues that could easily be applied in any number of directions. But according to Taylor's research, the psychic Norene Renier had actually provided some valuable insight into several cases. Robert Ressler, the FBI criminal profiler, had been impressed enough with Renier to invite her to speak at the Academy in Quantico.

Hoping against his hunch that it was probably a waste of time, Taylor sent Renier the items she requested. In the meantime, he put into action his plan to intercept Harold Whitlock as he brought his little girl to California to spend some time with Jacque.

In the summer of 1993, Harold Whitlock was openly hostile toward Taylor's insistence on another interview, although he did acquiesce. Taylor needed it to happen at the station. He needed the added stress that the official interview room would induce in Whitlock, and Detective Taylor had also asked a well-respected psychologist from the state capital to witness the interview through a one-way window into the room. Together, Taylor and the psychologist would rely on everything they knew about latent signs of guilt and stress in order to determine, once and for all, if Harold Whitlock had been involved in the murder of his wife.

In the interview room, Taylor opted to skip any initial chitchat and instead started to apply pressure immediately.

"Harold, I've worked this case extensively over the past year or so, and here's what I know. I know you were involved in Debi's death. What I don't know is exactly how you did it. And you're not leaving until we've got the finer details worked out."

Harold looked stunned, then angry. "I told you before, I didn't kill her."

Taylor figured Harold was probably already mad and feeling

betrayed by Jacque, realizing that she had to have cooperated with Taylor. But he wasn't mad enough for Taylor's purpose. "Come on, Harold. You told your friends you wanted her dead. You got her blood on you that morning, even though you say you didn't touch her—"

"I touched her," Harold shot back, "but I didn't kill her. She was already dead."

Taylor pressed on. "You left the party at Ortega's and went to Heather Barnett's house, but the problem is that you didn't go straight there."

"I told you—"

"Yes, you said you stopped somewhere. Where was it?" Taylor knew exactly where Harold had said he stopped. He wondered if Harold would remember.

"I stopped—just for a minute—at a stop sign. It's at the corner of Braden and Haun. I was just, just thinking about some things—"

"Except." Taylor interrupted again. "Except that your friends from the party saw you leave at midnight, and Heather says you didn't get to her house until closer to one o'clock. That doesn't sound like a minute to me."

Whitlock crossed his arms. "So maybe it was longer than a minute, but Heather is mistaken about one o'clock, if that's what she even said."

"Heather said that when you finally showed up, you told her you'd been sitting at a park, in your car. Do you recall that?"

"No. You've asked me this before! You've asked her before! We're talking about one night three years ago—"

"A night when your wife, who was divorcing you, who was cheating on you, whom you had threatened to kill, was murdered. A night when you are totally unaccounted for during the time of your wife's murder."

"I sat in the car, OK? I was—I was sitting there, mad about some coworkers, and I was trying to figure it out—some things out." Whitlock was twitching now, his eyes looking from his hands to the wall.

"So you expect me to believe that at twelve o'clock in the morning you drove to a children's park and thought about work-related matters? Does that sound right to you?"

Harold kept his gaze on the table. "I don't have to tell you that I was also deciding where to spend the night. You are perfectly aware of that." Whitlock looked at the detective, then away. "That's part of the reason we're sitting here, right? I know that."

"You were angry with Debi about her affair—"

"I was hurt. But I don't think she meant for it to happen. Even then, I realized that—that . . . It's not like we weren't having problems. But I was only at that stop sign for a minute. Maybe two."

It was these moments, when Whitlock seemed almost chivalrous about his wife, that kept an inkling of doubt about the widower's guilt in Taylor's mind. Still, he was here to get a job done. He continued his questioning.

"Here's what I think happened, and you let me know how I'm doing. You left the party and met the killer you had hired at a prearranged location. You finished your transaction, maybe showed him the house—"

"That's absurd."

"—and you waited while he killed Debi." Taylor rose, maintaining eye contact. "Maybe you helped, or maybe you just got blood on you because the place was a mess. Hell, maybe you changed your mind and went in to stop him, but it was too late. So you panicked. Debi's blood was on you, so you used the towels in the guest bathroom and left them in the truck. That was sloppy, by the way."

"You're insane!"

"It was about one o'clock. Then you went to your mistress's house. Heather heard you, you know that? She heard you mumbling, 'How am I gonna explain this?' She heard you wondering how you were going to explain your way out of murdering your wife. Then Heather watched as you came up with the solution." Taylor's eyes opened in mock inspiration. "An out-of-town phone call from Heather's house! Of course! Thank God the people from work gave you some minor excuse, right? Otherwise, what would you have used as a reason to call a store manager in the middle of the night?"

Harold was bristling. "You're out of line! I told you why I called Al Bates! He was a friend *and* a manager. He told you it wasn't unusual."

"But you know what, Harold? Now Al's thinking a little differently. Now he's remembering some other things, and he's thinking, *Hey, you know what? Maybe Harold Whitlock did kill his wife after all, and I was just blind to the evidence.*"

Harold looked stunned but was silent.

"I'm going to leave you in here for a minute to think about things. Maybe you want to change your story. Maybe you want to finally put this behind you. I'll give you a minute to think it through."

Ray Taylor turned on his heel and walked purposefully out of the room. He made a sharp turn to the right, then another, and entered a nondescript door. The interior of the room was murky with weak light, but Taylor could see the man in the chair, scribbling in his notebook. The psychologist looked again through the one-way glass at Harold Whitlock, still sitting shaken in his chair in the room where Taylor had left him.

"What do you think?" Taylor asked.

"I saw some definite discomfort about that missing block of time. He's being purposefully evasive."

Taylor nodded. "I think so, too."

The psychologist checked his notes. "This, um, Al Bates. He was a friend of Whitlock's?"

"Hard to say. At the time they were pretty close, but he's been distancing himself. Kind of remaking the relationship, saying now that they weren't that close, even though they took some vacations together."

"I understand," the psychologist nodded. "The subject seems to have hit Mr. Whitlock pretty hard. I think you should pursue that."

"Let him wonder how much his old buddy is revealing now?"

"Couldn't hurt," the psychologist agreed. "You might also use other outside relationships. It would help me to see him when he's very uncertain about how to answer your questions, uncertain about what exactly you know about him."

"I can do that."

Taylor grabbed a sheaf of notes and walked back to the interview room. Harold would have had a chance to catch his bearings. Taylor was going to have to undo that.

"So, we were talking about your former friend, Al Bates. You have anything to say about that?"

"Not really." Taylor didn't expect he would.

"Well, Mr. Bates is wondering a lot about you these days. He's thinking back to when you had him take your mistress to your wife's funeral. You remember that?"

"We were friends. All of us. Heather and Al were there for me, and they rode together. That's all."

"That's not what he told me. Mr. Bates said that you and Heather had this planned, and he went along with it, even though it made him very uncomfortable."

"Then he shouldn't have agreed to ride with Heather. And at the time, I don't think it really bothered him at all."

"He disagrees with you."

Harold shrugged. "Well, he'd be the one to know how he felt."

Taylor plowed on. "In fact, he's wondering about a lot of other things, too." Taylor pretended to check his notes. Let Harold wonder. Let him worry. "Ah, yes. He's wondering about Callie Smallwood. You remember her? The coworker you followed home after she told you to leave her alone? Do you remember Callie, Harold?"

Harold sat upright now, panic coming into his face. "No, no. That was a misunderstanding."

"Ms. Smallwood doesn't think of it as a misunderstanding. She viewed it as threatening. Why did you follow her?"

Harold was shaking now. "I didn't follow her! I mean—I mean—it was an innocent action of concern. She misunderstood my intentions, that's all."

Taylor switched lines of questioning. "Let's leave Ms. Smallwood out of it, for the moment, and get back to you establishing your alibi, then going home and pretending to be shocked by your wife's death. You know, some of the first responders say you were faking your shock that morning."

Harold put his head in his hands. "They're wrong."

"But you messed up," Taylor continued. "Somewhere along the line you changed your clothes. You showered, and you changed your clothes. You weren't in the same clothes that you left Heather's house wearing. What did you do with the other clothes, Harold?"

"There were no other clothes!"

"Here's an idea: You realized you'd left evidence in the house linking you to the murder. Handprints? The second knife? You were covering your tracks, and you got blood on your clothes. Your hand. Your hair."

Whitlock was shaking his head emphatically. "No. No."

Taylor drew his breath and fired with precision. "What did you do with the clothes you were wearing when you killed your wife?"

Harold Whitlock slammed his hand down on the table. "Damn it, there were no other clothes! I didn't kill her!"

"How did you pull this off, Harold? You're wasting my time here. Everybody knows you had Debi killed. Was it for the money? Big disappointment then, since the life insurance had lapsed."

Whitlock was shaking now, biting back his answers. Was he afraid to incriminate himself? Taylor was close now.

"Did you know," Taylor said, feigning a glance at his watch, "that at this minute I have a crew of detectives in Miner's Cove?"

Whitlock looked up at him, color draining from his haggard face.

"That's right. Two of my guys are in Oregon with Heather right now, getting some answers. Finally! I've got people talking to your neighbors, your friends, your coworkers. Even your damn mailman. And they're going to find what they need, and we're finally going to swear out a warrant for your arrest."

Harold was standing now. "You son of a bitch! I didn't kill her! Get out of my face! Get out of my life! I didn't kill Debi!"

"Sit down, Mr. Whitlock!" Taylor stared down the enraged man until Harold sat back down, panting, his eyes glaring defiance.

Looking at him, Taylor knew that Harold was acting just like someone who had not, in fact, killed his wife. Still, the detectives in Oregon would leave no stone unturned. If there was evidence to find, the Modesto Police Department would have it soon enough.

Detective Taylor wrapped up the interview and left Harold shaken and angry. After he left, Taylor returned to the observation room and flipped on the overhead lighting.

"That was interesting," the psychologist said, still in his chair.

"It took me a while to get him angry, but it finally worked."

"Yes. Definite stress going on there."

"So, what do you think?"

The psychologist steepled his fingers together in front of him and bounced them together several times. Taylor suspected they taught this gesture at all schools of psychology.

"Well, this is a difficult person to read. He's definitely acting guilty. He's under an incredible amount of stress, and I would even say he's harboring some secret information, if you will, about which he feels exceptional guilt."

Taylor waited. He knew it was coming.

"But he didn't kill his wife."

"You're sure?"

The psychologist sighed, parting his hands in a near shrug. "I wish I could say yes. But what I can say definitely is that he is not exhibiting any signs that would tell me he was a participant in his wife's death. He feels guilt, yes. Even extreme guilt. But he is not guilty of this crime. That is my strong belief."

During the next week or two, Taylor studied the reports from the detectives in Oregon and found no new leads. He hadn't expected any.

How preposterous. With so much evidence pointing to the widower, it was practically inconceivable that he was not involved. And yet, no matter which way Taylor put the pieces together, they never made a solid, seamless case against Debi's husband. Harold Whitlock was guilty of being a strange man with questionable judgment and horrible luck. That's as far as it went.

Ray Taylor was out of ideas, and he dreaded telling Jacque. On the other hand, the timing was perfect. She was thrilled that Debi's case was going to be shown on *America's Most Wanted*, and right now all of her hopes and energies were pinned there.

THIRTEEN

New Suspects

Jacque had called *America's Most Wanted* for years, but Debi's story was getting old, and there were always new, equally tragic unsolved homicides. A journalist who had covered Debi's story in the *San Francisco Chronicle* told Jacque she needed to come up with a new angle; that same week Jacque ran across an article about the famous crime-solving psychic Norene Renier. With Renier on board, *AMW* agreed to profile Debi's case.

In August of 1992, four years after Debi's murder, Norene Renier received a package from Detective Taylor containing the knife, Debi's wedding ring, and the butterfly key chain. Prior to filming she wanted to run some of her impressions by the detective, and he was frankly amazed.

During their phone conference, Taylor listed the information Renier provided about the victim and the murder, making his own notes after each item. Among those were facts of the investigation never before released to the public:

The Victim

- Had a cut on her lower wrist and left rib (yes)
- Strong social routine (yes)
- Had taken a trip prior to death (yes—with boyfriend, Bloomberg)
- Pain in temple or eye (hit or grabbed on top of head)
- Long, thin scar on torso from prior incident or surgery (yes)
- Had received telephone calls (yes—hang-ups)
- Was fearful and scared that "he would hurt me again." (First husband supposedly abusive; Bloomberg said Harold hit Debi)
- Had shared her fears with another person, probably a woman (Paula Thompson, Bloomberg's friend, who said she tried to get Debi to leave "before it was too late")
- Had relationship with suspect, had lived together or were married, so that he was familiar with and comfortable in the residence where the murder occurred (first husband? Whitlock? Bloomberg? Someone else?)

The Murder/Scene

- No sign of forced entry; the suspect just came into the residence (yes)
- The murder weapon belonged to Debi (yes—kitchen knife)
- After the murder, the victim was dragged or dragged herself (yes)
- Lots of blood (obviously, since weapon=knife)
- Renier saw blood on shoe, tennis shoe (possible sneaker tread found)
- The murderer wanted to hurt Debi (excessive violence, posing of the body)

- The suspect wiped or washed off blood from the attack (second knife in sink? Harold Whitlock's shower? Missing towels?)
- Killer was anxious about the murder, but he could think (car keys in a nearby yard=false clue?)
- Left the residence through double sliding doors, outside of which is a concrete slab (yes)
- Has remarried or is living with someone else (Whitlock living with Heather Barnett)
- Has a daughter
- Waited for a long enough time and then got out of the area (Whitlock now in Oregon)
- Police have already spoken with him but don't yet realize he's the killer (over two years of extensive interviews)

Jacque called Detective Taylor that same day, as he knew she would.

"So? Did she tell you who killed my daughter?"

Taylor thought about the list of factors Renier had correctly identified. How much should he tell Jacque, knowing that anything he recounted may only set her up for more disappointment? "She didn't name anybody, but I'm willing to participate in the reading for the show."

The following month Jacque flew Taylor to Florida to meet with Norene Renier in person. The detective was intrigued if not exactly hopeful.

Taylor looked forward to meeting the show's host. In 1981, John Walsh had lost his six-year-old son through an unspeakable nightmare of abduction and murder. Years later, the grieving father-turned-crusader began hosting a national television show devoted to tracking down criminals.

Now, Taylor realized, Jacque MacDonald may be following in

Walsh's footprints. She had already learned so much about both the police and civilian sides of criminal investigation, and she was active in several local survivor support groups where she seemed intent on sharing what she had learned. Bonded by their mutual pain and desire for justice, Jacque would promise to help other families in any way she could. Often this meant asking Taylor to encourage the officer on the other case to be more communicative with the family. Like Walsh before her, Jacque was turning her personal tragedy into a crusade for others.

Taylor was happy to cooperate with the *AMW* profile of Debi's case, and he sincerely hoped it would become one of the numerous success stories of the show's history. However, he was in uncharted territory with the psychic component of the show. He had to meet with Renier in a quiet room with soft lighting, and he could only talk to her through her assistant. This, the assistant explained, was to help the psychic cut down on distractions and "outside influences," which sounded a bit hocus-pocus to Taylor. Still, he played along. After all, she'd already come up with several unknown facts that she simply couldn't have gotten elsewhere.

As he told the other detectives back at the Modesto Police Department when he returned, he'd never experienced anything quite like the psychic session. "You should have seen her," he said, shaking his head. "She sort of closed her eyes and started going through the murder. Sometimes she was the victim, and sometimes she was the killer. And I was supposed to ask her questions like she was each of those people."

Some of the detectives guffawed, but Taylor shook his head. "No, listen. What really freaked me out is that she said something like, 'I'm dead now, but I get cut again.' And then she touched her side." Taylor mimicked Renier feeling her left rib. "She said, 'I'm cut right here,' and I thought I was going to fall on the floor. That's exactly where Debi received a postmortem cut! She even positioned her hand at the most likely angle of entry for the wound! And nobody knows about that." Taylor looked around at the other detectives with amazement. "I mean *nobody*."

Dick Ridenour listened with interest. In addition to being the crime scene manager on the Whitlock case and the department's hostage negotiator, he had been on the victim's side of violent crime. Only a year or two into his role as detective, Ridenour had been called to the scene of a shooting in one of Modesto's city parks. A group of young men had opened fire on three teenagers who had been sitting in a baseball dugout and were unable to escape the gunmen. It wasn't until he arrived at the scene that Ridenour recognized the one fatality among the victims as his own nephew. The family had been grief stricken, and then victimized again when the killer escaped from San Quentin four years into his sentence. Finally, Ridenour's brother (who would one day be mayor of Modesto) landed the case on *America's Most Wanted*, and Detective Ridenour was working the *AMW* phones when the tip came in. The fugitive was recaptured shortly thereafter. Needless to say, Ridenour was a big fan of the show, and he hoped for the best for Debi's family.

"Earlier, you said something about a sketch," Ridenour prompted. "Did she come up with a suspect?"

Taylor nodded. "That's the weird thing. She comes up with this guy who looks Cuban or African-American, thirty-something, no one I've ever seen or even heard of. And it's like I'm supposed to be impressed or go, 'Aha!' but all I can think is, 'Now who the heck is this guy?' "

Although the show wouldn't air for several months, Taylor had been given a copy of the sketch, and he passed it around the group. The suspect had a high forehead, broad nose, and kinky shoulder-length hair. Bill Grogan stared at it for a long time. "I'm with you. Who the heck is this guy?"

"Exactly." Taylor turned to the case's former lead investigator. "But this psychic was right about so many other elements of the scene that, frankly, I hate to discount it." He glanced around and was met with nods of understanding. Encouraged, he turned back to Grogan. "Also, I wrote down what she said about the suspect, and I want to run it by you to see if it rings any bells." Taylor looked at the eager faces around them and realized no one was going anywhere. He laughed. "Fine, why don't we all go over it?

"Renier said that the killer was a white male but with a dark complexion—"

"But the guy in the picture is obviously black," said Jon Buehler, Ridenour's new partner. Next to Ridenour, Buehler was the most outgoing detective in the unit. The two men working together were like a social club in a squad car.

"Maybe mixed race?" suggested someone else.

Taylor cleared his throat. "—white male but with a dark complexion, possibly mixed race, five foot ten, one hundred and sixty-five pounds, tattoo on his shoulder, possibly representing military service."

Grogan started. "That's what the first psychic said! Remember that psychic the family brought into the house a week or so into the case?"

Taylor nodded and turned back to his list. "The killer also wore a ring that has something to do with the letters *SK*, and maybe a work uniform or else athletic clothing. He's a private person, likes books—"

"I think she picked up on your vibes there, bookworm."

"—and he is very image-conscious. He had a working relationship with the victim. He has no conscience."

"No kidding?" That was Buehler again, and Ridenour laughed appreciatively.

The detectives went over the list again. Many of them had

been at the house that morning, and in spite of the occasional joking and pantomimed palm reading that the moment inspired, they all felt personally invested in this case. Many of them had met Jacque, and they respected her efforts to bring publicity to her daughter's case. They had heard about the case in workshops, and Taylor had interviewed those who had been on scene numerous times. But their discussion of the psychic's information netted no new suspects.

Debi Whitlock's episode of *America's Most Wanted* finally aired in November of 1992, four and a half years after Debi's murder. Jacque MacDonald sat in her living room in Merced, along with her friend and grief counselor, Midge, and her daughter, Karen. The producers had told Jacque that the final edit of the show was "a tasteful representation" of the case. Jacque was pleased by the news, but with Dennis flying out of the country, she had been sure to have a support network around her just in case she became too emotional while she watched.

The three women sat side by side on Jacque's plush couch as John Walsh's voice narrated. "March 1988. Debi Whitlock seemed to have it all . . ."

Jacque's friend Midge patted Jacque on the leg encouragingly when Jacque's face appeared on the screen a few minutes later. Dressed stylishly but with great reserve, one of her ever-present angel pins on her lapel, Jacque MacDonald spoke with complete confidence. She had long since lost her nervousness in front of the cameras. "Debi was vivacious. Ambitious. She was always full of hopes and dreams. When I think of Debi, I think, *A joy for all seasons.*"

Watching at home, Jacque said quietly to Midge, "That's what's written on Deb's grave marker, you know."

Now the camera was back in the interior of the home, where the actors pretending to be Debi and her little daughter were engaged in a tea party with plastic teacups and plates piled on a small table. Then the actor hired to play Harold Whitlock entered the frame.

He was, in a word, creepy. Tall and gangly, the man lumbered into the living room, the low camera making him loom menacingly over the happy tea party like a storm cloud settling over a metal Ferris wheel.

Debi looked up into the camera from her position far below her husband. "Don't be the *last* to leave the bachelor party, Harold," she said with a strained smile.

Harold stood there expressionless, then finally said in a flat, humorless way, "You know me . . . I'm always a *good boy*." The actor was haggard, his eyes wild, his voice falsely low in a misguided attempt to emulate Harold Whitlock's deep tones. The upshot of the look, the sound, and the bizarre script was that "Debi's husband" looked like Jack Nicholson in *The Shining*, minus some spittle and a bloody ax.

The next cut revealed the real Harold Whitlock, his pale skin looking blemished in the harsh lights. He exuded nervousness, his voice shaking and his face twitching as his eyes constantly roved the room. His thinning hair was fashioned into an early-stage combover. He was talking about his conversation with Debi prior to leaving the house. "She was aware, of course, that we were having this bachelor party, and had made some joke about 'be home early.' You know, just some offhand remark. And then I kissed her and I left."

His words were straightforward and simple, but his body language coupled with the creepy actor playing his part combined to form a menacing psychopath who looked guilty as hell.

Watching from home, Detective Ray Taylor sighed heavily. He

knew what was coming: hundreds of calls from viewers saying, "Just look at the husband! He had to be the killer!"

Walsh related that the Whitlocks had received months of "late night anonymous phone calls," and the reenactment moved inexorably closer to the kill.

The director pulled out all the stops at the entrance of the killer. Eerie notes from a keyboard laid the soundtrack as a shadow stalked stealthily through a room lit bizarrely by pale blue lighting. A lone spotlight shone on a pale figurine on a coffee table, casting across the ceiling a hulking humanoid shadow, its arms raised in a threatening gesture.

"This is a *tasteful rendition* of the crime?" Jacque's friend asked incredulously, as the camera zoomed in on a knife block atop a tiled counter. "I don't know if you should watch this."

Debi's sister had covered her eyes several minutes ago, but Jacque was staring intently at the screen. "No, it's fine," she said. "That's not Debi. Did you see? She's right-handed. Deb was a lefty. I just keep telling myself that."

The eerie background noise faded just enough to make room for the exaggerated sound of the knife being pulled with excessive slowness from its wooden holster, resonating with an incongruous metallic *zing*. The gloved hand tilted the knife back and forth fractionally until light glinted off its blade.

"Oh, honestly!" Midge said in undisguised disgust.

At home, Jacque watched the footage of the psychic reading with interest. Norene Renier was dressed in a violently purple skirt and matching suit jacket over a plum colored silk top. Her beaded earrings rattled as she moved, talking to Debi's killer in the voice of a lifelong smoker. "You didn't just want to kill her outright. You wanted her to suffer. You know you did." She chastised him, listing the steps he took leading up to the murder. "The phone calls. The little touches. Yes, the little touches."

Midge glanced sideways at Jacque, whose hand was covering her mouth. "Are you doing all right with this?"

"Yes," Jacque mumbled.

"OK. You let me know if . . ." Midge's voice trailed off as she saw the gleaming knife back on the screen. Renier's gravelly, otherworldly voice narrated as the killer: "*Hate. Anger. I've got to mess her up some way.*" Now the actress playing Debi was on the floor beside her bed, scrambling to get away and shrieking at the top of her lungs.

"Good God," Midge said, mesmerized.

A wicked smile played coyly under Renier's closed and heavily shadowed eyes. "I enjoy . . . I enjoy . . . I'm enjoying this. I'm enjoying this a great deal."

Debi's sister Karen had already left the room, and Jacque closed her eyes. "I might get sick." She opened her eyes again briefly to see Renier holding the knife, making exaggerated sweeping motions as she chanted, "Debi, Debi, Debi, bitch, bitch, bitch."

Now that the "killing" was done, Renier's body language changed subtly. Then, as Debi, she wailed, "Didn't want to die! Didn't want to die!" She waved her arms despondently, completely at a loss.

Jacque was given the last word to address her daughter's loss. "You can keep saying, '*I'm not a victim; I'm a survivor.*' But we are victims, because we don't know who killed Debi. And we will continue to be victims until we find out. *Then* we'll be survivors."

Jacque was shaken by the show, but she was also glad that another set of viewers had heard Debi's case and her own plea for information. Norene Renier's sketch of the killer was picked up by newspapers and televised news shows across California, and Jacque hoped he would be recognized. Also, she hoped that the show would dispel some of the suspicion still surrounding her son-in-law. Jacque had appeared with a psychic on *The Jerry Springer Show* previously, and that woman—and now Renier—had told the nation that Harold Whitlock had not killed his wife.

Detective Taylor was exceptionally busy in the weeks following the show. Over four hundred viewers had called, half of them naming a suspect. Setting aside those who named Harold Whitlock, Detective Taylor called in reinforcements to help him check other names through criminal and facial recognition databases, local microfiche, CLETS (California Law Enforcement Telecommunications System), and DMV to determine if they had any association with California. If the name made it through that screening process (meaning they had a chance of legitimacy), Taylor himself examined booking photos or license photos and had prints sent from the Department of Corrections so that he could compare them to latent prints found in the Whitlock crime scene. If blood typing was in the file, he used this information to rule out suspects as well.

After this process, Taylor looked at his small list of possible perpetrators. Taylor conducted interviews and ordered basic blood tests for his five "finalists."

From the four hundred phone calls, two names were added to Taylor's ongoing list of possible perpetrators: one was a former violent sex offender living in Modesto at the time of the murder and the other was a longtime felon currently incarcerated in Arizona. Both had blood types matching the drops found on the Whitlocks' kitchen counter and patio.

A call from a Southern California prison revealed that the sex offender had been in jail on the night of Debi's murder. That left one guy: Edward Cunningham.

The tip had come from an Arizona convict named Jackson Lee, who was in the next cell. Lee claimed Cunningham was a violent offender who had bragged about pulling off a Modesto murder sounding very much like the one profiled on *America's Most Wanted*. According to Lee, Cunningham identified Debi Whitlock as his victim.

Taylor discovered that Cunningham had ties to Modesto and had been through the area several times during the late 1980s. Based on this and an initial blood type match already on record, Taylor felt confident enough to make a trip to Arizona. He invited the case's first lead detective, Bill Grogan, to accompany him.

Together the two Modesto detectives traveled to a prison outside Flagstaff. They interviewed the two convicts extensively and felt hopeful they were on the right trail. Cunningham was telling them things about the victim that had not been publicly released and, given his history of violence, it was entirely believable that Cunningham had been Debi Whitlock's brutal killer.

Taylor and Grogan spent an entire week in Arizona, securing eight different search warrants and a full blood screen on Cunningham. They went through seedy apartments and became physically ill from heat exhaustion in a storage unit that had an inside temperature of over 130 degrees. They interviewed dozens of people familiar with the convicts. Over the course of the week, their enthusiasm waned, then died entirely. Taylor and Grogan ultimately realized they had been scammed. Lee had offered several incentives to Cunningham if the latter would help Lee receive early parole. Since there was no chance Cunningham would ever be paroled, he had agreed to the plan.

Dispirited and frustrated, Ray Taylor compiled a forty-page report summarizing all of the evidence in the Debi Whitlock case and took it to the Sacramento office of the California Bureau of Investigation. Top CBI agents went through all of the evidence, piece by piece. The most likely scenario, according to one crime scene reconstructionist, was that Harold Whitlock had returned early from the bachelor party and caught his wife with another man, the breather in the master bedroom. Angered, Harold likely returned to the bar or called someone he knew from there, and then hired someone either to kill his wife or to help him do the deed.

Taylor nodded tiredly. Yes, he'd been through both of those scenarios, but there was simply not enough evidence to support it. Furthermore, Taylor believed in light of his recent confrontation with Harold that the man was not involved in any way.

Take out Harold Whitlock, and who was left?

The Bureau could offer no other plausible scenarios, given the information at hand. They all reached the same conclusion: Ray Taylor had done all there was to do. There was no hope for a resolution to the case, short of a miracle.

Taylor went back to the department and asked that the case be reassigned. Jacque was getting slow but steady media attention for the Whitlock murder, and it needed to be assigned to someone who could juggle other assignments and follow up on the Whitlock case on short notice. That no longer described Ray Taylor. He was still the sole crime scene manager for the department and, based on his frustration with Debi's case, had established the department's first CSI Unit. Modesto's growing homicide rate made those duties more demanding.

He was also becoming more involved in domestic violence issues, where his particular skills were needed by the many women in Modesto who were beaten, and increasingly killed, by their abusive boyfriends and husbands. Hundreds of women put their faith in the wrong men, much like Debi Whitlock had done in her first marriage and, some believed, her second. It was a problem that Ray Taylor was anxious to tackle. He was optimistic that he could make a difference, and his supervisor agreed. In the winter of 1993, the chief authorized Ray Taylor to set up MPD's Domestic

Violence Unit. Within a few short years, Modesto's homicide rate from domestic violence would drop to zero.

On December 3, 1993, Debi Whitlock's case was reassigned to its original lead investigator, Bill Grogan. It was the Christmas present nobody wanted. There were no new leads of any substance. The neatly organized notebooks lay on a dusty shelf, waiting for the miracle the CBI had mentioned and that Jacque was positive would come.

FOURTEEN

Weddings

In the fall of 1992 I was living in Chapel Hill, North Carolina, while my boyfriend, Ira, attended law school at UNC.

I wanted to invite my father to our wedding the following May, although I felt certain he wouldn't attend. Our relationship had been sporadic and guarded since I moved away from California four years earlier. He, too, had relocated with Jessie and Heather Barnett to Miner's Cove, Oregon. However, during our infrequent phone conversations, my father sometimes mentioned his desire to return to the East Coast. "Miner's Cove reminds me so much of home," Dad told me. "One side of the town is on the coast, but you drive ten minutes and you're suddenly in these beautiful rolling hills." He sighed. "I still think about moving back home to Virginia."

But in spite of his talk, my father showed a reticence to return that bordered on dismay: ghosts waited for him in Virginia: phantoms of a troubled childhood and, conversely, of a gloriously promising adolescence. They were equally difficult for a broken man to face. I hoped that if I could entice my father to come for a visit, he would discover that the ghosts of the past could somehow minister to the hollowness of his spirit now. Perhaps together they could form a new and improved Harold Whitlock. If not, at least my sister would be within a few hours' drive.

With this plan in mind, I called my father, and we spent a few minutes catching up. "You still working at the lumberyard?" I asked.

"Yep. They keep asking me to take an office job, but I told them I spent enough years in an office. Now I like the pure pleasure of pounding a nail into a piece of wood." He paused, considering. "You know, you get up on a roof and you lay a line of shingles, and you stand back and say, 'I did that, and now it's done.' I've discovered an incredible satisfaction in that."

I could almost see my father up there on the roof, the Oregon coastline violent and beautiful behind him, but my father in complete control of this handful of shingles. Laying them into place one at a time, an anonymous guy and the task at hand.

My father interrupted my thoughts. "You know, I'm fairly certain I had a breakdown after Debi died. It's hard to tell when you're in the middle of it, but looking back, I'm pretty sure I was just about out of my mind."

The thing about talking to my father was that I never knew which version of him I would get. Would he be distant? Or comic? Or, like today, would he talk like we had been confidants for years? At a loss for what to say, I fell back on Paul Simon. "Hey, breakdowns come and breakdowns go."

My dad supplied the next line of lyrics. "But what are you going to do about it? That's what I'd like to know."

We stopped, both of us thinking of the next line but refusing to say it: *You don't feel you could love me, but I feel you could.*

My father cleared his throat. "So, you didn't call to hear my book report on *Zen and the Art of Roof Maintenance*."

"No, but I'm enjoying it," I answered truthfully. "It's been too long. And that's one reason I'm calling. Ira and I are getting married next May, and I'd like for you and Jessie to come."

"Wow. Married, huh? You sure know how to make a guy feel old."

"Sorry. How selfish of me." I laughed. "We've planned to get married pretty much since our first date two years ago, but we decided Ira should get through his first year of law school. He needs to concentrate on that."

"Ira's going to law school?" My father sounded incredulous. "But lawyers make money, am I right? And I thought Ira only did bleeding-heart, no-paycheck stuff." I heard the smile in his voice.

Ira had spent the last year working with Savannah's inner-city homeless population in conjunction with the Catholic Church. He'd slept at an abandoned church retreat in the marshes, and drove a donated, clunker of a car to and from the soup kitchen downtown. His sense of doing good had been his only compensation.

"Well, maybe he'll only do *pro bono* stuff."

My father laughed. "You know *pro bono* is Latin for 'I just made a million bucks by screwing the little guy, so now I'll do one hundred dollars of work for free to make myself look good.' "

"Wow. All of that?"

"Yeah. Latin was a very economic language. Not like German. If I said the same sentence in German, it would take me two and a half days."

"Bummer."

"*Ja*. On the plus side, it would probably boil down to two or three really, really long words."

Our chitchat eventually returned to the subject of the wedding, and I tried to allay any fears he might have about his reception by my mother or her family. "You know Nana has always loved you. And Mom is dating someone, so I doubt she'll be upset. Why don't you come?"

He considered. "It means a lot to me that you want me there, but it's bound to be a crazy time. Why don't I fly you and Mr. Do-Good out next year for your wedding present? That way we'll have more time to visit."

I almost dropped the phone. "That sounds great, Dad. Whichever way you prefer. I'd just love to see you and Jessie again."

"Same here," he said, almost tenderly.

"So what about you and Heather?" I asked, changing gears before things got too maudlin. "You thinking about getting married again?"

"Who, me?" His voice suddenly became sad. "No. I mean, I've thought about it. I owe her a lot, you know, so I guess that's one reason to marry her. And an even better reason not to." Then he sighed. "You know what they say: if at first you don't succeed, try, try again. Then, if you still don't succeed, give up and stop making an ass of yourself."

My father had never been very forthcoming about his relationships after he divorced my mother. I once met a woman he dated during the separation; I can't remember her name, but she gave me a diary with a little golden lock and matching key. She claimed she had been dating my father "for a while now." He looked horrified when she said that. I never saw her again.

And then one day, Dad took me to his new house. A woman's clothes hung in the closet. During the next visit, I met Debi.

In the summer of 1984 I was fourteen, and Mom and I were preparing to move from California back to my parents' home state of Virginia. I was visiting Dad and Debi over the weekend, and Debi called me into the living room. I sat on the couch and looked at them, my father looking embarrassed in his chair and Debi standing behind him with her hand on his shoulder. It was a strange tableau—the first time they had ever sat me down to have a talk. I didn't know what to expect.

"Um," my father began. "How do you feel about . . . you know, me and Debi living together?"

"OK, I guess."

"OK, you guess," my father repeated tonelessly.

Debi made a sort of huffing noise, and I was afraid I'd said something offensive. "I mean, all my friends know you guys are living together, so, you know, it's OK."

"Well, how would you feel if we maybe got married?" Dad asked.

"Great!" I hoped they would get married before Mom and I moved. Would I get a new dress? Would there be a big party?

My father didn't say anything, so Debi took over. "You know, don't you, that I would never try to take the place of your mother?"

"Yeah, I know." I practically laughed. They'd been living together for years, and Mom and I were moving away. Why would this worry Debi now?

She nudged my father.

"OK," he said, taking a deep breath and staring into his clasped hands. "The thing is, Debi and I are married. I mean, um, already." He glanced up at me. "Already married," he repeated.

"You already got married? When?"

My father looked at his hands again and Debi said his name. He looked away. "Over a year ago."

"What?" I tried to keep the disappointment out of my voice.

Debi answered. "We got married a year and a half ago. We were just . . ." She glanced irritably at my father. "We were waiting for *the right time* to tell you." She said it in a way that made it clear she had heard the excuse many times.

My father stood up. The discussion was clearly over.

"Well, um, congratulations," I said lamely.

Debi stared at my father, clearly irritated. Then she turned to me. "Thank you," she said briskly and walked toward the back of the house. She seemed upset. I didn't know there was more he wasn't telling me. Debi was three months pregnant.

That incident should have clued me into the possibility of serious marital discord between my father and Debi. However, four years later, while living with them, I was so busy being a big sister that I was largely taken unawares the night Debi told my father their marriage was over and all hell broke loose.

Ira and I were married in May of 1993, and that winter Dad called to finalize plans for my husband and me to visit him for our first anniversary. That settled, I mentioned that I had heard Jacque got Debi's case onto *America's Most Wanted*. "Did anything ever come of that? Or have you heard?"

My father laughed derisively. "Of course I've heard. Me and the investigators, we're tight."

My dad went on to explain that he had driven Jessie down to Merced a couple of months ago to spend her summer vacation with Jacque and Debi's sister. "Next thing you know, I'm back in the interrogation room."

"I don't understand," I said, genuinely perplexed. "Everyone knows you were at that bachelor party at Ortega's."

There was a pause. "Well, I had to take care of some business outside the room that night for a few minutes."

"Some business?"

"Yeah. I think I fell asleep in another room or something. It was so long ago, I don't really remember."

He was being evasive, but I passed it off. Maybe he had passed out in Jerry Ortega's office. Whatever he had done in that other room wasn't any of my business, and it certainly didn't make him a murderer. Then a thought struck me.

"Wait. This new detective asked if you slipped out and killed Debi? Doesn't he know the other detectives cleared you a long time ago?" So far as I knew, any doubts the police had about my father were cleared up before I left California. Yes, I had seen some of that suspicion myself when the investigators interviewed me at school shortly after the murder, but that was over five years ago. Surely everyone had realized by now there was no way my father was involved. For God's sake, the man was at a well-attended bachelor party at a popular bar until five o'clock in the morning!

Then I remembered the only crime show I'd seen about the case. *Missing: Reward* had cast a lot of doubt on my father. Suspecting the worst, I asked, "Did someone watching *America's Most Wanted* tell this Taylor guy that you were the killer?"

"Ah, an interesting question! Actually, some voodoo woman on the show sacrificed a chicken and read in the entrails that I didn't do it."

"Voodoo woman?"

"OK, so she was supposedly a psychic, and no poultry was harmed during her spectacular performance. But the point is that she went into her purple haze and said some guy had called Debi, then come over and killed her. She made a sketch of the guy. Looks black to me."

"So . . ." I was still trying to make sense of it. "So the detective wanted to know if you recognized the guy in the sketch?"

"It was more like, '*Tell us about your homeboy accomplice here.*'"

"Seriously?"

"He did one better than that," my father said vehemently. "While I was in Modesto, he sent a Gestapo team up here to terrorize Heather."

Dad rarely mentioned Heather, and given how he guarded his privacy, it was equally possible that they had broken up or, conversely, gotten married and produced a household of kids.

"They grilled Heather, the guys at the lumberyard, our neighbors. They cuffed some of Jessie's Care Bears. We're talking full-scale invasion. Scared the crap out of this small town, I'll tell you that. Most of these people are still living in the 1950s, and all of a sudden they're invaded by the Central California National Guard."

I felt sorry for my father. He had finally found some anonymity and a quiet life in Oregon, and now that had been taken away from him.

"I'm sorry, Dad. How have . . . How have people handled it there?"

He sighed. "These are good people around here. And you know, some of them have run away from their own demons. They know me here. They know what they need to know. In a town like this, it's sort of live and let live as long as you treat folks respectfully. So they've really—" His voice cracked, and I felt a lump rising in my own throat. We were both quiet for awhile. When he spoke again, my father sounded weary. "Sometimes I feel like the stupidest hooker in town: I keep getting screwed, but somehow no one ever pays me."

In May of 1994 my husband and I flew into San Francisco and drove up the inland highway through mining country, then cut to the Oregon coast. We arrived in Miner's Cove at midday and made our way to the rustic lodge where Dad had booked us a room. He had very thoughtfully left a large cooler there with some soft drinks, crackers, cheese, salami, and some other munchies. I called him to let him know we had arrived. "Thanks for the cooler," I said. "You're full-service around here!"

"I guess." His distant tone threw me off.

"So where would you like to meet up?" I asked.

"Why don't you meet us at the house around dinnertime? Then we'll go out with Bob and Doris."

"Oh. OK." I tried not to sound disappointed. It was hours before dinner, and we only had three days in town.

My father gave me directions and hung up. He sounded more distant than he had in a year. What was going on? We had been speaking so freely on the phone with each other since I had invited him to the wedding. Was he having second thoughts about our visit? Had I made a horrible mistake by coming here?

I pondered the situation as I walked through the pine trees outside the lodge. I listened to the waves crashing against the nearby coastline and caught glimpses of white foam through the pine boughs. Ebb and flow. Ebb and flow.

I thought back to the friendship my father and I had shared after Debi left, of his bizarre and cruel response to my sexual assault, and how after six weeks of silence, he had called me "honey" as he told me of Debi's murder. I thought about his empty hug in the San Francisco airport when I returned a week later, and how he would not meet my eyes when I told him I was moving back to Virginia. I recalled our infrequent, stilted phone conversations since then—sometimes distant, sometimes confessional, but always exhausting. Now here I was in Oregon, hoping for a new beginning but realizing, too late, that it was just the same old ebb and flow.

My husband and I drove the rental car to my father's house a few hours later. Dad, now balding, opened the door. I was pleased to see he had put on a little bit of weight, and I knew it was Heather's doing.

"Hi there!" I chirped determinedly.

"Hello." He extended his hand self-consciously to shake mine. I ignored it and hugged him, feeling his hand pat my back in an awkward staccato. I didn't care. I was going to get through this if it killed me.

I introduced my husband and headed for my sister, now a little girl of almost eight. Though we only spoke a couple of times a year, my sister and I shared a connection that would always allow us to pick up right where we had left off.

"Sissy!"

"Hey, Jess," I said, giving her a big bear hug. "Look at what a beautiful girl you are!"

"You have long hair!" she squealed. "I can braid hair pretty good now!"

"I don't know about that." Heather Barnett walked into the living room, still slim and sporting short hair. Only her eyes looked older. Much older. "Hi," she said, smiling.

"Hi," I replied, introducing her to my husband.

I let Jessie 'braid' my hair before we left for dinner, and within minutes I had upwards of twenty different plastic barrettes stuck haphazardly in my mostly knotted hair.

"That's probably enough," Heather said to Jessie, laughing good-naturedly.

"Aw, Mom!"

"It's almost time to leave," Heather replied. "Uncle Bob and Aunt Doris will wonder where we are. Go to the bathroom, and let's get going."

"I should probably go, too," I said, putting a hand to my hair.

"Why don't you use the one in the back?" my father said from the couch, where he and my husband had been trading trivia about Isaac Asimov.

I walked down the hall and into the master bedroom. The restroom was located on the other side of a tall chest of drawers, on top of which was a framed certificate of marriage. My father had married Heather Barnett over a year ago. Two months before I married Ira. Three months after he had told me that, even though he "owed" Heather, he would never marry again. I went to the restroom and returned to the living room, never mentioning the marriage certificate.

"You're keeping your hair like that?" Heather asked with a smile.

I looked at her. My father's wife. "Of course!" I smiled at Jessie. "People at the restaurant are going to be so jealous!"

"Sure, *you* don't care," my father said, "but we have to live here." He wasn't looking at me, but at least he sounded a bit friendlier. I could live with that.

Over the next two days Dad settled into the role of tour guide, and as long as I didn't ask for more, he seemed relaxed and comfortable. I spent as much time as I could with my sister, drawing in the sand with sticks and exploring lighthouses and rocky coastlines.

On my last night there we stood together at a scenic overlook, silently watching the sun sink into the Pacific Ocean. Jessie slipped her hand into mine. I gave it a squeeze and smiled down at her, and her return grin was toothy and mischievous. Then she ran back to Heather, the woman she called Mom, and stood wrapped in her arms as the temperature began to drop.

Looking at them, I knew they shared a love as genuine as any mother and daughter. I hoped my smile to Heather conveyed the thanks in my heart.

FIFTEEN

A Mother's Voice

Shortly after Jacque moved back to California the year following Debi's murder, the grieving mother had found comfort from the Stanislaus and Merced County Victim/Witness Assistance Offices. These offices were attached to the District Attorney's Office for each county and provided crime victims with a variety of different services including counseling referrals, financial aid, and help in understanding the legal aspects of their family tragedy.

The counselors knew that speaking to other family members in similar circumstances would help Jacque. A local chapter of the national organization, Parents of Murdered Children, had recently disbanded—a happy circumstance because it indicated that the need was not great in the community. And yet there was no general survivor group to take its place.

Not long after, a woman named Jean Hoover called Jacque. Jean had recently lost her son, Kevin, a twenty-five-year-old Army veteran who had been awarded one of Germany's highest honors for his rescue of a German civilian. Kevin was killed in a brutal act of violence on January 19, 1989, and Jean was devastated. She had gone to the Victim/Witness outreach coordinator looking for parents who had suffered a similar loss. The coordinator gave her Jacque's number.

Jean Hoover and Jacque MacDonald found comfort and understanding in each other's company and, with the assistance of the Victim's Outreach Office, they decided to form a new support group. Jacque had named the group, Survivors of Sorrow (SOS), and Jean organized the first meeting. An advertisement in the *Merced Sun-Star* drew a small, sad collective to a nearby church fellowship hall one evening in the spring of 1990. The group grew each month.

Participants were dealing with a wide range of losses. Loved ones had been murdered or had died through illness or accident. Children had run away or been victims of kidnapping. Among the Central Valley's growing immigrant population were those whose family members had been deported. Jacque and Jean never turned anybody away.

Members found comfort and understanding in one another's company, and Jacque was pleased to have helped found the group. Still, sharing her own sadness and listening to the heartbreak of others often left her shaken.

"You'd think we would all feel better," she explained to Debi's sister, Karen, who was not interested in attending. "But sometimes I think it actually makes me feel worse."

The two women were enjoying a day of shopping, and Jacque had stopped by the See's Candies store in the Merced Mall, where she knew all the staff on a first-name basis. Now mother and daughter were seated side by side on a wooden bench near the center of the mall, eating truffles and watching other shoppers wander by.

"Then why go, Mom? Why put yourself through that?"

"Because they understand." Jacque licked a bit of melted chocolate from a finger. "You know what it's like. People who haven't experienced this, they want to be sympathetic, but they don't really know what to do or say."

"I guess that's one reason I just don't talk about it," Karen replied. "I mean, except for the family." She paused, struggling to form the thought into words. "Since Debi died, I just feel like I . . . I don't connect to people. I don't trust people anymore. I'm afraid to let my guard down, because then I don't have anything protecting me. The way I feel about Debi—well, that's mine. So I just don't talk about it."

Jacque took her daughter's hand and squeezed it as Karen blinked hard, trying to discreetly clear her eyes. "I can't *not* talk about it. I am the mother of a murdered daughter. I don't know how to not be that. And even though *some* people"—she arched an eyebrow at her daughter—"might suggest that I get on with my life, I just can't. I'm not even going to try. Can you understand that?"

Karen considered. "Well, that's not how I am, but I think I understand." She straightened her shoulders and reached for her bottle of water. "So what are these meetings like? You just tell your stories?"

"That's mostly what we do."

"I think that would be too sad for me. I'd just sit there and cry the whole time. I do that enough on my own, thank you."

Jacque shrugged. "For a lot of people, talking about it helps. Especially for the new people. They can see that the rest of us are making it. We're still sad, and we're still angry, but we're making it." Jacque patted her daughter's leg, and both women stood. "Sometimes, though, I think I get in trouble."

Karen, considerably taller, looked down at her mother and laughed. "You?"

"Yes. People will come in to the group and say, 'I just can't do this! I can't live like this!' And I come very close to saying, 'Yes you bloody well can!' Honestly, sometimes I have no patience with these people, even though I know exactly how horrible it is."

"Deb wouldn't want you fussing at them," Karen said. "She was so tenderhearted."

"Are you kidding? Debi would tell them exactly the same thing!"

Karen smiled, remembering a trip to Europe that she and Debi had taken as teenagers. At one point the sisters were on a boat overcrowded with surly and sweaty tourists. The girls were famished, and they had to stand in an incredibly long line waiting for a table in the boat's dining area. They finally reached the front of the queue when a large man, radiating self-importance, stepped in front of them.

"Hey! Excuse me!" Debi was determined to get the man's attention, although he was equally intent on ignoring her. "Excuse me!"

The hostess was now at her station. "One, sir?"

"Yes."

"Hey! He just cut in front of us!" All of Debi's fatigue had vanished, replaced by outrage at the man's rudeness.

The harassed-looking hostess glanced at the slight, angry redhead and then at the businessman. She seemed to reach an internal compromise. "Right this way, sir."

"No, wait!"

Karen watched in mortification as her sister followed them. It would do no good to call Debi back. She never backed down from a challenge.

"You know what?" Debi was tailing the man. "My sister and I have been waiting in this line for almost an hour, and you have no right to cut in front of us." The overworked hostess was trying to shush Debi, but she continued, gesturing back toward the line.

"In fact, all those people have been standing in line. And just because you're in a designer suit doesn't mean we owe you anything."

"That your sister?" An older man with a strong Irish brogue stood behind Karen. He was wiry with strawberry blond hair and beard, and fierce green eyes. 'As Irish as Patty's pig,' Jacque would say affectionately. He was watching Debi and smiling broadly.

Karen turned again toward her sister, who was now stomping back toward the line. "Oh, yeah, that's my sister."

"I'd hate to cross that one."

"Yes, you would. Believe me."

Karen turned from the memory and looked at her mother, who was still worrying aloud about her strong opinions getting her into trouble. "You know, Mom, in some ways Debi was just like you."

Jacque continued to look for local avenues to bring Debi's unsolved case to the eyes of the public. Sure, she felt blessed to have landed the story on national talk and crime shows, but Jacque believed that the answer lay closer to home. Jacque's "one person who knows" (as she now called him) was probably still in the area. Because of that, Jacque's first target was always the local media.

Daryl Farnsworth at the *Modesto Bee* had been a true friend over the years, using almost any excuse to mention Debi's case. "I don't have to find an excuse to include you in the paper," Daryl told Jacque whenever she thanked him. "I just have to follow you around, and news *happens*."

And increasingly, that was true. A few years ago, Jacque had talked a regional manager at Pizza Hut into putting a flier on their take-out boxes. From Merced to Stockton, every person who ordered a pizza opened the door to find a photo of Debi Whitlock and a plea for information tacked down to their delivery box. Of course Daryl had covered that. Who would have ever guessed that a major corporation would acquiesce to having information about Jacque's murdered daughter hand-delivered to their customers? Then Jacque had used the money from her mother's meager estate to place the same picture and reward information on grocery carts at the largest supermarket in the area. And just a few months ago, in December of 1994, Jacque was able to secure two giant billboards: one on I-99, the major thoroughfare through the central valley, and the other on Modesto's famous McHenry Avenue.

Daryl and Jacque spoke after the billboards went up. "Now when you write about this," Jacque said, "please make sure you say that Citizens Against Homicide helped me get them. Because I tried for five years, but nobody ever told me I needed a tax-free ID number. Nobody ever said, 'You have to be part of a nonprofit group.' I've been a member of CAH for years! I could have done this years ago!"

"So," Daryl said, "this is the first time any victim has appeared on a billboard. Is that right?"

"That's right. But I've already told several other families how to do this, so you'll see more in the future." Jacque considered. "You know how miserable I am every Christmas." It wasn't a question. Daryl did know. "I always sit around thinking, *Is the killer celebrating right now? Is he with his family? Did he give his mother a present? Did he hug her when he gave it to her?* Because he took away every hug I would have gotten from my daughter. He stole that."

"Yes he did," Daryl agreed.

"But this Christmas—this Christmas I was happy! I got a present I'd been trying to get for five years. My Debi's face is on two billboards! And now the one person who knows—he's going to see her picture, and he's finally going to come forward. I know it."

Daryl scribbled notes on the pad in front of him. Five years.

She'd tried to get those billboards for five years. You had to admire that kind of tenacity. And now, six years after her daughter's unsolved murder, Jacque was absolutely positive that the case would be solved. Daryl Farnsworth had seen so much heartbreak during his time as a crime reporter, but listening to Jacque made him believe that her miracle might come after all.

When speaking to other victims' families, Jacque always gave Daryl the highest praise. "He's one of my angels," she'd say. "He's a good man. I'll talk to him for you." And Daryl had learned early on that being one of "Jacque's Angels" carried a certain amount of responsibility with it. The frail, grieving mother who had written him a plea for help six years ago had transformed into a fiery and increasingly outspoken advocate, not just for her daughter but for other victims as well. As such, she frequently called Daryl to ask him to profile other cases or to bring attention to even the most minor development in an ongoing case so that the full story could be presented again to the public. "We can't let them forget about these victims, Daryl," she'd say. "Look at everything you've done for me—for Debi. I just know you're going to help this family, too. Because the truth is, there's no one else to help them right now."

And Daryl would. Not because Jacque had pressured him, but because she had a unique gift for inspiring people to be a better version of themselves. He always maintained that Jacque Mac-Donald had a glorified vision of him. Secretly, that very vision often stirred him into action.

Daryl and other area journalists from Merced to Sacramento had been terrific friends to Jacque and other families in pain; however, it increasingly irritated Jacque that there weren't other, easier venues in which families could talk about their unsolved cases. What these families needed was their own forum, like a local version of *America's Most Wanted* or *Unsolved Mysteries*.

That way they didn't have to experience what Jacque had been through: the hours and days and years of phone calls, fighting for a spot on a national show. Just as important, these families also needed the freedom to talk about not just the crime but also their loved ones. These were more than just a set of horrible facts about how each person was murdered, or abducted, or suddenly missing. They were real men and women, boys and girls. The families needed to share memories and stories about how the tragedy had affected them all.

Jacque started watching the local cable station to see what shows were already on the air. Farmers talked about their crops and cattle. Doctors and lawyers dispensed free advice in hopes of sounding knowledgeable and friendly, thereby drumming up more business. Jacque particularly watched the hosts of a few local-interest talk shows. Could she do that?

"Of course you can do that," Carol Benson assured her. Carol had been a news editor for a local radio station that covered Debi's murder in 1988. Since that time she had started teaching media classes at Modesto Junior College, and she was also Jacque's unofficial media advisor. "I know what it takes to talk to people, and you can talk to *anybody*."

"I think most people consider me friendly," Jacque conceded.

"And well-spoken. A British accent is a bonus in this market. It adds a patina of sophistication and believability. Besides, this has become your passion. You're not just after salacious information. You actually respect these people. I think you'd be terrific."

John Kano hosted one of the local shows Jacque had watched, and she remembered meeting him in the past. She called, and he invited her to appear on his show. She agreed, and in return invited him to go with a group of survivors to the annual March on the Capitol. Together they boarded a local bus, one of many such buses leaving from all over the state in order to take participants to the rally. Once they arrived in Sacramento, they listened to the speakers and viewed with quiet respect the seven hundred coffins lining the capitol building lawn, each one a silent symbol of a homicide victim. On the way back to Merced, Jacque confided her idea to Kano.

"I want a show, John. I want a show so victims can be heard."

"Then let's do it. You can use my studio."

The Victim's Voice was filmed live on a small sound stage within the Assyrian Cultural Center in nearby Ceres. Victims Against Homicide agreed to provide funding for the first three months; after that, Jacque would pay for the show personally. Kano agreed to act as a temporary cohost until Jacque got the hang of it. They decided each episode would feature one or two unsolved crimes, with a follow-up time for viewers to call in.

Jacque invited California Assemblyman Dennis Cardoza to be her first guest. The two had met years before at a hospital fund-raiser when Cardoza was a Modesto city council member. Since that time, they had become friends. Jacque told the councilman about her daughter, and in turn Cardoza told her about an event that had changed him forever.

When he and his brother were young, their mother owned a police scanner. One day she heard a call go out about a young girl who had been abducted from a neighborhood bordering a nearby park. The Cardoza brothers knew every inch of the park and decided to investigate. They arrived a few moments later, and within an hour they heard frantic voices. Stepping as quietly as they could, the brothers edged closer to the noise. Finally they saw two teenage boys accosting a young girl. The brothers rushed into the clearing. After a scuffle, the Cardozas took the traumatized girl back to her family, then delivered the culprits to the local police station. The event continued to spur now-Assemblyman Cardoza to use his growing influence to bring attention to victims and their families.

Dennis Cardoza had been a true friend to Jacque. He had helped her speak to government officials about upcoming crime legislation, and he did the same for the many families Jacque introduced to him. He had personally contributed money to the reward for information leading to the conviction of Debi's killer. And he was genuinely pleased and honored to be chosen as Jacque's first guest.

During the first show, Jacque alternated between explaining her hopes to the viewers ("I'm going to be turning this show over to a lot of families, and hopefully you viewers can help them.") and chatting with Cardoza about possible solutions for the area's escalating crime statistics (Cardoza favored early intervention coupled with tough repercussions for offenders).

The first several episodes of *The Victim's Voice* were full of good intentions. Jacque had met so many grieving families that she had no problem finding guests. She profiled some of the area's most puzzling unsolved crimes against persons—a police term that included murder, assault, and abduction. She invited only one or two representatives of the family to appear on the episode, having learned this the hard way after sitting squeezed between eight different family members as they gamely attempted to talk over one another.

It was equally important to Jacque to have a member of law enforcement on hand, preferably a detective who was working the case. The family was often uncomfortable talking to the officer, chiefly because they sensed the police were withholding information. Perhaps if she facilitated the conversation, Jacque could help the family realize that the officers had to withhold certain information in hopes of one day using it to help identify the culprit. On the other hand, she hoped to help law enforcement understand that a family in pain needs to know that the officers working the case view their loved one as a person, not just as a file folder on the officers' desk.

While she was shooting the shows, Jacque felt very satisfied; however, viewing the final product was more than a little painful. Because Jacque left her guests so much leeway to say whatever was on their mind, the shows sometimes dragged on a bit. And while the Assyrian Cultural Center had high-quality equipment, the operators were not well-versed in how to use it. This meant that sometimes the guests were telling their stories while the camera focused on Jacque jotting notes to herself or making tick marks on her list of points to cover. Occasionally the camera would jostle for several minutes, making the viewers at home have to look away in order to avoid a headache or motion sickness. And the lighting was terribly inconsistent.

"I look purple!" Jacque complained to John Kano, calling him from in front of her television set at home.

"Now, Jacque."

"I'm serious! I'm watching the bloody thing right now, and everybody looks purple! Can't we do something about that?"

Before he could answer, she groaned. "Now the screen is blank. *Totally blank.*"

Later, Jacque listed her complaints to Dennis. "It's not that I'm not grateful for this opportunity, but we're using our own money for this! Can't we get better people behind the camera?"

"Maybe they just had an off day," Dennis replied charitably. He was standing at the kitchen counter, preparing salmon for the grill. Jacque was beside him, carefully polishing some of the miniature perfume bottles she'd begun collecting in Minnesota.

"No. These mistakes are happening every time. I don't even

know which camera to look at, or when it's safe to check my notes. John said he'd talk to the production crew."

Dennis slid his hand under the plate of fish and vegetables and headed toward the door. "You might also tell the crew to watch that banner in the background."

Jacque lowered the delicate blue bottle in her hand. "What do you mean?"

"You know, that big seal behind the table that says Assyrian Cultural Center." He waved the grilling tongs in an arch, mimicking the wording on the banner. "I was watching the show the other day, and I noticed that the camera was positioned so that one of your guests had the word 'Ass' hanging over his head. You might want to mention that."

Jacque almost dropped her bottle in the sink. "Oh, God!"

"Don't worry, honey. It will all work out. I have faith in you." Dennis smiled and headed outside.

In spite of the production difficulties, Jacque began hearing positive feedback from the community almost immediately. Her friends behind the counter at the local chocolate shop congratulated her when next they saw her. "That's really great, what you're doing for those families."

"I just want them to be heard," Jacque answered, sidestepping the praise but accepting a free truffle with a smile.

Local merchants began to contribute money to help sponsor the show. The Sears where Debi had worked was one of the first sponsors, soon followed by car dealerships, drugstores, and law enforcement organizations. Local celebrities and politicians such as Fresno Mayor Alan Autry, who once played Bubba on the television show *In the Heat of the Night*, and female boxing champion

Jennifer Alcorn, whose husband was a homicide detective, recorded commercials for the show.

In spite of the growing support, Jacque yearned to move out of the studio. She told Kano, "I want to shoot cold cases on location. That's the most likely way to jog people's memories."

"Jacque, the cost is going to be astronomical on that."

"Then I'll raise more money."

Jacque began soliciting items for an auction. She included some personal items from home but also received outside donations. Tom Selleck, Jacque's favorite American actor, sent a signed photograph, and Jennifer Alcorn helped out again by donating a pair of autographed boxing gloves. The auction brought in enough money for Jacque to shoot a few shows on location, but at two thousand dollars per episode, Jacque had to admit that she was bound to the studio.

Meanwhile, families across the valley were turning to Jacque to find organized assistance for their case. She invited the cofounders of Citizens Against Homicide to appear on her show, since that was the organization that had most helped her.

President Jan Miller had lost her daughter Veronica in 1984, just after the girl had finished her first year at Chico State College. Veronica was found murdered in her dorm room. The case was still unsolved.

CAH Vice President Jane Alexander was a widow in 1983 when her boyfriend bludgeoned her aging aunt to death. "It took thirteen years to get a conviction," Jane told Jacque's viewers, "even though I knew who it was for eight years. The only reason they finally arrested him was because I was a total pain in their side." She smiled unapologetically.

"Learning to live through this type of tragedy is like learning to live without a finger," Jan explained. "You wake up every morning, and you miss your finger, and your hand doesn't work as well without it. But you learn to manage. You learn to live without it."

This was a message that Jacque found herself relating time and again. Even those survivors who didn't want to be on her show still wanted to talk to her, if only because she had lived through years of the pain that they were now experiencing. In the grocery store or the shop where Jacque regularly purchased flowers for Debi's grave, people would stop to ask when their own pain would subside.

"I'll be honest with you," Jacque would say. "My daughter has been gone for over five years, and I still can't go to weddings, or funerals, or baptisms. On Mother's Day I skip church because the choir is singing 'I Was There to Hear Your Borning Cry.' When you lose a loved one to sudden violence, it always just happened yesterday."

Many people were taken aback at Jacque's words, especially those who wanted to compartmentalize their emotions and pretend their loss would eventually be roped off from other areas of their life. Jacque knew there were no compartments. She wasn't going to lie about it.

At the same time, Jacque took precautions to keep her show from being too maudlin. She always encouraged guests to share a happy memory about their loved one. "Don't be afraid of the pain of remembering," she told one woman. "You've lost your future with your husband. Don't lose your past."

Jacque maintained her belief that Debi's murderer would be found, but now she was fighting the apathy of the public. There were new homicides every day. The Central Valley was being claimed by competing gangs who ran drugs up and down the highways of California, and the attention span of the public was shortening month by month. Jacque secured more reward money for her daughter's case, but where could she put her daughter's picture now? She considered this as she walked toward Merced's farmers' market, and the next moment she stopped short in front of a bus bench. Of course. The city buses. Forgetting her shopping, Jacque went home and called Jane Alexander at CAH.

"Jane! How can I get reward posters on the Modesto city buses?"

"I don't know, but I'm on it."

Within two months, Debi's photo and the enticement of reward money was on every Modesto city transit bus, as well as at several terminals.

Jacque called Daryl Farnsworth at the *Modesto Bee*. "Now I've done everything I can," she said. "Debi is everywhere. The one person who knows—he'll see her over and over and over again." Her voice was warm and insistent. "You watch, Daryl. Now the miracle is going to happen."

She was absolutely right.

SIXTEEN

Mr. X

The temperature was dropping quickly, although it still wasn't particularly cold at 11 p.m. on November 11, 1996. The lights from the fast-food restaurants and strip malls along Tully Road hid all but the brightest stars in the clear evening sky. It was a nice night for a walk. Good thing, too, since Michael Warnell's bike was broken.

He hoisted his backpack higher up his shoulder and walked on. A few cars passed. Somebody honked, but Michael didn't recognize the car. Probably wasn't for him. A nondescript black man in Coke-bottle glasses, Warnell was used to blending into the scenery.

A black-and-white patrol car passed him on the other side of the street. His mind didn't really register it until a few seconds later when the same car pulled up next to him. He stopped walking.

An officer got out of the car. Warnell knew him immediately. It was the officer who had busted him for burglary back in 1990. Since that time, Warnell had seen him at the Chevron station on

Sisk Road where his girlfriend worked. Warnell often hung out there when she was getting close to clocking out, and Officer— Steele, was it?—sometimes came by about that time for a tank of gas and a coffee. The two men always nodded to each other on sight and often exchanged hellos. Looking at the officer now, Warnell wondered what this was about, but he wasn't particularly concerned. The officer was always polite, and Warnell was clean. Had been for three years now.

The officer walked toward him casually. The nameplate on his uniform read Steele. "Hey. Kind of late to be walking, isn't it?"

"Yeah. Bike's broken."

Steele nodded. "Where you headed?"

"Home." He gave his address: 2101 Vera Cruz, just off Coffee Road. He shifted his backpack. "Just finished up a class."

Steele recognized Warnell's address as the Ensenada Apartments: moderately priced, fairly well-maintained, with a burgeoning criminal population. Officer Steele glanced at his wristwatch. "Late class."

Warnell returned the smile. "Night class, then I went over to my mom's for awhile."

"Trying to be a good son, huh?"

"Trying." He shrugged. "You know how it goes."

The officer seemed to believe that explanation. "You're going to MJC?" Modesto didn't have a university, so locals often went to the junior college before transferring to a four-year school.

Warnell told Steele he'd been taking classes over there for a few semesters. Steele was familiar with the campus, and they chatted amicably for a few minutes.

Shifting topics, Steele gave Warnell an appraising look. "Mind if I take a look in the bag?"

The other man crossed his arms. "What are you gonna do if I say no?"

"Drive away, I guess," said Steele, nonplussed.

"Drive away, huh?" The neon lighting flashed off Warnell's teeth when he smiled. "Man, you're all right. I don't care if you look in the bag." And he didn't. He'd dealt with cops most of his life. Michael Warnell was a large black man with a criminal record and some hard time under his belt. He got stopped a lot. Factor in the late hour, Michael on foot, and the backpack. He could see why this combination would raise suspicions. But Steele was always pleasant and respectful. Didn't give him any crap. Warnell extended the pack. "Go ahead. It's clean. Things are different now."

Steele glanced inside the bag, nodded, zipped it up, and handed it back to Warnell. "I'm glad to hear it. Good for you." Warnell took the pack with a told-you-so grin. A smile flicked at the corner of Steele's mouth.

The two men talked about common acquaintances, mostly folks who had run into trouble with the law a few times. Since his parole in 1993, Warnell had cleaned up his act, and now he was taking classes, living with the nice girl from the gas station, and keeping his nose clean—in every sense of the word. But he still had friends who were in and out of trouble. The occasional disturbance or possession charge wasn't uncommon.

Steele heard a crackle on his radio. "Well, I better head on. Stay out of trouble. I'll see you around." Steele lifted his hand in farewell and headed back to his car.

"Hey, wait!"

Officer Steele turned at the sound of Warnell's voice, and Warnell drew in his breath. Was he finally going to do this? Yeah, what the hell. Too late now, anyway. Steele was looking at him with growing curiosity. "I got some information for you."

Steele took a step toward Warnell. "What kind of information?"

"You've always treated me real nice," Warnell said, warming up to it. "Some of the other cops, they treat me like garbage, you know? I know I've messed up and all, but . . . I don't know, you've always treated me like a regular person. Respectful, I guess." He paused.

Steele looked at Warnell curiously. "Well, thanks. I guess I feel like people make mistakes, but that doesn't mean they can't start making better decisions down the road." He smiled. "Like you seem to be doing."

Now Warnell was starting to think twice about this. The fact was, his life was going really well now. He was out of jail, out of trouble, and enjoying a normal, boring life. And here he was, about to screw that up by getting into somebody else's business.

Steele seemed to sense his hesitancy. "So you know something, but you're not sure you want to say it?"

"Nah, I wanna say it. I just don't want . . . You know, it happened a long time ago, back when I was . . ." his voice died away.

"You're worried that it might reflect badly on you—whatever this thing is?"

"Yeah, I guess so."

Ed Steele put his head to one side, thinking. "OK. Well, I'm happy to work with you. But I don't really know what we're talking about, so it's hard for me to say exactly how to handle this."

Warnell watched Officer Steele, could see that he really was trying to be helpful. Michael had seen his share of cops with chips on their shoulders, guys who went into law enforcement as a legitimate way to bully others. Ed Steele wasn't like that. And besides, there was a family in pain out there, and Michael could help them. If he really was walking the right path now, shouldn't he help people when he could?

"Let's just say, I know something that's been weighing on my mind."

Steele was coming closer, nodding encouragingly, and Warnell already felt better about it. "Something happened a long time ago, and I sort of forgot about it. It was back when I had troubles of my own, you know? But now I'm driving around, and there's these billboards and all these posters and stuff."

Steele looked puzzled.

"Look, I trust you, so I guess I'm going to tell you something I should have said a long time ago."

Twenty minutes later, Ed Steele stood beside his sergeant's Ford Explorer. Their cars were parked bumper-to-bumper by the sidewalk on Rumble Road, and Michael Warnell waited patiently in the front passenger seat of Steele's squad car. Steele held the sergeant's cell phone to his ear, adrenaline humming through his body. The ringing on the phone gave way to a sleepy male voice.

"Hello?"

"Sergeant Harden? This is Patrol Officer Ed Steele. Sorry to call so late."

The sergeant's voice sounded groggy. "Why didn't you go through dispatch?"

"I thought it best not to, sir," Steele answered. "It seemed like I should call you personally."

Harden's tone lost its sleepy quality and took on a note of interest. "Oh? What have you got?"

"You know the Whitlock case? You worked that, right?"

"Yeah."

"Yeah, I thought I remembered you were there." Steele had been on patrol that night and heard some of the radio traffic about Debi Whitlock's murder. "Sergeant, you're not going to believe this. I think we just got a serious lead."

On November 19, Detectives Bill Grogan and David Trogdon arrived at Michael Warnell's residence on Vera Cruz Avenue.

Trogdon had interviewed Michael Warnell a week earlier regarding a recent homicide at the Ensenada Apartments. They had had a pleasant conversation, and Trogdon had agreed to come along with Grogan to help facilitate today's interview about the Whitlock case.

In his hands Grogan carried the memo generated by Ed Steele, detailing his conversation with Warnell from a couple of nights ago. The memo was heavier than its one sheet of paper might otherwise connote: it carried Grogan's desperation to be rid of this unsolvable case, an albatross that had weighed him down for years. Grogan folded the memo, put it in his breast pocket, and stood uncertainly before Michael Warnell's door.

"You know, this woman's mother still calls me almost every week. And when I hear her voice on the phone, it's like my heart sinks. Because I'm wondering, *What can I tell her now? What can I say to make her think there's still some hope that her daughter's killer is going to be found?* And now I'm standing here . . ." There was no need to finish the sentence. Grogan drew a breath and knocked.

"Is this the residence of Michael Warnell?" Grogan asked the young woman who answered the door.

She nodded.

"Bill Grogan," the detective said by way of introduction. "And David Trogdon of the Modesto police. Is Mr. Warnell in?"

"Are you here about Giovanni again?" she asked.

Trogdon turned to his fellow officer and supplied, "That was the victim downstairs last week."

Grogan turned back toward the young woman. "Actually, we're here on a different matter today."

"Oh. That old murder, right? Mike figured you'd be coming by or something." The woman stepped aside and ushered them into the small, neat apartment. "I'll go get him."

A moment later, Michael Warnell walked in. "You mind wait-ing in the other room?" he asked the girl quietly. She said she didn't and left.

Warnell smiled at Detective Trogdon. "Hello again."

"Hi, Michael," David Trogdon said, extending his hand. "This is Detective Bill Grogan. I was just telling him about Giovanni Moore downstairs."

Warnell shook Grogan's hand, then sat down. "Yeah, that was a bad scene. You guys wrapping that up?"

"We're trying," Trogdon answered.

"Too bad about this place." Warnell gestured expansively, taking in the neighborhood. "These were nice apartments. Now you got these guys running around. Gangs or whatever." He shook his head. "I mean, I'm not saying I didn't do some bad stuff in my day, but not like gangs. That stuff can kill you."

Soon the conversation ranged to the Whitlock murder. Grogan needed to verify that Warnell had information and then needed him to go downtown for a taped interview. Warnell agreed, and the three men got into the detectives' unmarked car. Grogan turned the key in the ignition. "Mr. Warnell, if we drove by your old apartments, do you think you could point out the apartments where you and your neighbor lived?"

"Sure," Warnell said. "I did that the other night with Officer Steele, too."

Grogan drove in silence, listening as Warnell chattered about the night his neighbor came into his garage confessing to murder. When they arrived at the 1800 block of West Rumble, Grogan slowed as they passed building after building of nearly identical duplexes. Warnell pointed out his old address at 1815, then pointed to another across the street. Chipped wooden numbers read 1810.

"I think that was it, right there. Scott—I still can't remember his last name—and his mother and stepfather lived there. They used to keep a big blue pickup in the driveway."

"That was Scott's truck?"

"No. I think it was his stepfather's."

"And the stepfather—do you know his name?"

Warnell thought about it. "Nah. I never really talked to the parents, you know? Just Scott. But there were some other guys who used to know him, too. Scott, that is." Warnell paused for a minute. "Hey, you guys aren't using my name, right? Because Officer Steele said I could be anonymous."

"That's right," Grogan said. "I can't guarantee no one will find out your name. This case has had a lot of publicity through the years. But as far as we're concerned, you're an anonymous informant."

"Can I be, like, Mr. X?" The moniker would keep his identity a secret, plus it had an air of intrigue about it.

Grogan smiled to himself. "Sure. We can call you Mr. X."

Warnell then pointed out a few neighboring houses and mentioned the names of young men who had lived there at the time. "We all used to play basketball. Well, not Scott. He wasn't interested in getting into the game. Kind of a loner, you know? And he was also kind of . . . not fat, really, but sort of heavy."

Grogan turned the car east and headed downtown as Michael Warnell relived the old days. As he listened, Grogan surely began to feel the stirrings of hope. The pressure in his chest, where the albatross had hung for more than eight years, must have lightened just a fraction.

Over the next two years, Michael Warnell would tell his story over and over again—to police officers, to investigators, to reporters, to talk show hosts. Sometimes he was asked to dwell on one element or another. Tangential threads of the story might come and go, but except for these slight variations, the story was always the same.

In March of 1988, Michael Warnell lived with his mother, whom everyone called Curly. He'd just recently gotten out of the California Rehabilitation Center, a juvenile detention center of sorts. His mom lived in a duplex on Rumble Road, about a mile from the home of Harold and Debi Whitlock.

March 24 was just another day. Michael Warnell sold marijuana out of his mom's garage, and he had seen quite a few customers that day. He'd also had some friends come in, smoke a joint or knock back a few beers, and just hang out. An acquaintance came by to borrow his bike, and even though Warnell let him use it, it was the general consensus of the guys in the garage that Warnell would never see that bike again. There were jokes and stories, bags of weed and small stacks of cash. Just a normal evening in the neighborhood.

In the early morning hours of March 25, things had quieted down. Warnell was at a table cutting and bagging more marijuana, stopping every now and then to take a swig of beer and maybe change the station on his clock radio. The lights were on, the side door cracked very slightly so friends and customers would know he was in.

At 3 a.m., there was a knock at the door. Warnell opened it and saw his neighbor, Scott.

"Hey, can I come in?" Scott glanced nervously over his shoulder.

Warnell stood aside as Scott walked in. Well, walked wasn't exactly right. More like he bounced in. Scott was Warnell's neighbor and sometime customer, and he had a habit of dropping in almost every day. He was usually pretty laid back—a high school dropout with a laconic sense of humor. They shared the hobbies of burglary and smoking pot. Both close to twenty. Both in the same crappy apartments. They were friends, but not particularly close. Warnell didn't even know the guy's last name.

But something was definitely different about Scott tonight. He was practically jumping out of his skin. His eyes were huge. Probably meth, thought Warnell. He knew Scott used methamphetamine sometimes, and he had all the signs of a major high.

"Hey, man," said Warnell. "What's up?" He followed Scott with his eyes as his friend paced the floor, his hands clenching and unclenching against his dark blue sweatshirt. This looked intense.

Scott eyed the dope on the table. "I need some of that."

"You know the price."

"I'm busted," Scott replied, then went silent. He obviously wasn't in the mood to talk. Instead he continued pacing, his eyes wild, his body twitching beneath the camouflage clothing he always wore. Every now and then he'd rub his hand across the top of his short-cropped hair. Michael went back to work at the table and decided to wait it out. It didn't take long.

"Man, I just stabbed this girl."

Once Scott started talking, the words tumbled out of him like they were making a fast getaway. He told Warnell he'd broken into a house nearby, looking for valuables he could steal. He thought the place was empty, but while he was in the kitchen, a woman surprised him. "She was just standing there all a sudden, and she's asking me what I'm doing there, and—I don't know. I just freaked out." His eye picked out the shape of a knife block on the kitchen counter. He grabbed a knife and lunged at the woman. "I stabbed the lady," Scott said, more to himself than to Warnell. "I think I killed her."

Warnell listened with barely disguised suspicion. This was just a drug fantasy. Scott was tweaking. Warnell knew several people who did crank, knew they tripped out of their minds sometimes.

One user had recently confided to Warnell that Hitler lived in his coat closet and sometimes came out for a chat. What Scott was saying wasn't all that alarming. Maybe even tame, by comparison. Warnell sighed. What was it with guys freaking out and then coming to him?

Warnell rolled a joint and handed it to Scott, who tried to light it with shaking hands. Warnell watched Scott fumble the lighter once, twice. Reaching over, Warnell took the lighter and lit the joint for him. As Scott inhaled deeply, Warnell looked him over. No blood, but would it show up on camouflage pants? Probably. Anyway, the story seemed pretty far-fetched. Warnell held out the lighter to return it, but Scott was up and pacing again, jittery. Warnell laid the lighter on the table.

Scott was talking again, taking long drags on the joint. "So I was freaking out, right? And I ran out the door, and I'm running, and all a sudden I've got the keys. The keys from the house! I don't even know how I got them."

"Uh-huh, keys," said Warnell, not even looking up as he sorted the marijuana into small piles and reached for a box of Ziplocs.

"So I throw them on the grass outside, and just keep—Oh man!"

Warnell looked up.

"My prints are on the keys! I'm screwed!"

Now Scott's story was sounding . . . very coherent. Warnell laid his plastic bags aside. He started to speak but was unsure what to say. He decided not to open with "If this really happened . . ." and instead jumped right to his question. "Wouldn't your fingerprints be in the house already?"

Scott slumped onto a stool in the garage. "Oh man, oh man, oh man. I am so screwed. The knife. The—the—I don't even know. Other stuff. I was—I touched—Oh, man!" Scott looked up toward Warnell, who was now studying him frankly. "You can't tell, OK? Mike? Don't tell." Now Scott was standing up, still agitated, walking closer. "Don't tell! You gotta swear!"

"Sure, Scott. Sure. I swear." Warnell leaned back slightly. Drug fantasy or not, Scott was suddenly looking crazy. Maybe dangerous-crazy.

Scott lapsed once again into silence. Warnell wanted to know more, but he didn't want to be involved in this. He lit another joint and handed it to Scott. After a moment's consideration, he rolled one for himself. "Where did it happen?"

"Down the street." Scott gestured east toward Davis High School. "Not far." Scott shook his head, trying to clear his thoughts. "I didn't mean to do it. I thought the house was empty. I just went in to see if there was stuff I could take, you know? And then she was just there."

Scott talked and paced some more, then headed back to his place, again swearing Warnell to secrecy. No problem, thought Warnell. He only half believed Scott anyway, and if it was true, Warnell wasn't getting involved. He had burglarized the same area of town in the past, although now he was making plenty of money with just the dope. But he had a police record. He was staying out of it. Still, he marveled at the story Scott told him. There were too many details, and they sounded too real.

Later that morning, Curly Warnell ambled into the kitchen and saw a most amazing sight. Her son, Michael, had brought in the *Modesto Bee* and was poring over it, a warm beer forgotten by his side. She knew something was wrong. Her son didn't read the paper. In fact, he couldn't even read all that well. The only thing Michael excelled at in school was slipping out the back door.

"What are you looking at?" she asked.

"Nothing."

"Don't tell me 'nothing.' You never read the paper. What's going on?"

Warnell looked up at his mother, her arms now crossed on her old terry cloth robe. "I need to ask you something, but you gotta promise not to freak out."

Curly Warnell had been through a lot with her son, and she had a sinking suspicion that more was to come. "I ain't promising nothing. Now tell me what you've got to say."

"Well, if a woman was stabbed or something, what part of the paper would it be in?"

Curly sat heavily in a chair. "Sweet Jesus—"

"No, it's not me! This isn't about me! I'm just asking—"

"Who's it about then?"

"I'm not supposed to say." He cringed as he said it.

His mother's eyes glared levelly across the table. "The devil you're not! You tell me what's going on right now!"

Michael told his mother a pared-down version of Scott's visit earlier that morning, repeating his suspicion that the story was probably a hallucination. Together Curly and Michael searched through the paper, but there was no news of the murder. They sighed in relief, chalking it up to the drugs.

Had they turned on the radio or the local televised news that day, they would not have reached the same erroneous conclusion. But no matter. They learned the truth the following morning, when the front page of the *Modesto Bee* sported a full-color, above-the-fold picture of the draped body of Debi Whitlock being wheeled down the driveway of her nearby home.

Curly read the article aloud to her son, then she read it again. "I don't think you should say anything," Curly told her son. "You get in enough trouble as it is. Scott said he left fingerprints, right?"

"Right." Warnell looked distracted and distraught. "But he said they were on some keys outside. Did they say anything about keys?" He gestured toward the paper.

"I just read it twice. It didn't say anything about keys, but that don't mean they didn't find them."

Michael Warnell shifted uneasily in his kitchen chair.

"You wanna tell them?" Curly asked.

"No."

"Then don't." She nodded with finality. "It's none of your business. You already get in trouble with the police, so why won't they point the finger at you?" She considered a moment. "Besides, we don't know what this Scott kid would do to you if you did tell."

"I've got a record, and the cops know it," Warnell echoed. "I don't need any more trouble."

Curly Warnell nodded and reached for a box of cereal. "That's the truth. God knows we got enough of that already." She poured some cornflakes into a bowl. "Let's just wait and see what happens."

Michael looked at his mother. "You can't tell anybody, OK?"

Curly looked at her son. A thief. A drug dealer. But he'd never hurt anybody—she knew that. Would the police believe it?

"You ain't gotta worry about that, son," she said, putting a hand on his shoulder. "I ain't gonna say a word."

Later that week, the newspaper reported that the woman's keys had been recovered, and Warnell and his mother agreed that the fingerprints would soon lead to Scott. They put the matter out of their minds.

By summer, Scott was gone. Warnell barely noticed. After that night in the garage, he hardly ever saw Scott. And anyway, Warnell had started using crack cocaine. Because he had a growing habit to support, his own illegal activities picked up. Warnell gained short-lived notoriety as a gifted cat burglar when several local businesses were robbed without sign of entry, their electronic alarm systems miraculously bypassed but still operational the next morning. Within months, Officer Ed Steele and several detectives apprehended Michael Warnell. He was back in jail, this time at an adult facility, which was so much worse than juvie. Life went on. Warnell didn't think about Scott or the dead woman. In jail, he was isolated from the frantic and fruitless investigation to find Debi Whitlock's killer.

When he got out on parole three years ago, Michael Warnell decided to make some changes in his life. No more drugs, taking or dealing. No more theft. He realized he'd spent more of his life in jail than living it. Things had to change. He'd gotten his GED, and now he needed a straight occupation. He started taking classes at MJC, met a nice girl, and moved in with her. They even started going to Modesto A's baseball games together. And that's when he saw something that took him back to a scene he'd completely forgotten.

Warnell was driving toward the baseball field on Highway 99 when he saw the face of Deborah Anne Whitlock smiling down at him from a huge billboard. Memories came rushing back at him—a neighbor pacing in the garage and muttering, "I stabbed a lady."

Huh. So Scott had never gotten caught. Or maybe it wasn't even him. Michael Warnell averted his eyes and kept driving, ignoring the stir of his conscience. Every time he made the drive, it got harder to look away.

A few months later, he was at the grocery store when he walked by a shopping cart. There was Debi's picture again.

Her picture was on the city bus.

Her picture was on another billboard downtown on McHenry Avenue.

She was on his mother's television set.

The eyes of Debi Whitlock were following Michael Warnell everywhere he went, and he couldn't get away. She was smiling at him with encouragement. She was chastising him. She was challenging him. And if he wanted any peace, he was going to have to tell the police what he knew.

"I talked to my mom about it, maybe a year ago. My girlfriend, too. They were both saying I should tell what I knew. Or thought I knew. And I was feeling that way, too. So that's why I told Officer Steele last week."

Warnell was sitting in an interview room in the detectives' building downtown. Across the table, Detectives Grogan and Trogdon took notes and flipped through files. A tape recorder sat on the table midway between all of them, its spooling tape capturing every detail of Michael Warnell's story. It was just before noon on November 19, 1996: eight and a half years after Debi Whitlock's murder.

The guys in homicide knew Bill Grogan was working the Whitlock case again, but he kept it very quiet. He was making discreet inquiries, researching databases, and having confidential discussions with the captain.

"What you got?" an officer would occasionally ask Grogan.

The answer was always the same. "I don't know yet."

Rumor around the department was that Ed Steele had gotten an incredible tip, and that rumor made its way back to Jacque. She called a friend at the department. "I understand you got a tip in Debi's case."

"How did you hear that?"

"I have a bloody crime show! I hear stuff. So what can you tell me?"

"Nothing yet. Nobody is talking."

"But I'm her mother! This is my life!"

"Jacque, I want to, but I can't. You know how this works."

It struck Jacque that she did, in fact, know how this worked. After years of single-mindedly focusing on finding Debi's killer, of learning how police officers investigate crimes against persons, and having now spent a couple of years hosting a show that addressed both the family and law enforcement aspects of countless crimes—well, Jacque had gained a very thorough education. One she never wanted.

Eventually Grogan confirmed to his coworkers that he had secured permission to travel out of state to question somebody about the case, and excitement spread like wildfire in the dry California foothills. No one wanted to inform the family, especially Jacque. The last thing they wanted to do was set her up for more heartbreak.

Michael Warnell's information had proven invaluable. Detective Grogan spent hours poring over records of blue truck registrations from 1988. He questioned anyone he could think of who could have had ties to Scott. The detective's diligence was unmatched, and eventually he called Michael Warnell to come down to the station and examine a table full of head shots from DMV.

"That's him," Warnell said, pointing to one of the photos.

"Are you certain? Absolutely certain?" Grogan needed there to be no mistakes.

"Absolutely certain," Warnell said. "That's Scott."

Warnell had picked out a photo of Scott Avery Fizzell, one-time resident of a duplex on Rumble Road. His stepfather had owned a dark blue pickup truck.

Now Grogan had a name. It would take another full-scale effort to track down Fizzell, who had left the area long ago. His mother and stepfather were gone as well. And even as Grogan's search brought him closer to finding Fizzell's current whereabouts, he had to caution himself against excitement. What if Scott Fizzell was only repeating something he'd heard from the real murderer?

There were so many unanswered questions. In either case, the next step was obviously to get to this Scott guy, hoping that the element of surprise might lead him to give up any information he knew— whether about his own guilt or someone else's.

On January 12, 1997, Detective Bill Grogan typed an affidavit for arrest, listing all of the evidence he could think of to prove to a judge that there was finally a viable suspect in the long-ago murder of Deborah Anne Whitlock. He took the affidavit to Stanislaus County District Attorney Tom Brazelton, and together the two discussed the evidence. Within the hour, Grogan had his warrant. He was headed to Arkansas.

SEVENTEEN

The Arrest

On the morning of January 21, 1997, Detective Bill Grogan of the Modesto Police Department drove into Flippin, Arkansas. With him were Sergeant Mike Harden, who had also worked the Whitlock crime scene, and Stanislaus County Deputy District Attorney Mike Stone.

Flippin was a small town in the north part of Arkansas, "one hundred miles and twenty years from the nearest big city," according to the locals. Situated on the intersection of I-62 and Highway 178, the town's 1400 or so residents were mostly Caucasian factory workers who had completed some if not all of their studies at Flippin High School, where football was big and the school band was the best in the state.

The Modesto delegation parked on Main Street next to City Hall. The morning was cool and humid, and the slight breeze felt like a plant mister. The men entered the two-story brick City Hall and were directed upstairs.

The amiable face of Flippin's Chief of Police Frank DePriest peeked into the stairwell at the sound of so many shoes on the wooden stairs. The chief had thinning brown hair and authentically scuffed cowboy boots.

"How you all doin'? Hope you found your way all right." DePriest's accent was thick and slow, his body language casual. He had been chief for over four years, and his laid-back manner put the residents of the town at ease. DePriest was the leader of a five-man force, and the work was pretty easy. Talking people down off a drunk, calling folks to say their kids had been caught hot-wiring a car . . . if both happened in the same night, DePriest could call it a crime wave.

"Which one of you gents did I talk to last week?"

Grogan stepped forward. "That was me." They shook hands as Grogan introduced his two traveling companions.

"So how do you want to do this?" Chief DePriest asked, once the pleasantries were observed.

"We just drove by the suspect's residence," Grogan answered, "and it looked pretty quiet."

DePriest rubbed his chin. "Well, Scott works nights at the plant—that'd be Micro Plastics—so he probably just got in a while ago. Wouldn't surprise me none if he was asleep."

"Didn't you mention a girlfriend who lives there, too?"

DePriest nodded. "Yep. Name's Becca. Rebecca Halog. She's from your neck of the woods, by the way. Moved out here with him, from what I understand. Anyway, she works days, so she's probably not there."

"Sir?" This question was both a greeting and announcement, proclaiming that Flippin's new assistant chief was reporting for duty. Steve Smothers's uniform was pressed and starched, his shoes were polished, and his back was ramrod straight. His gray hair was neatly trimmed. Everything about Assistant Chief Smothers proclaimed *retired military*.

Chief DePriest, suddenly frumpy by comparison, smiled. "This here's Steve Smothers. Former chief of police from over at Diamond City, and I guess you could tell, lifelong Coast Guard man."

"Pleased to meet you," Smothers barked.

Chief DePriest made introductions all the way around, then turned back to the matter at hand. "So I was thinking that it'd probably do you boys the most good if Officer Smothers and myself were to go and get Scott and bring him up here. That way y'all could use the mayor's conference room. I'll make sure the table's cleaned off for you."

Grogan thanked the chief for his offer, and DePriest waved off his thanks. "Not a bother. This is a small town. We usually handle things kind of laid-back. And like I told you on the phone, we never had a problem with Scott before, other than that time he got a pretty bad whuppin'." DePriest chuckled. "Thought about pressing charges, too, but these things tend to blow over around here."

Chief DePriest and Assistant Chief Smothers helped Grogan secure a search warrant for Fizzell's premises and another warrant for a blood draw at the local doctor's office. The closest hospital was twenty miles away in Mountain Home, but DePriest assured them they wouldn't need to transport Fizzell. "We only got one doctor, but he's a good one."

It was after lunch by the time DePriest and Smothers climbed into the chief's red Jeep Cherokee and drove six blocks to 202 North Sixth Street. The trailer was quiet, the curtains drawn. Chief Smothers knocked on the door.

Scott Fizzell was a large man in his late twenties with long, unkempt hair. He was wearing sweatpants and a white T-shirt, and a fair amount of fat poked out between the two. He rubbed sleep from his eyes.

"Hey, Frankie."

"Hi, Scott. Guess I woke you up, huh?"

"That's OK. What's going on?"

"Guess you haven't heard from Miss Pearl lately?" Fawn Pearl was a friend of Scott and Rebecca's who had run afoul of the law. There was a warrant out for her arrest, but Miss Pearl had disappeared.

"Nothing lately," Fizzell answered, "but I'd guess she went back out to California. You still looking for her?"

DePriest chose his words carefully. "Well, let's just say we're working on a bit of an investigation over at the station, and I was hoping you might help us out. If you've got some time, that is. We'll give you a ride."

Fizzell scratched absentmindedly at his chest. "Sure, no problem. But like I said, I don't know where she is."

DePriest continued to stand on the front stoop, a benign smile on his face. Officer Smothers stood warily at attention behind him.

Fizzell shrugged. "OK. Let me grab a jacket and some shoes."

Fizzell and DePriest exchanged small talk during the ride to the station. Nothing about the moment let Scott Fizzell know how drastically his life was about to change.

Five minutes later they were back at City Hall. DePriest had grown suddenly silent, and Fizzell followed the chief up the stairs and down the hall to a large room crammed with furniture. The center of the room was heavily occupied by a massive oak table with assorted chairs tucked around it. DePriest pointed toward the far side of the large table. "Now Scott, why don't you sit down right over there, and we'll get started. Steve?" This last remark was directed at the assistant chief, who nodded curtly and left the room. Scott made his way around to the side of the table, pulled out a chair, and eased himself in. He leaned back lazily.

Officer Smothers was back at the door, standing aside to allow others into the room. Three men in suits entered, the first one vaguely familiar. Fizzell sat up. He had seen the big guy's picture years ago. Newspaper? Television? He couldn't quite place it. The guy was stocky and sizing him up frankly. "Scott Avery Fizzell?"

Fizzell wasn't tired anymore. "Yes?"

"I'm Detective Bill Grogan from Modesto, California." He flashed his badge, then gestured to his colleagues entering the room behind him. "This is Sergeant Mike Harden and Deputy District Attorney Mike Stone. We're here to talk to you about a murder that happened in Modesto in 1988."

Fizzell crumpled into his chair, his strength suddenly gone.

At that moment, any doubt vanished. Everyone present knew they had finally found Debi Whitlock's murderer. Bill Grogan, haunted for almost a decade by the image of Debi Whitlock's body, allowed himself a moment of self-congratulation. "I guess you didn't expect to see us."

Fizzell held his head in his hands. In a ragged voice he answered, "I hoped I never would."

Modesto Homicide Sergeant Mike Harden turned on a cassette tape recorder and placed it inconspicuously on top of a filing cabinet as he made his way to a seat next to Detective Grogan. Flippin's Assistant Chief Smothers placed his recorder atop a table at the far side of the room, where he sat near enough to Fizzell to head off any trouble. Chief DePriest sat on the other side of Fizzell, looking as detached and unruffled as if he was listening to some neighbors having a twilight talk on the front porch. Only a trained eye would notice he had placed himself between Fizzell and the door, or that his legs were placed so that he could spring from his seat in a moment.

For benefit of the record, Detective Grogan recapped the situation. "Scott Fizzell, we need to talk to you about a homicide that occurred in Modesto in 1988. Right now you can consider your-self under arrest, homicide, OK? We need to sit down with you and talk to you. Do you understand this?"

Fizzell, still cradling his head, replied, "Yeah, I understand."

Glancing at the Deputy District Attorney, Grogan continued. "Since you're under arrest, I have to advise you of your rights prior to us talking." Grogan read Fizzell his Miranda rights, and Fizzell's resolve seemed to gather. He sat up straighter and af-fected a look of defiance. The officers in the room noted the change. The *Innocent Man* show was about to begin. When Gro-gan asked if Fizzell was willing to talk, he answered, "Sure. I have nothing to hide." And thus began the performance. But the show was short-lived. Fizzell, it seemed, couldn't help but to incrimi-nate himself at every turn.

Officer Smothers drove Fizzell and Grogan to the office of Dr. Roland Bailey, where a nurse carefully extracted a blood sample from Fizzell's arm. Then he was transported to the Marion County Jail in nearby Yellville, entered into the record, fingerprinted, and photographed.

Fizzell said he would fight extradition to California unless he was allowed a private audience with his girlfriend, and Grogan agreed. Assistant Chief Smothers returned to Flippin, where a shaken and tearful Rebecca Halog waited. Later, Smothers re-called driving Halog toward the jail and explaining that, while she would be able to talk to Fizzell privately, they would be sepa-rated by a glass window. Once they arrived, Smothers waited pa-tiently in the lobby while Halog and Fizzell conversed. The woman reappeared thirty minutes later, her eyes wet and glassy and her face streaked with tears. Smothers led her back to his car, helped her into the passenger's seat, and shut the door. Once he was seated behind the wheel, he asked if he could take her to a friend or relative's house.

Halog shook her head. "Just home," she gulped. She turned her head to the window, fighting unsuccessfully to control her emotions.

Yellville's version of rush hour traffic had begun as Smothers merged onto the highway. Rebecca dabbed at her eyes. "I can't believe it."

She began crying hysterically, all hope of composure gone. "How can I marry a murderer? I can't believe it! How can I marry a murderer?"

Smothers tried to comfort her, listening as she struggled to come to terms with the news Fizzell had wanted to tell her himself, in his own way. Smothers felt sorry for her. Her world was shaken. The man she intended to marry had done unimaginable evil.

Jacque received the call from Police Chief Jefferson early on the morning of January 21, 1997. She was still in bed, having been unable to fall asleep until late the night before. Dennis was out of town, flying the Northwest route between San Francisco and Hong Kong. He'd be home in two days.

"Hello?" she said sleepily. The bedside clock read 8:10.

"Jacque? This is Chief Jefferson in Modesto. Did I wake you?"

"That's OK. You know the dogs would get me up soon anyway."

"Well," the chief continued with the air of one making an important announcement, "I wanted you to be the first to know. We're making an arrest in the case today."

Jacque sat upright. "Debi's case?"

There was a smile in the chief's voice. He had rarely made such a joyful phone call, and he was absolutely tickled that he was about to make Jacque happier than she had been in nine years. He savored the moment. "Yes. I've got a team arresting the man who killed Debi. Detective Grogan just called me. They're out of state but awaiting extradition to bring him back here."

Whatever frustration she had felt with Bill Grogan during his years on the case suddenly melted in a glow of thankfulness and goodwill. But Jacque still needed to hear the answers to the questions that had driven her for years.

"Who is he? Why did he kill my daughter?"

"Well, the facts are still coming in, but the man appears to have been a burglar."

Jacque was stunned. "A burglar? You mean he was trying to rob the house?"

"Apparently so. He came in the backyard through the alleyway and entered the house through the back door."

"The sliding glass door was unlocked?"

"That's my understanding."

Jacque fought to make sense of this information. "So he—he didn't even know Debi?"

"I don't think so."

They had all assumed Debi knew her killer and had willingly let him into the house. The cops had been certain. Howie had been certain. Jacque had been certain. And now the scenario of her daughter's death was changing more quickly than Jacque could manage. "So this is the person your secret informant told you about?"

It was the chief's turn to be surprised. "What makes you think we had a secret informant?"

Jacque gave an exasperated snort. "Chief Jefferson, you know I know everybody over at that station. Some of them better than you do."

Jefferson laughed. "You don't know how much power you have, Jacque. You could be dangerous."

He cautioned her not to tell anybody about the arrest. It was vital not to jeopardize the case against the man they had sought for so long. Jacque was equally adamant that she be allowed to tell Debi's sister, Karen. And surely Jessie could know that the man who had taken her mother away from her was finally going to be held accountable.

There would be a press conference that evening, broadcast live across the valley. Since this victory belonged in part to Jacque, Jefferson said he'd be honored if she would attend. Of course, she replied. She wouldn't miss it for the world.

Jacque called Northwest and left word for Dennis to call her as soon as possible. Then she called Karen. "They've got Debi's killer! They've found him!"

Mother and daughter talked for a while, both of them feeling shocked and overwhelmed. They had been waiting nine years for this moment. Now it was here, and they didn't know how to react. There was a sense of victory, but the devastation of losing Debi felt once again fresh and new.

Jacque also called Harold Whitlock in Oregon. He was clearly overcome and had to call her back after regaining his composure. He called a half hour later. "I told Jessie that Gran is our hero," he said, choking on his tears.

After hanging up the phone, Jacque dressed hastily and got into her car. The morning air was bitter cold, and the frost made the cemetery's lawn crunch under her feet. Holding her coat around her, Jacque walked quietly to her daughter's grave. She removed her glove and pressed her fingers gently to Debi's photo on the marker, feeling the frozen condensation melt beneath her touch. The morning air fogged as Jacque whispered, "We did it, kid."

*   *   *

Despite everyone's precautions, by the time Scott Fizzell was finally unloaded in front of the Stanislaus County Jail, newspapers and cable shows from across the valley were staked out to record the image of the scraggly, disheveled murderer, still in the clothes he'd worn when leaving his trailer.

Debi Whitlock, and her mother's hunt for her killer, were constants in the lives of central California residents. Now, as Jacque arrived at the police department, clusters of news teams stood outside. Camera lights cast odd shadows against the towering eucalyptus trees planted by the Modesto Women's Improvement Committee over a century ago. Near the courthouse door Jacque saw Stanislaus County's Victim/Witness Coordinator Margaret Speed. "Over here, Jacque!" she called, waving.

Although Margaret was now the supervisor of the office, she and Jacque had developed a friendship through their mutual years as victim advocates, and Margaret had decided to handle Debi's case herself. She would be with Jacque through each step of the forthcoming legal process.

The ladies made their way to a table directly in front of the raised dais. Cameras turned toward them as Jacque was identified around the room as the victim's mother. She smiled, and reporters smiled back, hoping to look friendly and supportive in order to score an interview with her after the official announcement. *Join me for an exclusive interview with a Merced mother who found her daughter's killer.* That was worth smiling about.

Margaret explained that the killer was already in custody here, and many of these same reporters had already caught a glimpse of him. "His picture will be on the news tonight," Margaret said.

"You'll see him in person at the arraignment in a few days." Then, she explained, it would take months for the trial to occur.

Jacque nodded and made agreeable noises, but she found it impossible to concentrate.

Finally Detective Bill Grogan made his way to the podium. He looked pleased with overtones of exhaustion. "Today we made an arrest in the 1988 homicide case of Deborah Anne 'Debi' Whitlock," Grogan read from his prepared statement. "Scott Avery Fizzell was taken into custody in Flippin, Arkansas. He's charged with one charge of homicide and one charge of burglary."

"*Scott Avery Fizzell.*" Jacque said the name over again. This man thought he could kill her daughter and get away with it, but he couldn't. He would be held accountable for the wrongs he had committed against Debi. Jacque smiled grimly as cameras around the room captured the moment she had dared to believe in for so long.

A reporter called out from the back of the room, "Are there any other charges?"

"Yes," Detective Grogan replied. "One count of rape."

Jacque's smile crumpled. Cameras snapped as Jacque blinked into the glare of flashing lights.

No one had told her Debi had been raped.

That raised podium became the epicenter of a violent shock that radiated out across the valley. Friends and family reeled at the news of Debi's rape. Some cried. Some simply buried their head in their hands. Driving in her car, Debi's sister, Karen, swerved dangerously as the news was broadcast over the car stereo; her daughter, Megan, tried to comfort her.

Debi's rape was not the only surprise of the press conference.

Many people had long believed Harold Whitlock had killed his wife, and the news of another person's arrest flew in the face of the death scenario they had long ago come to accept as true. For some of them, there could be no other truth.

"This is such good news. Such wonderful news. So why am I so angry?"

Jacque MacDonald was talking on the phone to Cathy Wood, her Irish friend in Minnesota who had been the first to arrive at the house after Jacque found out Debi had been killed.

"You don't sound angry."

"I'm bloody furious! Why didn't they tell me my daughter had been raped? They lied to me! They all lied to me!"

Jacque had originally called Cathy to tell her that the police finally had Debi's killer in custody, but the joy of victory had been stolen from her. In its place was the terror of knowing everything her daughter had faced at the brutal end of her life.

"She didn't cry out," Jacque said, weeping. "I always knew my daughter died a hero, because she didn't scream. She didn't want him to know Jessica was asleep in the next room. She died defending her daughter. And now I know what that must have cost her, and it's . . . it's horrible!"

Jacque fought down the bile rising in her throat. For the last nine years, she had learned to live with a version of her daughter's death that was horrifying but somehow kinder than the truth.

On the morning of January 24, 1997, Jacque prepared to lay eyes on the man who had raped and murdered her daughter almost nine years earlier.

"He's in my power now," Jacque said aloud. "The courts, the law. That's my territory, because I live by the rules!"

Dennis watched as she slammed her coffee cup into the dishwasher.

"This man thought he didn't have to live by the rules. He thought he could make his own. But now he's going to learn just how wrong he was!"

Jacque and Dennis arrived at the Stanislaus County Courthouse thirty minutes before Fizzell's arraignment. Walking through the large glass atrium, Jacque looked up at the tall white figure towering over them. The goddess of Justice. She had been placed atop the original 1872 courthouse, holding her sword and balance high above the growing frontier town. Strong winds had toppled her two years later, but she had been restored and placed upon her tall pedestal inside the new courthouse in 1960. Jacque, too, had been toppled in the stormy aftermath of Debi's murder. But she was back on her feet. And justice would come to her family inside these same walls.

This was Jacque's moment of victory, and she was determined to relish it. She sat at the front of the courtroom near the aisle. Margaret Speed was on her right, just as she had been at the press conference. Dennis was on Jacque's left, clasping her shaking hand.

Suddenly a tall, slim man in a suit and tie was standing in the aisle near Jacque. He leaned across Margaret. "Here's how we're going to do it," he whispered urgently. "They're going to bring the scumbag in through that door next to the judge's bench. I have a handgun on my side holster—it's unclasped, and the safety's off. You grab it, walk toward him, and just keep firing. Then I'll wrestle the gun away from you."

Jacque stared at him blankly, and his face split into a wide grin. "Too late. You missed your chance." He disappeared up the aisle.

"Who was that?" Jacque asked Margaret, whose shoulders were shaking as she tried not to laugh.

"That was Jon Buehler. He's a homicide detective and a friend of mine. And he's a fan of yours."

"Was he serious?"

"No." She smiled. "But the whole city is so impressed with what you've accomplished here. I guess if you were going to do something like Jon said, you'd have a lot of people ready to jump to your defense."

Jacque started to reply, but the bailiff was telling everybody to stand as the judge entered the courtroom. And then, suddenly, there was Scott Fizzell.

His lanky hair partially obscured his face and fell around the tattoo on his neck. (Jacque remembered with a jolt that all three psychics consulted about the case said the killer had a tattoo on his arm or neck.) He wore the standard red cover-up, and his arms were cuffed in front of him. Jacque willed him to look at her as her eyes burned into him. He glanced around timidly, and Jacque was pleased to see fear in his eyes. Then he looked down.

"He won't even look at me!" Jacque hissed to her companions. "He doesn't dare look at me, because he knows what he is."

The judge was talking to Fizzell now, asking him if he had representation and then referring him over to the public defender's office. The whole scene lasted less than twenty minutes, and then he was gone.

"That was it?" Jacque asked Margaret.

"That's it for now, Jacque. He'll get whoever's up at the public defender's office, and then the pretrial conference is in a month. That's when the judge sets bail and puts the trial on the calendar."

"Bail?"

Margaret patted her arm. "Don't worry, there won't be any. This guy isn't going anywhere."

"Dad?"

"Yeah. You heard about the arrest?"

"I heard."

My grandmother had long since moved from California back to Virginia, but she still had plenty of friends in Modesto. And the arrest of Debi's murderer had been front-page news.

"One of Nana's old bridge buddies called her and told her about the arrest. I'm floored."

"Tell me about it." He sounded defeated and exhausted, but I chalked it up to shock.

"How does Jessie feel about it?"

"I don't know, really," my father answered. "She's twelve. I think she'd be more likely to turn to her friends on this one."

"So the guy—he really was a stranger?"

"That's what I hear. We'll learn more later probably, but so far it sounds like he just happened to go into our house to rob it, and Debi was there . . ." He was silent for a moment. "I used to go in and out of that door all the time."

I realized he was talking about the sliding glass door the killer had used to enter the house. "Me, too."

It was obvious to me that my father didn't want to discuss this, and although I didn't understand why he wasn't more elated, I respected his need to sort through his feelings on his own. I scrambled for another topic, anything, but all I could think of were unanswered questions. *If it was a random burglar, then who did I hear breathing in the master bedroom? Who put blood in*

Jessie's baby pool? Who had called and left the creepy threaten-ing message on my grandmother's answering machine? Who had tried to break into her house?

My father noted my silence. "I guess you're wondering why I didn't call you days ago and tell you about the arrest myself?"

Yes. "No."

"I would have. I just wasn't sure what to say. I still don't un-derstand it all myself."

"You say that as if something like this can eventually be un-derstood," I observed.

"True. You may be on to something there."

Something else occurred to me. "I bet Debi's mom is thrilled."

"That doesn't begin to cover it. People used to say she was crazy—Wacky Jacque—but she never gave up." He explained to me that a tip had come in from the constant publicity Jacque had brought to the case. "Apparently the California State Legislature is going to honor her next month."

"Pretty cool."

There was no answer.

"Dad?"

But his mind wasn't on our conversation. Instead I heard him quietly repeat his words to himself. "I used that door all the time."

EIGHTEEN

Losing Ground

The evidentiary hearing began on December 11, 1997, almost a year after Scott Fizzell's arrest. Jacque and Dennis MacDonald ate breakfast across the street from the Stanislaus County Courthouse at Dewz Diner. From their table Jacque could see the Victim's Garden, a bronze statue of Chief Estanislao towering above its rocky fountain.

The preliminary hearing was expected to last at least two days, giving the prosecution a chance to lay out its evidence and the defense an opportunity to punch holes in it. At the end, a judge would decide whether there was adequate evidence for the case to go to trial. Margaret Speed had told Jacque and Dennis that the state would lead off with graphic testimony about Debi's murder, and she would notify them when it was over. That had been over an hour ago.

Jacque stirred her hot chocolate nervously and looked toward the courthouse. "I hate even thinking about what's going on in there right now."

Dennis looked at his wife. "You're not changing your mind, are you?"

"About being there? No. But I don't like her being displayed up there either." Jacque stirred some more. "Poor Howie. He already had to see her like that once. That changed him, don't you think?"

Dennis considered. "It would change anybody to see someone who had been murdered, even if it wasn't your wife."

"He feels responsible. Because he was with Heather."

She tried to say it casually. It had taken Jacque years to forgive her son-in-law after she learned Howie's real whereabouts that night. For years Jacque had told newspapers and television audiences that Howie had been at an all-night bachelor party at Ortega's. He had never told her differently. Eventually, years after Debi's death, Jacque had learned the truth from a detective familiar with the case.

Jacque looked out at the barren rosebushes in the Victim's Garden. "I try not to think about the fact that Debi might still be alive if he had only gone home. He left his wife and his daughter at home while he slept with his mistress. He has to live with that, but I do, too." She sighed heavily. "It doesn't matter how any of us feel, because that won't bring Debi back. But I know now why he always helped me on those crime shows. He felt he owed it to Debi."

Dennis took a swallow of his coffee. "Maybe he did."

Jacque thought back to the first time she met Heather Barnett. Seeing her in the role of Jessie's mother had made Jacque physically ill.

She hadn't spoken to Heather again until *Unsolved Mysteries* agreed to profile Debi's story. Jacque called Howie to ask him to participate, and Heather, intercepting the call, quickly became exasperated.

"You need to stop asking him to do these interviews," Heather insisted. "You don't know what they do to him. He gets so depressed."

"That's his decision," Jacque fired back. "I don't make him go on these shows. He does it for his own reasons."

"You know he won't say no. And this has ruined his life!"

Anger brought a flush to Jacque's face. "None of us deserve a life until this is solved!"

Sitting across the café table, Dennis noticed the crease in his wife's brow. He squeezed her hand tenderly. "This will all be over soon."

Department 3 was a dark-paneled courtroom with institutional fluorescent lighting and row upon row of wooden folding seats bolted to the tan tile floor. Every seat was occupied.

Public Defender Martha Carlton sat at the defense table with her assistant, Larry Cahill. Scott Fizzell sat between them, his hair now clean and cut short. Deputy DA Doug Fontan and investigator Alan Fontes manned the prosecutor's table. Behind them sat Bill Grogan, who had been promoted to patrol sergeant a month after arresting the perpetrator of one of Modesto's highest-profile cold cases. Judge Donald Shaver sat behind a massive desk, the American and California State flags on either side of him.

Judge Shaver asked Fontan to call his first witness, and Harold Whitlock made his way to the stand. Dressed in a suit and tie, Whitlock looked only at the bailiff as he promised to tell the truth. Then he shifted his gaze to Fontan.

Keeping his answers short and clipped, Whitlock stated that yes, he was Debi's husband, and that he had arrived home from work at 5:30 p.m. on the night of Thursday, March 24, 1988. At 9 p.m. he left again to attend a bachelor party at Ortega's

Cantina, and at midnight he went to a "friend's" house. The friend's name was Heather Barnett, and he stayed there until the following morning. Upon arriving home at 5:15 a.m., he opened the exterior garage door with the electronic opener and entered the house.

His answers were clear, and his voice and countenance were entirely devoid of emotion.

On a projected diagram of the house, Harold Whitlock marked his route from the garage into the kitchen, and how he had rounded the corner heading into the hall. "I looked directly down this hallway toward the bedroom and saw my wife lying in the hallway." Asked to describe the body as he found it, Whitlock ticked off the factors. "She was lying on her back with her head toward the bedroom. She was naked. There were bedclothes and items, linens from the bed, that appeared to be pulled in toward the hallway and by her head . . . I saw what I just thought was a blood smear on her throat but didn't really look." He had walked over to her, felt her unnaturally cold arm, and called the police.

"And what time was this?" Doug Fontan asked.

"About 5:45."

The attorneys at the defense table stirred. Whitlock estimated it took him a half hour to notify authorities of his wife's death.

The lights dimmed, a prelude to the grisly pictures to come. Harold was asked to identify a photo of his wife's body as it lay in the hallway, which he did haltingly. He then identified his wife's car keys, discovered the next day on a neighbor's lawn, and the butcher knife used to kill her.

Public Defender Martha Carlton stood. She was short and somewhat stocky, her blue suit highlighting the gray in her hair. She straightened her shoulders. Harold Whitlock would be ridiculously easy to discredit in front of a jury.

Within the first minute of his cross-examination, Whitlock said that he left his house for the bachelor party at "6:30 or 7:00," up to two and a half hours earlier than he had indicated just moments ago. The public defender glanced toward her assistant, who nodded imperceptibly. He'd caught the difference. She then established that Heather Barnett had been Whitlock's mistress.

Carlton thumbed through her time line of the evening of Debi's death. "When you left your home that night, was it your intention to sleep at your home that night?"

"Yes, it was."

"At what point did you decide not to return home?"

"When I left the party."

"And what time was that?"

"Eleven thirty, twelve, something like that."

Carlton checked her notes. Debi's time of death was listed at just after midnight. "Did you stop anywhere between Ortega's Cantina and Heather Barnett's?"

"No, I did not."

Carlton's assistant made more notes at the defense table. Whitlock had admitted earlier in a taped interview that he had stopped at a stop sign for "a few minutes" before going to his girlfriend's house, and Heather Barnett had put the missing time frame at almost an hour. Whitlock had been questioned about that missing period of time repeatedly. Now he was saying there was no missing time at all.

Harold Whitlock did not recall lying to the police or the press about being at the party all night. On the other hand, he was absolutely certain that the doors to his home were locked every night as a matter of habit.

Now Carlton had laid the foundation for foul play. If her client supposedly entered the house through the unlocked sliding glass door, then who had unlocked it? And could that person have been the killer? Perhaps her client had unwittingly stumbled into a crime scene. Anticipating this argument, Deputy DA Doug Fontan established that the Whitlocks' cat was let out through the same door, which was then occasionally left unlocked or even slightly ajar.

Then it was Carlton's turn again. Was the door customarily locked at night? Yes, it was.

She turned back toward Debi's widower, shifting topics again. "Do you recognize the name Steven Bloomberg?"

That was as far as she got. Fontan was up and objecting, requesting a conversation in chambers with the judge. Fontan and Carlton followed Judge Shaver out of the room, returning several moments later. Carlton resumed her questioning.

"Mr. Whitlock, it was your belief that your wife was having intercourse with somebody else besides you at that time, isn't that true?"

Harold Whitlock rubbed his hands together nervously and glanced at Debi's family. "I had no reason particularly to believe that, no."

The defense attorney set her mouth. "Isn't it true that you believed she had a boyfriend, who was an employee at the Sears store, named Steven Bloomberg?"

Whitlock considered a moment, then answered in a defeated tone. "Yes, I am sorry. I apologize to you. I just didn't connect the name there. It's been a long time. I do recognize Steve Bloomberg, yes. He was the store manager at Merced where Debi was employed."

Carlton nodded. Both marital infidelities were now in the record, which could help her build a case for reasonable doubt. That case would be strengthened by testimony from Harold's older daughter. The girl had moved out suddenly shortly before the murder. Further, she claimed to have heard someone else in the house on the night Debi was killed—someone Debi had claimed was her husband. Carlton glanced down at her notes.

"Mr. Whitlock, was your daughter Angela living with you at that time?"

Deputy DA Doug Fontan straightened. He knew what was coming.

"No, she was not."

"She had been living with you previously. Is that right?"

"Right."

"When had she moved out of the home?"

Whitlock seemed to consider. "I think she had moved, like, the previous September, and, again, I don't recall exactly, because part of the time she stayed with us, and her grandmother was here also. She stayed part of the time with her."

September. That was five months before Debi was murdered. Another blatant inconsistency.

The prosecution had to discredit Angela, and notes from one of Harold's early interviews provided the perfect avenue. Fontan asked Whitlock, "Now, did you ever have any problems with Angela sneaking in and out of the house through her bedroom window?"

"I think she did once or something. You know . . ." His voice trailed off.

"Was that at or near the time of the murder on March 25, 1988?"

Whitlock shook his head emphatically. "No."

Suppressing a grimace, Fontan sat down as the defense attorney prepared to do more damage to his case.

"Angela's relationship with your wife: how would you describe that relationship?" Carlton asked.

"It was good, I think. Not—I don't think they were antagonistic toward each other."

"Had they been antagonistic toward each other in the past?"

"Not to my knowledge, no."

She nodded. That made the girl credible enough.

Harold Whitlock was excused. He did not look at Debi's family on the way out.

Dr. William Ernoehazy was the medical examiner who had performed Debi's autopsy, and his testimony was absolutely critical in order to prove the assertion that Debi Whitlock was raped. DNA tests proved that semen found at the scene came from Scott Fizzell; however, according to California law, rape was a crime of sexual violence perpetrated against an unwilling, living victim. The prosecution would have to prove that Debi was alive at the time of intercourse. Dr. Ernoehazy's testimony could make or break that assertion.

Much of the doctor's testimony detailed Debi Whitlock's wounds. She had been held by the hair while her throat was cut, and she had tried unsuccessfully to block the knife. Blood smears on the soles of Debi's feet and the top of the right foot indicated that she was dragged by her feet into the hallway *after* her lethal wound was inflicted. Ernoehazy explained that after the artery in her throat was severed, Debi would have lost consciousness "anywhere within a minute" and would have died from exsanguination, or blood loss, within three or four minutes.

"Can you say whether or not intercourse occurred before or after death?" the defense attorney asked.

"I can't tell you that," Dr. Ernoehazy answered.

"You can't say one way or the other?"

"I cannot."

At the prosecutor's table, Doug Fontan must have known that his rape charge was in serious jeopardy. If Debi's throat was cut in the bedroom, could Scott Fizzell drag her into the hall, remove her clothing, and commit his sexual act within three minutes? It was possible, but would a jury see it that way?

Jacque and Dennis came into the courtroom after the morning recess. Fizzell entered with his attorneys, and Jacque was deeply offended to see Martha Carlton smiling at Fizzell and patting his arm in a comforting way.

"Has she been doing that all morning?" Jacque asked Margaret Speed, who was once again by her side. "I know she had to represent him, but does that mean she has to be nice to him?"

"It's a performance, Jacque. She's trying to say, 'Look at me! I'm not afraid of him. I don't think he did this.'" Margaret looked toward the defense with barely disguised disgust. "Just don't look."

Jacque averted her eyes only to hear Carlton chuckle.

"He raped and murdered my daughter!" Jacque whispered in outrage. "Does she have a daughter?"

Doug Fontan called Michael Warnell. He had long since lost his anonymity in the press, so there was no need for the court to make special arrangements for his testimony. Because Warnell knew Scott Fizzell only by first name in 1988, Martha Carlton was voracious in making certain that all parties verbally distinguish between Warnell's neighbor, Scott, and her client, Scott Fizzell; she was not at all ready to concede that they were one in the same.

Fontan decided to cover Warnell's history up front and un-flinchingly. As a minor, Michael Warnell had been to a juvenile facility known as Boys Ranch; he earned his GED there and was released in 1985, just prior to his eighteenth birthday. He moved in with his mother, who lived in a duplex at 1815 West Rumble Road, just across the street from Karen Louchart, whose son, Scott Fizzell, would soon take up residence there. During the next four years, Warnell was arrested four times on theft-related charges. In 1990 he received a felony conviction for burglary and receiving stolen property and served two years at an adult facility. Since his release in 1992, Warnell had seemingly turned his life around.

Having laid out Warnell's tale of repentance, the prosecutor addressed the early morning of March 25, 1988. Warnell admitted that he was in his mother's garage "drinking beer and smoking some weed" before Scott's arrival. When Fontan asked how much beer Warnell had ingested, Warnell answered, "I drinked one and I had one in the refrigerator. And probably about eleven or twelve o'clock that night I dranked it and it was gone." Warnell also admitted that he had "two or three" joints during the day, then another one approximately an hour before seeing Fizzell. However, he didn't feel he had been at all incapacitated. "I could have rode a bike or, you know, walked down the street or anything."

Warnell explained that when Scott entered the garage, he was nervous and jittery. "He told me that he had went and tried to burglarize a house. And that he was in the kitchen and, when he turned around, some lady was standing there. And he said he found a knife on the kitchen counter, and he just grabbed the knife and he turned around and he stabbed her." After the stabbing, Scott told Warnell that "as he was running out of the house, he just noticed that he had a set of keys in his hand . . . [so he] threw the keys on the front lawn and came to my place."

The prosecution and defense both knew that Debi's butterfly key ring had been retrieved from a neighbor's side yard and not from the victim's front yard. Because of that, Fontan restated Warnell's answer. "So Scott said he dropped the keys on a lawn?"

Carlton didn't even bother to stand. "Objection. Misstates the testimony."

"Sustained."

Oh well, it had been worth a try.

Next Warnell related that Scott had pointed in the direction of Grace Davis High School and said the incident occurred "right down the street." That was roughly the direction of the Whitlock residence.

During Martha Carlton's cross-examination, Warnell admitted that at the time of the murder he regularly used marijuana and alcohol. A year later he became addicted to crack cocaine, and he increasingly stole from area businesses to support his habit. He was caught within two years and sent to prison.

"During all those times you were arrested between 1988 and 1990," Carlton asked, "did you ever tell anybody you had a Get Out of Jail Free card?"

"Objection," called the prosecuting attorney. "It's argumentative."

"Assumes facts not in evidence as well," Judge Shaver supplied. "Sustained."

Carlton rephrased her question. "You understand that information of this sort can help an individual who is charged with a felony, especially property thefts, don't you?"

Warnell furrowed his brow. "I was going to jail regardless. And I was a crack addict. I was loaded. It never came to my mind."

"You're saying you don't know that an informant on a, shall we say *famous* murder case might get some serious benefit from law enforcement if that informant revealed information that helped solve that murder case?"

Jacque was confused. Why would the defense attorney be pointing out that Warnell could have profited if he'd come forward with his information sooner?

"What's she doing?" Jacque whispered to her husband.

"I think she's saying he made it up recently," Dennis answered.

Carlton continued her questioning. "You say you were in your garage that morning. Why do you think it was three in the morning?"

"Because I stayed up every night selling bud out of the garage. I listened to the radio, so I may have heard the time on the radio." Warnell went on to admit he had "somewhere between ten and fifteen" customers that night.

Having established that on the night of the supposed confession the informant was drinking, smoking pot, and doing a brisk trade as a drug dealer, the defense homed in on the particulars of Scott's confession. "In this conversation, Scott did not say that he *killed* the woman. Is that right?"

"He never used the word 'kill,' no."

"Did he say it had just happened, or did it happen an hour before or two hours before or was it—"

"It had just happened."

Later, Carlton asked Warnell what year the murder had occurred. "Nineteen eighty-four," he said with assurance.

Jacque watched Deputy DA Doug Fontan turn pale. Michael Warnell had misjudged the time of Debi Whitlock's murder by four years and three hours, and had changed his earlier testimony from Scott killing a woman to merely "stabbing" her. Jacque wasn't a lawyer, but she could tell from the uncomfortable squirming at the prosecutor's table that Warnell wasn't doing very well on the stand.

Seemingly in an effort to bolster his informant's sinking credibility, Doug Fontan used his redirect to point out that Michael Warnell wasn't a user of "hard" drugs during the time of confession, and that he never used much meth. Trying to be helpful, Warnell agreed that he had only used meth "two or three times ever" but then added, "a lot of people used it in my garage. You know, my garage was—"

Fontan raised a hand to stop him, ignoring some chuckles in the courtroom. "Do you think Scott was on meth that night?"

"I think so."

Warnell did not come forward with the information at that time. "I was concerned . . . because I also was a thief, a burglar at the time, and . . . [I] thought . . . I might be accused."

"What ultimately convinced you to come forward and reveal what the defendant told you to the police?" Fontan asked.

"Because, you know, my life has changed since then." He gestured toward Jacque MacDonald, sitting on the front row of spectators. "The lady's mom was on television, and there was a lot of billboards and, you know, when I go to the store and, you know, like, the baskets, they would have a picture on it."

Dennis MacDonald put his arm around his wife and hugged her as she fought back her tears. She had done it. She had found her "one person who knows."

Back on the stand, Warnell said he had finally decided to come forward in 1997. "I talked to Officer Steele. He had been an officer who I had encountered in the past, and he was someone who had treated me fairly."

The prosecution had glossed over the particulars of Warnell giving his tip to the police, but the defense wanted to examine that further. Warnell admitted that Officer Steele was "possibly" concerned that Warnell was in the process of breaking the law that night, which was the impetus for the stop.

Debi's family and friends had followed all of this with great interest, but their hearts practically stopped when the Deputy District Attorney asked Michael Warnell about Debi Whitlock's little girl.

"Mr. Warnell, when the defendant was disclosing that he had

entered a woman's house and stabbed her, did he tell you that the woman's small daughter was sleeping in one of the bedrooms?"

"Objection," Carlton called out. "This is leading."

"I will allow the question," Judge Shaver replied.

Warnell nodded. "Yes."

Debi's family was horrified. What Scott Fizzell had done to Debi was unimaginably evil. They didn't want those same eyes to have viewed the innocence of their sweet, small Jessie asleep in her bed.

On the other hand, if the defense was actually going to posit that Scott's confession was about a totally different female stabbing victim who lived "down the street" and was attacked at 3:00 a.m. instead of midnight, they would now have to include a little girl sleeping in the next room.

If Martha Carlton was angry, it only served to make her sharper. She laid into Warnell with gusto. He had clearly learned about the little girl through recent media coverage. Otherwise, why didn't he mention it in his initial interview with Detective Grogan? Carlton put her full strength into hammering at the witness.

"You never, ever, ever heard about the girl from anybody anytime?"

"I never heard it from anybody. I never read it anywhere. I told the police what came out of his mouth. That's all. That's all."

"That's exactly all you told them?"

"That's all I told them. I never got nothing from no newspaper, radio, TV, hearsay! I got everything from his mouth. From his mouth!"

"You told Sergeant Grogan everything that came out of his mouth, right?"

Warnell slammed his hand against the witness box in total exasperation. "Man, I was on drugs at the time! Some things I forgot! Some things I didn't say! Some things I did! Some things I have remembered! Some things I didn't remember!"

Carlton barely hid her smile. "So you were on drugs on November 19, 1996?"

"I said I was on drugs at the time that this happened! At the time that *this* happened, I was on drugs!"

"Mr. Warnell, how much is the reward?"

"Ten thousand dollars."

"No further questions."

It was masterful. Carlton had the prosecution's star witness beside himself with frustration, shrieking that he had been on drugs on the night of the so-called confession, saying his memory was unreliable. There was, however, one thing he was very clear about: ten thousand dollars was on the line. The money was his if his testimony led to the conviction of Scott Fizzell.

Rebecca Halog did not want to be at the hearing. She wouldn't be, either, if the court hadn't compelled her to show. She bristled on the witness stand, radiating anger toward the prosecuting attorneys and frequently glancing at her former fiancé, sitting between his attorneys at the defense table.

Halog recounted that she and Scott had met on July 3, 1993, in Modesto, and that they had moved in together within a year. They had gotten engaged on December 22, 1996, exactly one month prior to Scott's arrest. At the time of the arrest they were living together in Flippin, Arkansas. They had planned to marry in December of 1997. This very month.

On January 21, 1997, Flippin Assistant Chief of Police Steve Smothers came to the residence Halog shared with Scott and transported her to City Hall. Once there, Halog met with Detective Grogan. "He told me about the murder, when it happened. And he told me that it was a weight off Scott's soul."

Sobbing on the witness stand, Halog recalled going to visit

Scott at the jail. Fontan waited for the witness to compose herself before asking how she felt about the proceedings. She was very angry, she said, especially with Sergeant Grogan. "I had been led to believe that Scott confessed."

"Did you believe it?"

"It was told to me by an officer of the law, and yes, I believed it."

Fontan shuffled some notes. "When you got to the jail and you saw the defendant, what did you and he talk about?"

Halog looked tearfully at Fizzell. "We talked about debts that had to be paid."

Fontan seemed utterly bewildered. "I'm sorry? You talked about what?"

"*Debts that had to be paid*," she reiterated. "There was a lot of crying. I think I remember asking him what I was supposed to do, and he told me the best that I could."

It was a good answer. Was Scott Fizzell talking about a debt he owed for a murderous impulse he had indulged long ago? Or merely an upcoming credit card statement?

"I knew what he was sorry about," Halog said, jutting her jaw out stubbornly.

Next, Fontan moved to the conversation Halog had with Assistant Chief Smothers as he drove her back home. "When you got back in the patrol car, did you tell Officer Smothers, 'He said he killed her'?"

"No, sir, I didn't."

"Did you say, 'How can I marry him now?'"

"Yes, I may have said that."

Fontan nodded. "Now, prior to coming to court to testify today, you were aware that the defendant's facing the death penalty, weren't you?"

"Yes."

"And you don't want him to suffer the death penalty, correct?"

"Well, of course not!"

"You don't want to be part of this proceeding at all, do you?"

"No!"

"And why not?"

"Because this is tragic," she said, melting into tears once again.

Assistant Chief Steve Smothers told the court his version of the ride back from jail with Rebecca Halog. "She just burst out crying, and her first words were, 'How could I marry a murderer? He said he killed that lady in California.' "

Smothers also confirmed that he heard Scott Fizzell say, on the day of his arrest, "I was young and high on crank all the time. It was a mistake. I didn't mean to kill her." Pressed to the point by Carlton, he admitted that might be more of a paraphrase.

The state's next witness was Sergeant Mike Harden, who had accompanied Bill Grogan to Flippin. During the return trip he heard Fizzell say, "I'd give anything to live my life over right now."

Stanislaus County Sheriff's Deputy August Gallasso testified that while in a holding tunnel for the jail, he saw Fizzell receive a copy of the official complaint form. After reading the charges Fizzell told Gallasso, "I wasn't in my right mind back then."

Finally Sergeant Bill Grogan took the stand, and Fontan walked his last witness through the particulars of the arrest. Yes, Grogan had traveled to Flippin with an arrest warrant for Fizzell. Yes, he had displayed his badge when the Flippin chief and assistant chief of police brought Fizzell in. No, he had never threatened Mr. Fizzell, nor had he made the suspect any promises. Grogan interviewed Fizzell for a half hour there in the mayor's conference room in Flippin, and yes, Grogan had the tape on him.

A hush fell over the courtroom as the tape played. At times the voices were almost unintelligible.

"I'd object to anything beyond this point," Carlton said. "At the point Sergeant Grogan says, 'Tell me what happened.' And my client answers, 'I think I need to talk to a lawyer.'"

A flurry of activity came from the prosecution table. "Your Honor," Fontan called out, shuffling through the voluminous paperwork in front of him, "I have a trial brief prepared on this issue. I'd like the court to review the law I have cited."

Martha Carlton looked cross. "Do you have a copy for—"

"Yes, I do." Fontan had located his brief and handed copies to Judge Shaver and the public defender.

Carlton laid the papers aside dismissively. "I haven't read the trial brief. It was not provided to me. This is an obvious issue. At this point in the interview there is an assertion of the right—the wish to talk to a lawyer. There is an attempt to talk him out of it. He continues to request a lawyer. From that point on, it's clear that it's his desire to have an attorney. He maintains that desire. There is some conversation back and forth that never should have happened."

Judge Shaver tried to call recess, but Fontan was half out of his seat and calling, "Your Honor? I have a comment." The judge looked toward the deputy DA, who was gesturing toward the defense table. "Counsel is wrong," he insisted. "The police are under no obligation to clarify an ambiguous statement." He rattled off several cases included in his brief while Carlton thumbed through her copy. "It's an ambiguous statement: 'I *think* I need to talk to a lawyer. I really need to talk to a lawyer before I go any further, I *think*.' The People don't feel those would normally be an indication of his right to an attorney, and investigators have no duty to stop and clarify it. However, the People will stipulate that Detective Grogan interpreted those two statements to be a clear and unambiguous implication of the defendant's Miranda rights. Those are—the People are not going to argue that point in this matter."

Judge Shaver blinked, sorting through this seemingly contradictory idea. "Okay."

Then Fontan was off again. "They are going to argue—and I do so in my brief—that there was no further interrogation after the first statement, 'I think I need to talk to a lawyer.' Simply a statement, 'Would you feel better if you cleared your conscience today and tell us what happened? Why it happened?' That's all. He doesn't ask him any questions that are relating to the crime."

Jacque thought she heard Carlton snort derisively. If so, Fontan ignored her.

"Now, the second statement, 'I really need to talk to a lawyer before I go any further, I think.' It's clear that Detective Grogan is simply telling him, 'I am going to leave you my card.' He is leaving at that point. He doesn't continue the interrogation at all. And then, without any kind of questioning from Detective Grogan, Fizzell starts in talking about the crime again. 'Oh, it was so long ago.' And then it's on again. So I think that's a reinitiation of the interview at that point."

"Okay," Judge Shaver nodded. "Let's take a short break, then, and I will take a look at the brief."

Martha Carlton was determined to have another say in the matter. "The transcript's clear, and it's obviously an attempt to get him to continue the interrogation after he has asserted his right to an attorney!"

"OK," the judge repeated.

"Perhaps," Fontan interjected, "we should have some testimony from Detective Grogan before the court goes in—"

Shaver gave a strained smile. "Let's take the break first."

"—or shortly after," Fontan continued helpfully.

After an hour recess, Judge Donald Shaver returned to the bench and notified all parties that he would have to spend more time reviewing the case law before he could make a ruling on Grogan's interview of Scott Fizzell. "Why don't we go ahead and continue with the balance of the case, and I will take that issue under submission?"

"You mean, leave the confession out and go on to other aspects of his testimony?" the prosecuting attorney asked with seeming innocence.

Martha Carlton's voice rang out, "I object to the characterization of the statement."

"Let's go on to other aspects," Shaver prompted.

It was obvious that Public Defender Carlton had some very specific ideas about how to defend her client. To begin, even if Scott Fizzell did stab the female resident of a house he intended to rob, that did not mean it had been Debi Whitlock.

"Sergeant Grogan," Carlton said, "did you do a survey between 1987 and 1989 to determine whether or not there were any burglaries, which turned into a robbery due to a stabbing that—"

"No, I did not," Grogan interrupted.

"So you don't know whether or not there is, in fact, a case out there where the woman of the house interrupted somebody in the kitchen and that individual was stabbed?"

"I couldn't say so now, no."

"That, in fact, is what Mr. Warnell told you; is that right? That the woman confronted the intruder in the kitchen and that the individual stabbed her in the kitchen?"

"He also said 'killed.'"

"I'll get to that in a minute," she replied coolly. "Now, you saw the crime scene on March 25, 1988; is that correct?"

"Yes."

"And based on your observations, it's clear that Mrs. Whitlock was killed in the bedroom, is it not?"

"Yes."

"She was not attacked in the kitchen?"

"No."

They went back and forth, Carlton pointing out the inconsistencies between Scott Fizzell's supposed confession to Michael Warnell, and the reality of Debi Whitlock's murder. She spent a lot of time establishing that Warnell said he had seen no blood at all on Fizzell that night in the garage. He hadn't noticed any scratch or injury to Fizzell either, although the police found foreign blood in the kitchen indicating that Debi's attacker had, in fact, received an injury himself. (That blood was a DNA match to Scott Fizzell's, a fact Carlton certainly did not mention.)

Now Carlton moved to the last person known to see Debi Whitlock alive.

"Angela Whitlock, in 1988, was the seventeen-year-old daughter of Harold Whitlock?"

"Yes," Grogan replied shortly.

"And she told you that Debi was awake and in a fairly good mood?"

"Yes."

"And there was a discussion with Angela about Debi saying that—"

Fontan interjected. "I am going to object to what Debi told Angela, because that is multiple hearsay."

Carlton turned toward the judge. "It's not being offered for the truth of the matter, Your Honor."

"Then what's the relevance?" Fontan asked hotly.

They argued back and forth until finally Carlton read loudly from her copy of Grogan's notes.

"Isn't it correct that Debi said to Angela, 'Well, your father called you, but now he is asleep in the back bedroom.'"

Fontan was on his feet. "I am going to object to that! I know that's where counsel is going. That is clearly hearsay! It's inappropriate for an attorney to get in inadmissible hearsay, and I want it stricken from the record!"

Carlton answered calmly, "I am not suggesting that it's being offered for the truth of the matter. I'm showing that Debi *told* Angela that there was somebody in the house, not that there *was* anybody in the house. And based on that statement, Angela then believed she heard somebody in the house."

Judge Shaver nodded. "If Angela then made a statement that you are trying to prove the truth of to Debi, that would be hearsay. I will go ahead and sustain the objection on the basis of relevance. That will be stricken."

Carlton paused, clearly formulating a different plan. "Sergeant Grogan, Angela told you that, as she kissed Jessica, who was asleep in the back bedroom next to the master bedroom, she thought she heard someone breathing from Debi's bedroom; is that correct?"

"Yes."

"And she told you she didn't think anything about it because Debi had just told her her father was asleep in the back bedroom—"

"I am going to object to that as being hearsay!"

"It's not being offered for the *truth* of the matter," Carlton reiterated, her eyes narrowing. "It goes to Angela's state of mind."

"Then there is no relevance!" Fontan fumed.

Judge Shaver raised his hand. "I am going to allow it in. The objection is overruled." He nodded to Grogan.

"She made the statement," Grogan replied. From her seat, Jacque saw Carlton smile and give her client a maternal pat on the arm.

At the end of the second day of testimony, both sides rested. Judge Shaver turned to the first issue at hand: whether or not to allow the part of Michael Warnell's testimony in which Scott supposedly said he saw a little girl asleep in a bedroom of the house. Fontan's position was that if the defense had bothered to interview Michael Warnell instead of relying on old notes, they would have learned the same information. Fizzell's attorney strongly disagreed. "It's another indication that this gentleman is making up this story as he goes along," Carlton insisted. Judge Shaver interrupted the mounting argument. The statement would be allowed to stand.

Next Shaver moved to the Miranda issue: the question of if and when Scott Fizzell's request for counsel was disregarded during his initial questioning by Sergeant Grogan.

"At the point where the defendant says, 'I think I need to talk to a lawyer,' that could possibly be viewed as an ambiguous statement, so the statement following by Detective Grogan would not necessarily be improper in light of that," Shaver explained. "When he gets down to, 'I really need to talk to an attorney,' as Detective Grogan has said, that's pretty clearly a Sixth Amendment invocation. At that time, Detective Grogan made comments about what he might feel like, some of the facts, circumstances that might have been going on to justify his conduct, and that sort of thing . . . I would have to conclude that was the functional equivalent of interrogation." Shaver sustained the defense's charge of Miranda violation. Everything after Fizzell's second mention of an attorney would be off limits to a jury.

The final issue was whether there was sufficient evidence for the suspect to be held on suspicion of the crimes indicated. Much of the state's evidence hinged on Michael Warnell's testimony, and the defense began whittling away at it now.

"Mr. Warnell's description of the crime simply isn't this crime," Carlton insisted. She referred to Warnell as a "career criminal" and said again and again that all of Warnell's correct details about the Whitlock murder had been in the media. "It's just not credible, frankly, that these statements were made to him ever, let alone during periods of time when he was being prosecuted and threatened with state prison and sent to the California Rehabilitation Center." Then, on a roll, she added, "I can't tell this court what I had to drink last week on Monday night, let alone that I had two quarts of beer and several cans, plus exactly four joints, in a specific period of time on March 24, 1988. That was *fascinating*."

Fontan jumped to defend his key witness. "It's obvious to me that this man was carrying this secret around with him all these years. It was a corrosive bit of knowledge that he retained. It was eating him up, and it was a conscience-induced act to disclose this information."

Carlton crossed her arms. "I would just bet that there is $10,000 in Mr. Warnell's bank account when this case is over."

With that, Judge Donald Shaver announced that "over the whole" he found Michael Warnell to be a credible witness. "I do believe there is sufficient evidence to hold the defendant to answer for the charges and for the special circumstances alleged."

The evidentiary hearing had damaged the prosecution. The DNA was solid, but taking scientific evidence before a jury was not a guarantee of success. Juries often responded first to the character of those who testified, and Michael Warnell's criminal past and history of drug usage would be used against him. Harold Whitlock certainly wasn't above reproach. Miranda issues threatened to nullify Scott Fizzell's most self-incriminating statements.

Fontan wanted Martha Carlton off the case.

NINETEEN

Murder and the Media

For years Jacque had sat by the phone, waiting for producers and editors to call with the news that they would profile Debi's case. Now that the perpetrator had been found, the phone wouldn't stop ringing.

Jacque had only called one person. John Downey was an actor who had produced *The Jerry Springer Show* when Jacque had appeared there. Downey and Jacque had kept in touch since then, and she had always promised she would call him once the case was solved. Within a day of the arrest, Downey had Jacque booked on Leeza Gibbon's show.

But now word was out about Jacque's long-sought victory, and suddenly everybody wanted to cover the story of "the avenging mother." *20/20, Oprah, Marie Claire, Geraldo*, the *National Enquirer, Dateline NBC*—Jacque could hardly catch her breath between calls. Two British magazines, the *Mail* and *Sunday: News of the World*, featured Jacque's heroic story while emphasizing that the heroine was a hometown girl.

Within weeks of the arrest, Jacque spent an afternoon with Keith Morrison, whose silver hair and matching silver voice made him her favorite *Dateline* anchor.

"Why did you do all of this?" Morrison asked, marveling at Jacque's tenacity.

"For love of Debi."

"And you?" Morrison turned to Dennis MacDonald. "You've been through so much. Why did you do it?"

Dennis shrugged. "For love of Jacque."

Morrison held an extensive interview with Detective Grogan, who described the crime scene as "very bizarre, one of the worst I've ever experienced in twenty-seven years of law enforcement." He admitted that "the police and a lot of other people felt it was a family member."

"Like the husband?" Morrison asked. He already knew. He'd conducted numerous interviews by this time.

Choosing his words carefully, Grogan answered, "The husband was questioned, and the physical evidence eliminated him."

The Victim's Voice had been on the air three years and was now broadcast on over forty television stations across the valley. Jacque stayed at the Assyrian Cultural Center for the first two, then used her own money to move out of the studio and shoot on location in partnership with local producer Tom Cusak. Assemblyman Dennis Cardoza, now running for a congressional seat, continued to support Jacque's efforts financially and politically. The scheduled speaker at the California State Fair, he shocked the crowd when, instead of delivering a self-serving stump speech, he thanked the fair organizers for inviting him and went on to make a few remarks about California's crime rate. "Crime is not about statistics. It's about real people in real pain. But it's also about people who vow to make a difference. I want you to meet one of them now." Then he turned the microphone over to Jacque.

Local radio stations had also taken note of Jacque's show. Angie DuBois, public service director at KYOS radio in Merced, offered Jacque a monthly fifteen-minute spot on the air. Jacque could choose the guest and the topic, as long it tied in to local interest. Jacque immediately agreed.

KYOS was located in a nondescript white building downtown. Inside, the walls were a dizzying hodgepodge of band posters, newspaper clippings, and political cartoons. Dennis Daly would record and produce Jacque's radio show and had followed the media coverage surrounding Debi's case for years. He was excited and honored to work with the long-crusading mother. "I've seen your show, and you're good. You're a liaison between the media and law enforcement. That's not always a great relationship. When I worked in L.A., if a dog pissed on the street the LAPD would call and ask if we wanted sound on it. But around here, the door is often shut. The police can't do it all on their own. We can help, if they'll let us. And you're the person who can open that door. You make people comfortable. And that's not an easy thing to pull off with police, and family, and the DA's office."

"Well, I've had a lot of help—"

"And I'll tell you something else. You encourage people to come forward with what they know. Sometimes people don't want to bother police, because they feel like the cops are always busy with big clues—some guy running down the street with the gun still smoking. And they feel like whatever they have to contribute isn't a contribution at all. But that's not true. You know that! Sometimes the most innocent observation can lead to a tremendous realization."

Jacque smiled at the man. He was enthusiastic and knowledgeable. Her first radio episode of *The Victim's Voice* was broadcast that month.

By this time, law enforcement from Modesto, Merced, and surrounding counties were calling Jacque regularly. She always told them the same thing: "This is your show. Profile whatever you want, but make sure you invite a member of the victim's family. It's their case, too."

Jon Buehler, the Modesto detective who had startled Jacque at Scott Fizzell's arraignment by pretending to offer her his gun, notified Jacque whenever he had a case that wasn't moving. "You're like our own John Walsh," Buehler said proudly. Jacque agreed to devote an episode of the show to a string of unsolved bank robberies Buehler was working. It wasn't her usual subject matter, but numerous tips came in from the show. Unfortunately, the case was never solved.

When seventy-four-year-old Merced resident Louise Melgoza Macias was beaten and choked to death in her apartment on May 29, 1997, her daughter Sylvia Mariscal called Jacque. Though Sylvia expected Jacque to be too busy to get personally involved in the case, what she discovered was both an advocate and a lifelong friend. Jacque had Sylvia on her next show, then helped her land spots on two national crime shows and numerous newspapers. She instigated a letter writing campaign that eventually helped Sylvia secure an additional $50,000 in reward money through the governor's office. And she included lead detective Scott Skinner and other representatives of Merced's law enforcement during every stage of publicity. "I know it's hard not to get upset with the police when a case stalls," Jacque told Sylvia as the case dragged on, "but they are good people, and they are our only hope. Think of them as family—you aren't always happy about what they do, but you always need each other."

Merced County Sheriff Mark Pazin also profiled cold cases regularly, as did local District Attorney Larry Morse. They also encouraged local groups to contribute to the show. Jacque was an additional resource—and a friend—for those working to solve and deter crime in the Central Valley. She followed crime legislation. She offered police officers working in local schools the opportunity to address parents about the specific challenges their kids were facing. And sometimes she allowed survivors to air their feelings about cases that had already been solved.

The Conrads, whose daughter Traci "Rene" had been killed in 1997 by a known child molestor and convicted felon residing in their neighborhood, wanted to appear on Jacque's show to thank the people of central California. "Losing Rene was the worst thing I've ever encountered," her mother, Traci, said tearfully, holding Jacque's hand. "But the bringing together of our community, and the entire valley, made it better."

My stepmother's murderer had been caught. His DNA and prints matched samples from the house. That should have been the end of the story.

I learned differently when the Stanislaus County Public Defender's Office called me a year after the arrest. The research assistant said he was reviewing my comments to police about the night of Debi's death. "You'll most likely be called to testify at the trial, and we need to check our facts."

I felt no particular animosity toward the defender's office. After my husband graduated from law school, we moved to a small town in the Smoky Mountains where he took on a variety of cases, including some criminal defense. I understood that defense attorneys must aggressively and ethically represent their clients, making certain the prosecution has competent evidence beyond a reasonable doubt for every assertion of wrong. It was all about ensuring due process, making certain that the particulars of the law were followed. However, the more the PD researcher talked to me, the more I realized my upcoming testimony could be used to cast suspicion on my father.

"So you did know at the time that your father and the victim were both involved in extramarital affairs?"

"Yes."

"And in fact we have some notes here saying that you had a conversation with your father's mistress shortly before Debi's death, in which the mistress became extremely distressed about a possible reconciliation between your father and stepmother?"

I didn't recall telling the investigators about my conversation with Heather that night at my father's house. Maybe they got the information from Heather.

"I guess so."

"So you would agree with the mistress being *extremely distressed?*"

I could tell his pen was poised, ready to record my exact response. "Well, she wasn't screaming or threatening to kill Debi, if that's what you mean. It was more along the lines of crying, dropping her licorice, that sort of thing."

"Her licorice?"

"It was in her purse. She was looking for a tissue."

"Ah." I imagined him writing down 'licorice' on a yellow legal pad. Maybe underlining it.

"And your father—how did he react when you told him about this visit from his mistress?"

"I don't even remember if I told him," I said, feeling defensive. "And you don't have to keep calling her 'the mistress.' Her name is Heather. They're married now."

"I don't think so. Not anymore."

"Oh." Well, why would Dad tell me if they had divorced? After all, he'd never told me they were married.

The researcher turned to the night of Debi's murder, asking about the number of lights that had been on in the house and spending an inordinate amount of time on whether the external garage door had been open or closed. Finally we made our way toward my conversation with Debi.

"And then she told you your father was asleep in the back bedroom?"

"Yes."

"And you later heard breathing coming from the master bedroom, is that correct?"

"I think so," I replied.

"Is that a yes? Because at the time you said you heard breathing. Do you recall telling that to Detective Grogan?"

"I don't know who I talked to," I answered wearily.

"I understand," said the researcher, continuing doggedly. "But at the time you did tell Detective Grogan—or a detective—that you heard breathing?"

"Yes. I told whoever first called me that I had heard breathing."

"OK. I'm just trying to make sure that we both understand what happened that night."

"Then you're wasting your time," I said, my patience running thin. "I don't understand what happened that night. Not at all."

"And you have no idea who was really back there?"

The question gave me goose bumps. "No, sir. I have no idea."

After we hung up, I mulled over our conversation, wondering how exactly I would be used by the defense. I couldn't be positive, but I suspected they were gunning for my father, and I was one of the bullets.

I dreaded telling my father that I would be called to testify in

Scott Fizzell's defense, but he took the news far more calmly than I had imagined. I, on the other hand, was frantic.

"I don't know what to do, Dad! It feels like I'm saying innocent stuff, and then they shout, 'Aha!'"

"Just tell the truth."

"Of course I will. But what if they use it against you?"

"Listen, I'm not perfect. Far from it." I heard him take a drag on his cigar. "In fact, in some ways I'm a real bastard. You know that."

It always threw me when my father denigrated himself. "I wouldn't say that."

"Because you're far too diplomatic."

"Because I love you."

"And I appreciate that. But what we've got to do—you and me both—is to be truthful to the extent that we can and trust that in spite of whatever is put out there, justice is done."

"But they're not going to let me put the whole truth out there," I insisted, near hysteria. "They only want part of the truth!"

His tone softened. "I know you don't want to testify. I don't want you to have to. But these guys, they're just doing their job."

"No, they're going after you."

"Well, yeah. It's a bitch, but right now they believe that's their job."

TWENTY

War of Words

Two months after the evidentiary hearing, Deputy DA Doug Fontan turned his attention toward having Martha Carlton removed from the case.

He filed a brief claiming that the Public Defender's Office had represented several of the state's witnesses. That, Fontan asserted, meant that any Stanislaus County public defender assigned to represent Scott Fizzell would have a conflict of interest. The issue was argued back and forth, but finally the court ruled there was no conflict since Carlton herself had not represented any of the witnesses named. Fontan appealed the decision, but the court supported the previous ruling. Martha Carlton would retain her standing as Scott Fizzell's counsel.

For her part, Carlton was trying to undermine the state's case in several ways. She challenged the DNA evidence, which is standard procedure in most cases that use such evidence. But the more promising paths to acquittal had already presented themselves at the evidentiary hearing: the defense would be targeting Michael

Warnell's tip to the police and Sergeant Grogan's potential disregard of Scott Fizzell's request for counsel during interrogation in Flippin, Arkansas. Casting reasonable doubt against Harold Whitlock was a solid plan B.

On September 2, 1998, Carlton filed a motion asserting that the arrest of Scott Fizzell was unfounded, and therefore everything that had happened during or after the arrest should be suppressed. Specifically, she wanted all of the following evidence against her client tossed out:

1. All observations of law enforcement personnel
2. All statements made by Fizzell and his girlfriend, Rebecca Halog
3. All other self-incriminating statements made by Fizzell after his arrest
4. Any statements allegedly made by Fizzell in the jail to other inmates since his arrest
5. Fizzell's blood test

In her brief, Carlton claimed that the arrest and search warrants affidavits (the reasons arresting officer Bill Grogan gave to a judge in order to get approval for the arrest and blood draw) were "based on uncorroborated information of a criminal informant" and "admitted drug addict" who had a "lengthy criminal record." Carlton doubted that her client had confessed the crime to Michael Warnell and insisted the witness had concocted his story recently in order to get the reward money: "Ultimately, the tale that Mr. Warnell told amounts to no more than information that was public knowledge and some additional 'facts' that were *inaccurate*," including Scott's address, how and where the victim was killed ("stabbed in kitchen" instead of throat slit in master bedroom), what was missing from the house (Warnell mentioned only the keys and not Debi's purse), the location of the house ("down the street" instead of on another street altogether), and the location of the discarded keys ("the front lawn" instead of a neighbor's side yard).

Carlton simultaneously launched an attack against the ethics of Sergeant Bill Grogan, claiming his affidavits demonstrated "dishonesty and/or disregard for the truth." She pointed out differences between the affidavit for arrest (made in California) and the affidavit for the blood draw (made in Arkansas): "It is clear that Officer Grogan's rendition of the 'facts' changes, with the shifting winds, to best serve his purpose. The record evokes the familiar maxim that, 'if you are going to lie, you better have a really good memory.' "

The public defender claimed Grogan purposely misled the magistrates by omitting that Warnell could have learned the facts of the attack from the media coverage surrounding the famous murder. Also, Detective Grogan did not mention that Warnell had admitted using drugs and alcohol on the night of the confession and therefore could only remember "some" of his conversation with his neighbor, Scott.

For his search warrant affidavit, Grogan wrote that the "perpetrator would necessarily have to have blood on his person and clothing," but neglected to mention that Warnell had said his neighbor "didn't look like he just got through killing somebody [because] he didn't even have blood on him . . . He wasn't ripped up or anything."

The search warrant also indicated that Detective Grogan was looking for an article of blue clothing he believed Scott had worn on the night of the murder, because dark blue fibers "apparently foreign to the victim's residence" were found on Debi Whitlock's body. In her brief Carlton noted, "This is a bold conclusion not supported by the record [and] apparently inserted to intimate that a nonresident was the killer. Undoubtedly because the victim's husband had been the prime suspect in this case for eight years, Officer Grogan was compelled to introduce some evidence that the perpetrator was not a resident of this household."

Further, Carlton claimed that the Whitlock case, originally assigned to Officer Grogan, was a black mark on his record. The unrelenting media attention surrounding the case may have compelled Grogan to apply "police pressure" to Michael Warnell in order to finally resolve the case.

Any way she looked at it, Carlton was convinced that Sergeant Grogan's conduct in this investigation was "far in excess of mere negligence [and shows] a pervasive pattern of deception." Because of this, "the warrants remain invalid, and all evidence seized pursuant to their issuance must be suppressed."

A month later, Deputy DA Doug Fontan fired back at the defense's accusations. Michael Warnell was a citizen informant (not a criminal informant) because he had been a productive member of society since his release from prison seven years earlier. He hadn't come forward with his information in 1988 because he had run afoul of the law himself and didn't want to be viewed as a suspect, but after rehabilitation he was motivated by the desire for a clear break from his past and also by sympathy for Debi Whitlock's family. "Such sympathy is a classic marker identifying the citizen informant," Fontan wrote.

Grogan had drawn heavily on Warnell's information in his affidavit supporting Scott Fizzell's arrest warrant, and Fontan now labeled that information as "essentially correct": the woman had been attacked with a knife in her home, which was located in the direction Scott Fizzell had indicated as "down the street," and her keys were taken from the house and later found on a lawn. And even though Mr. Warnell had indeed used the word "stabbed" in his testimony, "lay persons do not use forensically precise terms when describing trauma."

In her brief Martha Carlton had insisted that Sergeant Grogan lied when he included a "bloody knife" in his affidavit; now Fontan pointed to reports from four different officers at the house that morning, all of which mentioned the knife. If Carlton still doubted its existence, Fontan suggested she view the pictures from the scene.

Fontan agreed that Warnell hadn't seen blood on Scott Fizzell that night, but the three hours between Debi's murder and Fizzell's confession provided ample opportunity to clean up and change clothes.

Yes, Fontan agreed, Warnell had originally given the wrong address for Scott's duplex; however, the buildings were identical, and he had simply pointed out the right-hand apartment of the building *next door* to the right-hand apartment in which Scott Fizzell actually resided at the time. Further, Warnell had identified his neighbor, whom he knew only as Scott, in a lineup of similar DMV photographs. If Martha Carlton was actually suggesting that nobody should report a crime unless they knew the perpetrator's full name and address, then the deputy DA begged to differ.

Now Fontan's rebuttal turned toward a defense of Sergeant Bill Grogan, although it seemed to grant Martha Carlton some credibility when Fontan opened with the disclaimer, "every one of the purported misstatements or omissions made by Sergeant Grogan is at worst negligent or inadvertent."

Sergeant Grogan included a personal reply in Fontan's rebuttal, asserting that if any of Warnell's information from the confession was wrong, it was because Scott said the wrong thing. Grogan closed his remarks with a review of the defense's conduct. "Ms.

Carlton has chosen to attack my character rather than attempting to defend her client in a legitimate manner. By stating, 'if you are going to lie, you better have a really good memory,' her professionalism sinks to an all-time low."

If Fontan expected his rebuttal to deter Carlton's attack against his case, he was surely disappointed by her countermotion. "No court has ever suggested that a known convicted felon and drug dealer/drug addict is entitled to the presumption of credibility given to true citizen informants," Carlton stated. "Further, it is certainly novel to suggest an informant is a 'citizen informant' because he delayed reporting his information for eight years [due to] his fear of being considered a suspect."

As for Sergeant Grogan, Carlton maintained in a long tirade that he "intentionally misled" the magistrates. She barely dignified Fontan's assertion that the officers could have affected a citizen's arrest, since Sergeant Grogan *was* an officer and *acted* as an officer. Therefore, the blood extraction and all of her client's comments—in fact, everything after Officer Grogan walked into the room where Scott Fizzell was waiting—should be thrown out as "fruit of the poisonous tree," since they occurred because of an unlawful arrest.

These various arguments culminated in a hearing on February 5, 1999. After two days of heated testimony, Judge Al Girolami denied the motion of the defense to suppress evidence. Warnell, he said, was a citizen informant, and any omissions Sergeant Grogan made in his affidavits "were not material and were not intentional or recklessly false, and even if they were added there would still be considerable probable cause for an arrest."

However, Judge Girolami supported the earlier ruling of Miranda violations during Fizzell's initial questioning and proposed to throw out all of Scott Fizzell's testimony after his first mention of obtaining counsel: "I think I need a lawyer."

Fontan flipped frantically through his paperwork, scrambling to find the earlier court ruling that had allowed in all statements up to Fizzell's second mention of counsel. Now Fontan was in danger of losing even more of Fizzell's self-incriminating statements.

"Well," Girolami said, "what I would suggest then is that you notify her"—he indicated Martha Carlton—"at least two weeks from today as to what statements you want to put in as far as his statement, and then if she wants to have a motion we ought to do it well in advance of trial so you know before you're going to try the case."

Another round of appeals occurred in March of 1999. The Fifth District Appellate Court ruled that the DNA evidence linking Fizzell to the murder could be used in the upcoming trial. The jury would also hear the incriminating statements Fizzell had supposedly made to his girlfriend and in the presence of two or three other witnesses. However, the prosecution lost the most damning thing that Fizzell had said during his interview with Detective Grogan in Arkansas: "I don't know how I stand, probably not very good at all. But I know I don't want to go to jail. And I've changed a lot, I really have. But I know that don't make a difference."

In May of 1999, Doug Fontan called Jacque MacDonald and told her that the state was going to offer a plea bargain to Scott Fizzell.

"What? What does that mean?"

"It means we've got him on first-degree murder, plus burglary." He sounded pleased.

Jacque MacDonald did not share his elation. "What about the fact that that animal raped my daughter?"

"Jacque, we've been over this. It's not rape if the victim is already dead."

His words struck her like a blow. "But I don't want a plea! I refuse!"

"I'm sorry, Jacque, but you can't refuse. This isn't your decision."

"Will he get life without parole?"

"He's going to be in jail a long, long time. I can promise you that."

Jacque felt her hand gripping the phone. The District Attorney's Office had initially promised to fight for the death penalty. Then the promise was modified so that Fizzell would go to jail for the rest of his life. And now Jacque was being promised that the animal who killed and raped her daughter would be behind bars for a "long, long time." Jacque was sick of empty promises. She fought for breath.

"You know, Mr. Fontan, for eleven years I've had faith in the justice system, but this is not justice. And I'm going to hang up this phone because I don't trust myself to talk to you right now." She laid the phone down in its cradle.

Then she picked it up again.

Congressman Dennis Cardoza's top aide, Robin Adam, knew Jacque quite well. "I'm sorry, Jacque," he said. "He's on the House floor right now. Is there something I can help you with?"

Jacque struggled against the tears that were coming anyway. "Oh, Robin! They're taking a plea in Debi's case! The assistant DA just called me! And I just—I—" Jacque's voice sputtered and died.

"Oh, Jacque," Adam said, his voice full of compassion. "I am so sorry. Stay right there."

Five minutes later, Congressman Cardoza called Jacque. "Sorry, Dennis," Jacque said after blowing her nose. "I didn't know you were on the floor."

"Well, I'm not now. Tell me what happened."

Jacque recapped Doug Fontan's phone call. "That can't be right, can it? Doesn't the family get to say if we accept the plea bargain?"

"I'm sorry, Jacque," Cardoza said softly. "That's the district attorney's decision."

"But the people of Modesto wouldn't let this happen!" Jacque exclaimed. "I believe in them! They would convict him on everything! He admitted he killed her! The DNA evidence says he raped her! And the people from Debi's hometown wouldn't let this guy off! So why is the DA's office going to?"

"Jacque, let me make some calls. I'm just going to get a little more information, and then we'll talk some more. All right?"

"All right." Jacque hung up and reached for a new tissue.

Within the hour, Stanislaus County District Attorney Tom Brazelton called Jacque at home.

"I just got off the phone with Congressman Cardoza, and apparently you're pretty upset about this plea bargain."

"I'm bloody furious!"

"I don't understand," he said, genuinely puzzled. "I thought you'd be tickled pink."

On May 26, 1999, Scott Avery Fizzell pled guilty to the first-degree murder of Deborah Anne Whitlock, which occurred on March 25, 1988. His sentence would be six years for burglary and twenty-five years to life for murder. He waived his right to appeal.

In his written confession, Fizzell said he had entered the home in order to rob it, then armed himself with a kitchen knife and gone back to the bedroom where Debi Whitlock was asleep. He claimed he killed her as soon as she woke up, and that she never realized what was happening. He claimed he could not remember anything after that.

The detectives who had worked the case knew Fizzell's version of events contradicted the evidence. The defensive wounds on Debi's hands, and the fact that she was killed while kneeling next to her bed, proved Fizzell was lying.

In order to lobby for leniency in her client's sentencing, Martha Carlton prepared a sentencing memorandum. It was her intent to offer some reason for Scott Fizzell's murder of Debi Whitlock, and to explain why this action was, in her words, "a crime of adolescent sexual rage never to reoccur."

Richard T. Wood, a former probation officer and current educational doctorate candidate in psychology, compiled an in-depth biography of Fizzell to be included in the memorandum. According to Wood, Fizzell spent his early childhood in rural Michigan with his father, Ron, and his mother, Karen. When he was seven years old, Karen met a violent eighteen-year-old alcoholic named Ricky Louchart. They began an affair that continued until Ron Fizzell found them in bed together. Karen married Louchart as soon as her divorce was final, and Fizzell lived with his parents alternately until his mother and stepfather moved to Modesto, California. At that time Scott lived with his father.

Wood traced many of Fizzell's problems to his mother, who had practiced "emotional incest" on her son. "Through two failed marriages, Karen kept Scott close to her so that he could provide for her what her husbands could not: unconditional love and acceptance." Her insistent selection of distant and unhealthy partners had given Fizzell an abusive father who once denied the boy medical care when he broke his wrist due to a football injury, and an equally abusive stepfather who introduced Fizzell and Karen to methamphetamine.

After his arrest for murder, Fizzell claimed he had been sexually molested four times by either neighbors or relatives, beginning at age six. He also divulged that he was petrified of his father, who once shot a gun above his head as a joke. In high school, Fizzell rebelled against his father's strict rules and began hanging out with the "wrong" kind of kids. He and his father increasingly argued, until eventually his father hit him in the back with a baseball bat and abruptly shipped him off to his mother's house in Modesto.

By this time Karen had two sons with Ricky Louchart, and she and Ricky were "swingers." Scott Fizzell attended Davis High School in Modesto very briefly before dropping out. (The Whitlock residence was one block away from the route he would have walked to school.) Less than a year from the date he moved in with his mother, Scott Fizzell was a meth-addicted dropout who had murdered Debi Whitlock.

Following the murder, Fizzell moved in with his grandparents in Michigan, where he finished his high school degree in 1991. In July of 1993, he returned to his mother's Modesto duplex, which she now shared with her new but not improved boyfriend, Larry. Fizzell immediately began dating a neighbor, Rebecca Halog, who also moved into the house. All four adults started using crank.

Fizzell left Rebecca and his family and disappeared with an older woman the following year. A month later he came back alone, showing signs of severe drug addiction. Rebecca Halog "nursed him back to health," but he eventually started using drugs again. In April of 1994, Rebecca moved in with a girlfriend who had relocated to Flippin, Arkansas. Fizzell followed Rebecca to Flippin the following month. They moved in together and were joined a few weeks later by Fizzell's "emotionally incestuous" mother, her loser boyfriend, and Fizzell's half brothers.

Fizzell and Rebecca worked at Ranger Boats manufacturing plant during the week and, according to Wood, "partied hard" on the weekends. Fizzell had at least one affair while living with Rebecca, with whom he was "very controlling and critical."

Dr. Kathleen O'Meara composed a psychological evaluation of Fizzell for Carlton's memorandum, explaining that the defendant displayed "arrested psychological and emotional development." Long-term substance abuse had made it impossible for Fizzell to "process emotions in a productive manner." To O'Meara, Fizzell's murder of Deborah Whitlock could be traced back to his being "sensitive." Scott Fizzell feels things deeply, she contended, and his "containment of any strong emotion for any period of time contains risk [such as] emotional outbursts," murder and postmortem sodomy apparently being among them. However, O'Meara felt it probably wouldn't happen again. "The offenses of neurotic offenders such as Mr. Fizzell tend to reflect [a] psychological dynamic . . . fueled by emotional distress, internal conflicts, and unresolved traumas. These types of offenders tend not to be repeat offenders."

Finally, while Clinical Psychologist Gretchen White never spoke to Scott Fizzell, she nonetheless looked over the paperwork from his defense attorney and offered an opinion for the memorandum that "if" Fizzell perpetrated Debi Whitlock's homicide, it was most likely an act of "sexual rage." Careful to avoid the term *murder*, Dr. White explained that "the seemingly unprovoked explosion, accompanied by partial amnesia afterward, is most often due to a transfer or displacement of feelings to the victim from a significant figure in the perpetrator's life."

Dr. White did not identify who it was that Fizzell actually thought, or hoped, he was killing and raping, but her next few sentences offered a hint: "It is not uncommon to find a domineering mother, feelings of personal inadequacy, and sexual confusion in such a person. His age at the time of the crime, his heavy use of substances during this period, and the dynamics between him and his mother . . . support the finding of sexual rage."

In her summary of these three expert opinions, Public Defender Martha Carlton wanted to stress to the judge that Scott Fizzell's moment of "acting out" had victimized both him and his prey. "Scott Fizzell was an eighteen-year-old boy who acted in a fury of sexual rage, and, in just a few moments, killed Deborah Whitlock and condemned himself to a life in prison, leaving Deborah's family and his own family to grieve and wonder what might have been." It seemed Carlton wanted to convince the magistrate that Scott Fizzell had suffered a one-time trauma that turned out badly for everybody involved.

In a final attempt to secure leniency for her client, Carlton asserted that since murdering Debi Whitlock, Scott Fizzell "has proved that he is not a violent, vicious, predator. Rather, he is a man who is loved, really loved, by his family and a large circle of friends of all ages because he is hardworking, compassionate, caring person." She attached numerous letters of support from Fizzell's friends and coworkers, many of whom mentioned how "great" Fizzell was with their kids.

Now it was up to a judge to ratify the plea bargain.

TWENTY-ONE

Death Penalty

The last time I saw my father was at his mother's funeral in the fall of 1997, shortly before he took the stand at the preliminary hearing. I hadn't expected Dad to attend the funeral. He and his mother had a strained relationship at the best of times, with occasional years-long bouts of outright hostility.

Grace had been with abusive men much of her life, and it pained my father to see her put herself in that situation again and again. Grace's first husband, my grandfather, abandoned his family when my father and his sister were young children. Dad told me Grace had gone on to have bad relationships with two other men, during which time she became an alcoholic. My father had been raised by Grace's mother, a sweet-natured spitfire named Ruby, and she was his mother figure throughout the rest of her life. As for Grace, her last husband was rumored to have died in a drug deal gone bad, and she moved in with her aging mother shortly thereafter. It was at this point, after Grace had pulled her life together, that I met my grandmother. The years had made her tough but had also given her a compassionate heart and a sense of humor that was just the right mixture of naughty and fun. Grace cared for her mother until Ruby died of old age. Grace stayed in the house and grew increasingly ill. Her aversion to medical care led her to die of what my family called "cancer of the everything" in 1997.

At that time my husband and I were living in a small town in western North Carolina. Ira was an associate at a general practice law firm, and I was working toward my master's and teaching writing at a local university. We traveled to Roanoke, Virginia, for the funeral and to see my father and my sister, who were staying nearby.

When we arrived at my aunt's house, my sister ran outside and hugged me. Now thirteen, Jessie seemed happy and confident, and she chattered excitedly about her friends in Miner's Cove, her school, and her dogs. She and my husband fell into a conversation about soccer (he had just coached a group of teenagers to regional victory), and soon they were out in the freshly mown field, kicking a ball around like old pals while my uncle's cows looked on from the adjacent pasture.

I went inside the house, hugged my aunt, and chatted my way through the crowd. Finally I saw my father, alone and tucked into a corner of the kitchen. He sat on a barstool and stared glumly into his glass, speaking only when spoken to. He took no notice as I walked up to him.

"Is this seat taken?"

He looked up and smiled wanly. His eyes were distant, almost vacant. "Hello."

"You hiding?"

"No. I've been onstage since I got here. *The Return of the Prodigal Son.* I guess I'm just tired."

"Do you want me to leave you alone for a bit?"

"No, no." He put his hand on mine. It was cold and damp from his glass. "I'm glad you're here."

I slid onto the stool next to him. "What's good here?"

"If you like syrup on ice, I recommend the tea."

My aunt appeared with a glass full of ice and the tea pitcher. "It's peach," she said.

"Sounds perfect." I took a sip.

"How is it?" my aunt asked.

"Great! I think it just dissolved a filling!"

My dad snickered appreciatively as my aunt shot me a glare. "Yep, she's yours," she told my father, then turned to her other guests.

"How's the house coming along?" I asked. A couple of years ago my father said he had purchased some land and was living in a trailer on the property while he saved up enough money to build a house.

Dad's face darkened. "That's on hold. Indefinitely."

"Oh. Is there a new plan?"

"Not really."

During the rest of our conversation, it became apparent that my father had no plans, no hopes. He told me that Jessie still saw Heather frequently, which answered my unasked questions about his marriage.

"I noticed outside that Jessie still calls Heather 'Mom.'"

"Heather is the only mother she's ever known." He swirled the glass and watched the ice cubes revolve. "I would never take that away from her."

The look in his eyes spoke of guilt and incredible sadness, and I believed he was berating himself for another failed marriage. "Hey," I said softly, so others wouldn't hear, "people fall in and out of love. You know that. Sometimes it's nobody's fault."

He smiled at me and shook his head, like I'd just espoused

belief in Santa Claus. "It's always somebody's fault. You take any event, you trace it back, and the trail leads to somebody."

I was confused. "What are we talking about?"

"Everything. It's like that physicist said: a butterfly flutters its wing and causes a hurricane halfway around the world. Do I turn right or left at the light? Do I take my coffee with cream or without?" He shook his head, imprisoned in his own world of cause and unforeseen effect. "And then, years later, you find yourself asking, 'Damn it, why didn't I take the cream?'"

I was struggling to keep up. Was he saying that he had made mistakes with Heather that he now wished he could undo? "Can you start taking cream in your coffee now?" I asked, using his own analogy.

"Let me tell you something, as your father. The *wise* father." His voice was thick with sarcasm. "You can never go back and add the cream. In any situation, you can't go back. The coffee is cold. The cream is curdled. It's not an option."

I knew at that moment that my father was done. His return to Virginia was not to honor his mother but to see his family, to look upon the hills of his childhood, and to say good-bye to each of these things. Was it cancer, like his mother? Cirrhosis? I didn't know.

Just then my husband wandered in, followed by my sister. I noticed Dad was distant with her, too, although he teased her in a halfhearted attempt at humor. Jessie was used to navigating our father's moods. She drew closer or backed away with an agility I had never developed.

My father was quiet and withdrawn the rest of the day. Toward evening I hugged my sister good-bye and tousled her hair as I used to. Then I turned to my father. He submitted to my embrace, but I felt my arms would pass right through him. He was a wraith.

On the way home, my husband drove in silence, allowing me time to sort through my thoughts. Finally he asked, "How are you doing?"

"Pretty rough."

"It was hard to say good-bye to your dad and sister, wasn't it?"

"Heartbreaking."

Ira took my hand. "Jessie's doing really well. She seems happy."

"Based on my conversation with Dad, I'd say that's Heather's doing." I remembered his despondency. "I think he's dying."

My husband considered my comment. "He did look pretty bad. Is he still smoking?"

"Cigars. So yes, maybe it's cancer. He certainly seems to be deteriorating from the inside out." I blinked as tears clouded my vision. "I think he's pulling away. The Big Away."

I took the tissue Ira offered me and looked out the window at the darkening foothills. "Maybe Grace's funeral is making me imagine the worst, but at this moment I fully believe that the next time my father and I are together, I'll be standing over his grave."

But my father didn't die. Instead, the next month he admitted in front of a courtroom full of reporters something that he had never admitted to me: that he had been with Heather while Scott Fizzell was murdering Debi in their home. The story was re-counted in newspaper articles that never made their way to me. Maybe he thought I knew. Maybe that's why he withdrew from me. He wouldn't answer the phone. Sometimes he would call my house, say "wrong number" in a muffled voice, and hang up. At these times I was tempted to call him back, but instead I gave him his space. The motions and countermotions from both sides brought continual delays in the case against Debi's killer, and my father was dealing with them in his own way. I knew from experience that it would be disastrous for me to pressure him to talk to me if he wasn't ready.

Scott Fizzell's sentencing hearing took place on June 23, 1999. Jacque MacDonald sat in the first row of the same wooden and metal folding chairs she'd first sat in the day Scott Fizzell was arraigned. Dennis sat beside her in his usual spot, holding her hand. In the other hand, Jacque clutched her typed copy of her victim impact statement. She fidgeted with the blue ribbon on her lapel. Her friend Diana Ward had handed them to everybody entering the courtroom: the family, the police personnel, the press, and the gawkers.

"The pictures look nice," Congressman Cardoza said. He was seated on Jacque's other side, and he gestured at the large poster board covered in blue flowers and photos of Debi throughout her life.

Jacque smiled at her friend sadly. "Dennis helped me put that together," she said, patting her husband's hand. "I haven't looked at a lot of those pictures since before Debi was murdered. It's too sad. But Margaret said I needed to make Debi real to the judge, so that's what I'm trying to do."

Jessica Whitlock sat in the back row of the courtroom, sandwiched between her father and her Aunt Karen. Now fifteen years old, she had a fairly clear understanding of the proceedings.

Her mother's death was something that Jessie never discussed with her father. She remembered years ago that he used to ask her if she knew who killed her mother. It seemed so important to him that one day she had told him she did, and she concocted a wildly improbable description of the killer. Her father had known she had lied. More than that, he told her tearfully that he understood why she had lied. He thanked her and promised he would never ask her again. Since that time, they had never spoken of Debi's death. Gran mentioned the murder whenever a new television show or magazine profiled the story, but Jessie never saw any of the coverage. It wasn't a part of her life. But since the plea bargain was announced, her dad explained to Jessie that the rest of the family was going to court to watch as her mother's killer was sentenced. "You don't have to go," he explained, "but if you want to, I'll take you." Jessie had thought the situation through on her own for a while, then told him that she wanted to go. He nodded resolutely. Now here they were, waiting for the man to come in.

Jacque was pleased to have her former son-in-law in the room. Harold Whitlock had been suspected for so long by so many people, and Jacque saw this as an opportunity for him to finally be recognized as the victim he truly was. Howie sat with the family, with those who loved Debi. He sat exactly where he had been all along.

Jacque read through her typed copy of her victim impact statement. These statements were designed to allow the family to share how their loved one's loss had affected them and to ask the judge for a particular sentence. Jacque's statement did much more than that.

Suddenly Dennis squeezed her hand. "They're ready, sweetheart. It's your turn."

Every eye in the crowded room followed the petite woman as she made her way to the witness stand. Her search for justice had begun with an open letter to Debi's killer, printed in newspapers across the Central Valley almost exactly eleven years ago. Today, Jacque would read her letter to the murderer directly, staring at him, knowing that this time he would hear her words.

"I would like to start by thanking Your Honor for this opportunity to address the court with my thoughts and feelings. My name is Jacque, and I am the mother of Debi Whitlock. The past two and a half years we have heard of Debi referred to as 'the victim,' but today I would like to introduce you to my daughter."

Jacque talked about Debi as a mischievous and happy child, a successful businesswoman, and a loving sister and mother. "Jessica Jacqueline was the brightest star in Debi's life."

Next, Jacque turned to the day she learned of her daughter's murder. "From the moment I heard of her death, I began doing hard time. I ask Your Honor, how will I get parole for good behavior? How will I get a plea bargain to take away the pain? No court in the world can do that. Because of this plea bargain, we are sentenced to a life of not only parole hearings, but the fear that Debi's killer may one day be released. I ask you, sir, where is our justice?"

Fizzell stared directly at Jacque as she addressed him. "You felt you had covered all your tracks and could get away with murder. I know my daughter died a hero protecting her child, while for the rest of your life, wherever you may be, you will be branded not only as a sniveling little coward and murderer, but a necrophiliac, or one who defiles the dead. By taking the easy way out with this plea bargain, you have proved yourself to be the pathetic excuse for a human being that you are. In the final analysis, the day will come when you will have to face not only Debi, but almighty God, whose punishment will be swift and just."

Jacque turned toward Judge Al Girolami, who nodded. "For us, Debi's family, for the rest of our lives we are sentenced to live with only her memory. Time does not diminish the pain and sorrow. We are incomplete without her. Every holiday that was once a joy begins with the decoration of her grave. I only wish it were possible that the court could sentence this killer to life without parole and overturn this plea bargain."

Surveying the crowd, Jacque recognized so many people who had become friends and supporters through the years. She thanked them for all they had done for her and her family. Then she straightened and directed her full attention at the defense table. "I would also be remiss if I did not mention that I have been deeply offended by what I consider to be unprofessional behavior by the defense; namely, the smiles, the winks, the touching of the killer in this courtroom. I wonder, madam, if there is enough soap in the world to wash his stench from your hands?"

Jacque ignored the murmuring in the courtroom. She thought she heard someone clap, but they were quickly silenced. Beside her, Margaret Speed glanced at the defense attorney. She, too, believed the public defender had behaved insensitively and inappropriately throughout the hearings, and Margaret was immensely proud of Jacque for speaking her mind. She was equally thankful to the judge for allowing it.

Jacque turned back toward the judge. "In conclusion, I would like once more to thank Your Honor for finally being given the opportunity to speak about my feelings as a mother. To everyone in this courtroom, the next time you hear those three magical words, 'I love you,' from your child or grandchild that make life worthwhile, remember me. The only way I will ever hear them again from Debi is like this." She pushed a button on the tape recorder Margaret had placed beside her, and Debi's voice rang out in the last telephone message she would ever leave her mother: "Oops! I should have hung up. Oh, well. Hi, Mom. This is your daughter. I love you. I'll try back later."

Friends and family dabbed their eyes, and reporters scribbled madly on their memo pads. Scott Fizzell finally stood, and Judge Girolami sentenced him to thirty-six years for murder, with another six for burglary.

Now it was official. Scott Fizzell would be reviewed for parole in 2017, and no rape or sexual assault charge would appear on his record. Jacque was livid. Thirty-six years couldn't compensate for

Debi's brutal murder and violation. This part of the fight was over. There was one more battle Jacque was determined to win.

I called my father the day after the sentencing hearing.

"So, it's over," I said, skipping any preamble.

"I guess," he said dully.

"Aren't you relieved?"

"Actually, I don't know how I feel about it. It's just too much to process." He asked how I felt about Fizzell's sentence.

"I'm not sure," I admitted. "I know they were going for the death penalty at one point, but . . . well, no sentence is going to bring Debi back."

"I can't argue with that." My father started to say something else, stopped, and then started again. "You want to hear something crazy? I really did feel relieved at the very beginning. When I first heard about the arrest, I felt like, 'Oh, thank God it's no one I knew.' The cops even checked out Bob and Jerry. Made them give blood samples. One of them had the same blood type. I remember telling the detectives, 'These are my best friends! You're out of your mind for even considering them!' But the next minute I'm praying, 'God, don't let it be them. Just don't let it be them.'"

I knew exactly what my father meant. In the wake of Debi's death I had made lists in my head of her friends and sized each one up against my mistaken image of the murderer: a man Debi would care for enough to take as a lover, but who was also violent enough to kill her. We all had our theories, but at their heart those hypotheses always revealed a reason for Debi's death. She had angered someone. She had shown kindness to the wrong person. Now we all knew we had been wrong. There was no reason.

"It was a stranger all along," I said, thinking aloud.

"It was a stranger. He was in town, then he was gone. No

wonder they couldn't find him." Dad sighed. "I guess the guy was on drugs and just went nuts. They said he doesn't even have a record, although that sounds unlikely. If you had seen what he did . . ." His voice trailed off. My father had never told me about Debi's wounds.

"How's Debi's mom feeling about the sentence?" I asked, changing the subject.

"Mad as hell. She didn't want that plea bargain. You should have seen her at the sentencing hearing. Somebody with the Public Defender's Office said the guy didn't know what he was doing because he was high. And Jacque said, 'Well, he certainly figured out how to work his zipper.' I thought I was gonna choke."

I whistled appreciatively.

"I don't blame her. She's devoted her life to finding this bastard. People told her she was obsessed. Hell, she was. But she kept going." My father paused. When he spoke again, his voice was quiet and sad. "It's like she didn't realize that maybe people needed to put this behind them—try to build a life again."

I thought about the detectives questioning people in Miner's Cove. Dad had blamed Detective Taylor for stripping his family of anonymity in their new town, but he had already done that by participating in all those crime shows. What were the chances that no one in Miner's Cove would see *America's Most Wanted*, or *Unsolved Mysteries*? My father helped Jacque in spite of what it cost him. That had been admirable. Now he should be sharing in Jacque's victory. Instead, I sensed nothing in him but bitterness and despair.

"I couldn't tell Jacque to stop. Debi was her daughter," my father continued. "And no matter how I may have felt about it, I've got to admit she was right. She did the right thing. And now maybe she'll have some peace."

"How about you, Dad? Will you have peace?"

"I'd like to think so."

I remembered the crime show I had seen about Debi's case, and a new thought occurred to me.

"Well, if anybody ever thought it was you, I guess they know better now."

"Get real. People believe what they believe. They're not open to alternatives. It's better just to *know*." He considered. "OK, so there's this Fizzell guy sitting in jail right now, but that doesn't stop a lot of people from believing I should be in the next cell."

"I don't want to believe people are like that."

He laughed derisively. "Then don't! That's the point. Damn the evidence, and just *decide*. Be done with it. 'People are reasonable!' Check. Up next: achieving world harmony through Coca-Cola products!" My father caught his breath after his rant, and then added, "Of course, that would have to be old Coke. New Coke just pisses off *everybody*."

In spite of the jokes, my father's despondency upset me. Why was he saying "lots" of people doubted him? Surely his depression was causing him to exaggerate. "Dad, everyone knows you didn't do anything wrong. Forget the rest."

"Honey, there are things—things that—" He was tripping over his words, not sure what to say. Finally he settled for, "Thank you. That's very sweet of you to say."

"And anyway," I said, determinedly plowing ahead, "it's over now."

"It just doesn't feel over. It feels like it will never be over."

My father continued to be depressed and distant, but in May of 2001, I called to tell him I was pregnant. For the first time in years he sounded genuinely happy. He was now the office manager at Miner's Cove Construction, and we began using the company Web site to e-mail each other regularly.

I no longer thought my father's death was imminent. In fact, I was feeling better about his physical and mental health than I had in a long time. Maybe we could build from here. Maybe he would visit me after the baby was born in November. And Jessie was almost eighteen—maybe she could look at colleges on the East Coast, and I could start suggesting that my father finally move back to Virginia—something he'd been longing to do for more than a decade.

The nightmare of Debi's death was finally over. It was time for a new day in my relationship with my father. I could almost feel the sun.

"Hello? Angela?"

"Yeah?"

It was late in the morning on August 25, 2001, and I was exhausted. People always talk about sleepless nights with a newborn, but no one had bothered to tell me the sleep deprivation starts way before then.

"Angela, this is Heather. Heather Barnett." She could tell I was still struggling. I hadn't spoken to her since 1994. "I married your dad?"

"Oh, right. Sorry," I said, putting it together. Then the next part of the puzzle fell into place. She was calling because something was wrong. I was wide awake. "What's happened?"

"I have some bad news."

Suddenly I was once again on the phone in my aunt's guest room, and my father was bracing himself to tell me Debi had been killed. Just like I had then, I struggled for breath and asked, "Is it Jessie?"

"No. Jessie's fine. It's your father. He was in a bad car accident and . . . he died this morning."

According to Heather, my father had spent the previous night outside the house of a woman he hoped to marry, but who had broken off their relationship for reasons of her own. He sat in his car all night and headed for home in the predawn hours. On a curvy stretch of Oregon's coastal highway, his car hit a guardrail once, then twice. He suffered massive head trauma and was pronounced dead upon arrival at the local hospital. "I don't think he suffered," Heather assured me. "I think the impact probably concussed him seriously enough that he didn't feel the pain."

"*You choose your truth and believe it,*" my father had said. I chose this as my truth.

"I probably don't need to tell you . . ." Heather's voice trailed off.

"He'd been drinking?" I already knew the answer.

"Yes. But I think we both know that that wouldn't have affected his driving."

That was true as well. My father had been a functioning alcoholic for so long that I knew it wouldn't make him drive off the road. Not at the blood alcohol level Heather mentioned.

"So Jessie wasn't in the car?"

"She was at home asleep. The guys at EMT know me. I came over right after they told me what had happened."

"Thank you," I said, numb beyond crying.

I talked to my sister briefly, but we were both too overcome to stay on the phone. After we hung up, I grabbed my pruning shears, walked into the backyard, and butchered a butterfly bush that I had been meaning to trim for weeks. I cried and screamed and hacked away until all that remained was a misshapen stump. Then I dropped the shears into the mulch and turned into my husband's waiting arms.

* * *

The following week, my sister donated the wreckage of our father's car to Mothers Against Drunk Driving so that they could display it as a warning to others. I was exceptionally proud of her.

With her blessing, I had Dad's remains cremated and shipped home to Virginia. He had loved his grandmother, Ruby, more than anyone else in his life, and I made arrangements to have his remains interred with hers. The small graveside funeral at the old cemetery was attended by a smattering of family members as well as my mother, who had been devastated by news of my father's death. Several of my parents' former schoolmates from Oak Hill Academy were also in attendance, and one of them volunteered to have a "remembrance gathering" at his mountaintop cabin after the ceremony.

Clad in an ungainly black maternity dress, I clutched the eulogy and tottered unsteadily across the funeral home's Astro Turf to the podium. I placed the box containing my father's ashes on a small table surrounded by flowers, and I read my few meager words. After the funeral, I walked over to a stereo on the same table and played some Simon and Garfunkel. I knew my father would have approved.

At the gathering afterward, my parents' former schoolmates told raucous stories and passed around old black-and-white photos of Rocky Whitlock as a young man. He had been tall and handsome, with wavy black hair and a grin that said, *I can talk my way out of anything.* There he was at a formal dance in a suit and tie, his arm around my mother. And here he was in his basketball uniform, high in the air, his arm a perfect arc as he pressed the ball toward the hoop. I thumbed through the pictures of this boy who had been the most popular kid in his class and tried to concentrate on the conversations around me.

"Do you remember the night Coach said we weren't going to Regionals if we didn't bring up our math grades? Rocky stayed up all night tutoring us, and the next day we went to Regionals. Won, too, if my memory serves me."

"He was voted Most Likely to Succeed, you know. I'd have bet anything he would go on to change the world. *Change the world*. It's a damn shame, what happened to him."

I made my way outside, wanting some time with my thoughts. I would never know the boy who featured in the stories inside the house, but I tried to recall good times with the later version of that boy.

My mother found me outside sometime later with my feet propped up on a wooden porch swing overlooking the Blue Ridge Mountains.

"How are you doing?" she asked.

"I was just sitting here thinking about how dad had a different name for every phase of his life. Sometimes I believe he really was three different people. And I didn't understand any of them."

Mom picked up my feet, slid onto the swing beside me, and put my feet back on her lap. "I guess I hadn't thought about it like that."

"He was Rocky in Virginia and with you. Then he was Howie with Debi. Finally he became Harold in Oregon."

I watched a hawk ride the updraft where the Roanoke Valley met the mountains, following an ancient migration path. Its wings navigated the blustering wind with a skill that seemed effortless.

"The Rocky I knew was a really wonderful person," Mom said. "Deep down, he always was. He just had this habit of getting in the way of his own happiness. And the saddest part was that he knew it, but he couldn't stop himself."

She settled back into the swing, pushing her foot gently against the wooden porch floor to set the swing into an easy motion. "I always loved a part of your father. It was as if the boy I fell in love with was trapped inside of him. I'd catch a glimpse of him sometimes, and it broke my heart all over again. For all of us." Mom fumbled in her pocket for a tissue, then dabbed at her eyes.

We sat together in silence for a while, until the baby started kicking determinedly against my rib cage. I pressed my hand to my side. "When I talked to Heather last week, she said Dad could never accept being loved."

Mom nodded. "Your dad made mistakes. Everybody does. But he never learned to forgive. He used them against himself and eventually they destroyed him. And they destroyed his relationships with everybody who ever loved him."

My mother slid her hand underneath mine and smiled faintly at the feel of her granddaughter. "At the very least, maybe he can teach us something about the importance of forgiveness."

In the weeks following his death, I learned my father died in debt, with weeks' worth of unopened mail scattered around his trailer. He had allowed illegal logging on the land on which he was living—land he was only renting. Clearly he was beyond caring about consequences. He had even cut off his friendship with Bob Kramer, abruptly and without reason, though the two men had been as close as brothers.

The official cause of death was "drunk driving," but I have wondered many times if my father took his hands off the wheel that night. I think what happened in that car was only the lethal wound. The first blow happened near midnight on March 25, 1988.

TWENTY-TWO

Debi's Law

Debi's murderer would be eligible for parole from Ironwood State Prison in 2017. The defense's sentencing memorandum had labeled Scott Fizzell's crimes a one-time bout of "sexual rage," supporting this assertion in part through his claim of partial amnesia: he could not remember sexually defiling Debi's body. Now that the plea was in place and sentencing was over, Fizzell stated that he could, in fact, remember that part of his crime, but that Debi was "already dead." Jacque marveled that the California legal system could consider releasing Scott Fizzell without warning the public about his lethal sexual perversity. And how many other men like Fizzell were already back on the streets?

California law hadn't given Debi justice, so Jacque knew she had to change the law. As she had so many times during her previous battles, Jacque went to discuss it with Debi.

"You've got to help me," she said, standing beside her daughter's grave. The Evergreen Cemetery was deserted, and the mid-morning sun was struggling to dispel the Valley's thick fog. Jacque reached out and touched her daughter's smiling picture on the marker. "Mummy can't do this without you."

Jacque bent down to arrange the daffodils she had brought, then straightened as a memory came to her.

She and her first husband, Martin Garrett, had recently transferred to Merced when they decided to take a drive through the foothills. It was a warm afternoon, and a few hours into their exploration they stopped at a bar for a drink. It seemed like a nice enough place, even if the patrons did turn to check them out as they walked through the door. They ordered their drinks, and Martin excused himself to go to the restroom.

Immediately a large man in cowboy boots and a genuine Stetson hat walked over to Jacque. He hooked his thumbs on either side of a big silver belt buckle depicting two crossed rifles. "How you doing today?" he asked.

"Fine, thank you. Just waiting for my orange juice."

"A pretty woman with a pretty accent," the man continued unabashedly. "I bet you could do better than that guy you came in with."

"Thank you, but he's my husband. I think I'll stick with him."

"What the hell's going on here?" Martin was back and had sized up the situation in a minute. "Get the hell away from my wife!"

Martin was notoriously hotheaded, so Jacque was not surprised that he didn't notice several other men in the bar making their way over.

Minutes later, Martin was at the bottom of a pile of brawling cowboys. Jacque looked around, frantic for help, but the reactions of only mild interest around the room let her know this was one of "those sorts" of bars. If anyone was going to help her husband, it was up to her.

Jacque cast her eyes around the room, looking for anything

that might get the men's attention. Her gaze settled on a pool cue. Without hesitating, she ran across the room, grabbed the cue, and rushed toward the mound of writhing bodies.

Then she pulled up short. What exactly was she going to do? She was worried about her husband, but she was also placing herself in danger.

Holding the cue in her outstretched hand, she gingerly prodded the man on top of the pile. He glanced her way, and then did a double take. Jacque knew she must look ridiculous, a five-foot-three woman, slightly built, holding a pool cue above her head like Excalibur fresh from the stone.

Jacque fought to keep her voice from shaking. "My husband is at the bottom of that pile," she announced, her crisp British accent ringing across the bar, "and you better let him out of there right now!" She didn't say "or else." She didn't know what else. She prayed it wouldn't come to that.

Maybe because they were shocked, or possibly amused, or because another fight was always just around the corner in this place, the men stopped fighting. Jacque and Martin left, never to return.

Standing now by her daughter's grave, Jacque watched as one of spring's first butterflies flitted through the grass nearby. She could do this. She was a fighter. And there was no way she was going to let the law rob another victim of justice as it had robbed her daughter.

But how do you change a law?

The Victim's Voice was now underwritten by Comcast Cable and produced by Barbara Rodiek. Distribution fees came out of Jacque's pocket or through private donations. Over the years Jacque had grown close to many of the guests who had appeared on her show. Among them were Mike Reynolds and Marc Klaas, who had pushed through California's toughest crime legislation in decades: the so-called Three Strikes and You're Out law.

In June of 1992, eighteen-year-old Kimber Reynolds was outside a popular restaurant when two repeat felons shot her while attempting to steal her purse. Kimber's parents rushed to the hospital where Mike Reynolds held his dying daughter's hand and made her a promise. "If I can't save you, then I'll do my best to save other people."

The Reynolds family started researching California criminal law and was horrified to learn that it was standard practice for convicts to receive 50 percent time credit. "That's the way the law reads in this state," Mike Reynolds told Jacque and her viewers. "No matter what you've done to go to jail, half of your time drops away as soon as you begin your sentence. Then you can get that reduced further for things like good behavior."

"That's horrible," Jacque exclaimed.

"It's horrible, but it happens every day."

He went on to explain that almost 70 percent of California's murders were committed by repeat offenders who had already been to jail.

Reynolds and a small group of citizens, law enforcement personnel, and judges crafted the Three Strikes legislation aimed at repeat felons. Under this modified sentencing code, California's criminals had their sentences doubled with their second violent felony conviction, and served a mandatory minimum sentence of twenty-five years with their third violent felony. The battle for Three Strikes was just getting under way when one of California's greatest child tragedies struck.

Twelve-year-old Polly Klaas and her little sister were hosting a slumber party at their home in Petaluma, California, when a man broke into the house, tied up all the girls, and abducted Polly. The people of California banded together to find the man matching the sketch produced by the other little girls. Polly had been missing two months when a woman twenty-five miles from the Klaas residence found her tights and other articles indicating foul play. Within two days, police arrested Richard Allen Davis. The repeat felon admitted to molesting and killing Polly and led police to the girl's remains.

Mike Reynolds told Jacque's audience that Polly's father, Marc, joined the ongoing battle to pass Three Strikes, and together the grieving fathers put the measure directly before the California voters in November of 1994. It passed with the largest majority of votes for any California statute. Two years later, California's rate of violent crime had dropped to its lowest point since 1970. "We rolled crime back twenty-five years in twenty-four months," Reynolds said proudly.

At the end of his interview on *The Victim's Voice*, Reynolds encouraged the public to be vocal and active in pursuing justice for victims and potential victims. "If you think these common-sense laws are going to automatically be put into place, you've got another think coming. If you're waiting for political action to just happen, it's not going to. If you see something that needs to be done, get behind it!"

It was common sense to Jacque that postmortem rape should mean a harsher penalty for the murderer. But for whatever inexplicable reason, that law was not on record. Jacque was ready to fight for justice, but she was going to need some clout. She called her friend, Assemblyman Dennis Cardoza.

In February 2000, Cardoza introduced Assembly Bill 2826 (Debi's Law), seeking to amend California's penal code. Section 190.2 listed twenty-two categories of "special circumstances" that, when committed during the act of an intentional murder, could make the crime punishable by either life without parole or death. Cardoza proposed three new special circumstances, including murder committed in order that the killer could then perpetrate additional atrocities against the corpse, including sexual acts, dismemberment, or incineration.

The Assembly Committee on Public Safety reviewed Cardoza's bill in April of that year but decided to block its passage for several reasons. First, they believed those special circumstances already in existence could cover the other two circumstances proposed. Regarding the part of the law inspired by Debi's case, the committee felt Cardoza had not adequately defined the term *sexual acts*. "If a husband or boyfriend [intentionally] kills his wife or girlfriend and remorsefully kisses the dead body, is that a sexual act?"

Six years passed, and the Assembly seat vacated by Congressman Cardoza went to Barbara Matthews, a tenacious and often outspoken representative for her district. Matthews's office drafted a different version of the bill attempting to reach the same goal via a different avenue—this time by amending the Health and Safety Code section 7052, relating to treatment of human remains. Matthews proposed that if "sexual contact or penetration is found to have occurred after the person killed the victim, the punishment shall be imprisonment in the state prison for life without the possibility of parole." (Contention over the death penalty led Matthews to strike that from her version of the bill.) Within the language of the bill, Matthews defined *sexual contact* as "any willful touching by a person of an intimate part of a dead human body for the purpose of sexual arousal, gratification, or abuse." When she took it before the Public Safety Committee on April 4, 2006, Matthews included statements of support from Crime Victims United of California and Sergeant Mike Harden of the Modesto Police Department.

Several organizations were firmly opposed to the new bill. The Taxpayers for Improving Public Safety felt that "such an offense is so far outside of the realm of reality for an overwhelming majority of murders—so outrageously abnormal—that it is an anomaly which ought to be treated as a mental health issue long before it is addressed criminally." The California Attorneys for Criminal Justice claimed California's existing laws were sufficient, and that the bill was "a real threat to the good people who have to deal with the dead and their relatives in our state." The statement was confusing at best. Did the CACJ mean to imply that "good people" might intentionally kill people and then sexually copulate with their dead bodies? Or had they simply misread the bill? Jacque didn't know.

Assemblywoman Matthews's version of Debi's Law stalled, but the Public Safety Committee made a counteroffer: if Matthews would change the bill so that it merely increased the existing sentence for "sexual contact with, or mutilation or disinterment of, human remains" from a minimum of three years to a new high of eight years, then the Committee would pass the bill on to Appropriations. Matthews agreed, but even this watered down version stalled in May 2006.

Now Jacque is gathering her energy for another run. This time, California Assemblywoman Cathleen Galgiani is drafting a different form of the bill. When she feels the time is right, she and a new (and as yet unnamed) cosponsor will plead their case again. Jacque is doing all she can to get support behind the proceedings.

"I'll do whatever I have to in order to get Debi's Law passed," she recently told Congressman Cardoza. "I'll tap dance down the street in my knickers if I have to."

Of course he laughed. But he knew better than to doubt her.

Epilogue

In March 2007, Jacque called to tell me she would be awarded the National Crime Victims' Service Award from the attorney general the following month. Her local district attorney, Larry Morse, had nominated her.

The award ceremony was scheduled as a prelude to National Crime Victims' Rights Week, an annual commemoration first proclaimed by President Ronald Reagan in 1981. This year's observance was particularly poignant to those in attendance, as it fell just after the tragic shooting rampage at nearby Virginia Tech. I told Jacque I would meet her in D.C. It would be the first time we had seen each other since before Debi's murder nineteen years ago.

I stayed with my husband's aunt in Maryland and took an early Metro into Georgetown. The morning was beautiful, and spring flowers poked up jauntily outside the brownstone apartments I passed on the way to the Fairmont Hotel. Upon arrival I was told that Jacque and her "companions" were in the dining room. They weren't hard to find. They had taken over a small wing of the restaurant and were laughing as I rounded the corner.

Jacque and I recognized each other immediately and embraced. Any awkwardness we might otherwise have felt had been exorcised during our frequent phone calls during the past two years. Jacque was dressed in a tasteful blue suit. I knew an angel pin was on the lapel before I even looked.

Dennis walked up bearing a fresh cup of coffee, which he placed on the table in front of me. He had been up for hours, exercising in the hotel fitness center.

Slowly the ladies around the table introduced themselves to me. Donna Raley was a tall, slender widow whose stepdaughter Dena had been missing for eight years. "I guess you could say each one of us here has been through our own nightmare," Donna told me, grasping my hand with finely manicured fingers. "And at first, everybody wants to help. But as the case drags on and on, they go away. Jacque was the first one to come back on the scene." Jacque interviewed Donna on *The Victim's Voice* four years after Dena's disappearance, and that in turn helped Donna get another round of exposure for Dena's case.

Beside Donna was Linda Totty, a woman whose husband was murdered by an unidentified vagrant years earlier. The case was still unsolved.

Corrine Menzies had been Jacque's friend and confidant for years. Corrine's aunt had been murdered by a serial killer long ago, and since that time, Corrine had been reaching out to victims through a variety of different programs. "There's a need for a different kind of support group," she told me. "Most groups are founded by people in pain, and they are attended by people in pain. They tell their stories, and they find understanding and camaraderie in the first stages of their grief—and they need that desperately. But after a while, people start picking up their lives again, and that's when I try to help." She shook her head sadly. "People will never forget their loved ones, and they shouldn't. But some people lock away their pain instead of learning to walk with it." She smiled at the guest of honor. "Jacque walks with it."

"I stumble, darling," Jacque quipped.

"Yes, but you stumble with style."

Next was Kaysie, whose adult son had been stabbed to death at a Modesto park. She was concerned about the welfare of her young grandchildren, but Kaysie had little legal ground to do anything. "We've got to do something about grandparents' rights in this country," Kaysie said, looking angry and determined. "And Jacque said she'd help me."

"I told you," Jacque said with a reassuring smile, "we're going to see Senator Feinstein and Dennis Cardoza, and whoever they can send us to from there."

There were others there as well, each with their own pain, and each now tucked protectively under Jacque's wings. Surveying the group, I realized that they were more of a political action committee than a fan club. They already had a full day scheduled, and it would begin at Congressman Cardoza's office.

"Jacque's helped me pass several crime bills by bringing them to the attention of the public," the congressman later told me. We were sitting in his office at a large round table just minutes before he was scheduled to preside over the House of Representatives. "She's been very instrumental in ways she doesn't even realize." He smiled and patted her hand. "For example, Jacque helped us pass a bill that gave us the ability to prosecute child predators even if the parents don't want to prosecute personally."

I knew that Congressman Cardoza had donated his entire midterm pay raise to various charities, among them *The Victim's Voice*. "Jacque is one of those people who thrive by fighting back," Cardoza said, by way of explanation. "She fought back for Debi, and when she gave her victim impact statement at Fizzell's sentencing, it was one of the bravest things I've ever seen. Now she uses her bravery to help other people fight their battles."

He sat back, choosing his words. "Jacque and I share a belief that things are not as they should be but that we can create a better society. And we try to help each other do just that."

Merced District Attorney Larry Morse caught the red-eye into Washington the following morning in order to attend Jacque's banquet. He was in the middle of prosecuting a man who had shot and killed a Merced police officer, and the trial was extremely intense. When I saw Morse at an opening ceremony for Crime Victims' Week, he looked dog tired but insisted he wouldn't have missed Jacque's award ceremony for the world.

"You may not be aware of everything Jacque accomplishes in our community," Morse explained to me. "She operates outside the system, but she has amassed this incredible network of victims and law enforcement. Being in Jacque's network gives you credibility." He took a gulp of coffee, and I strongly suspected it was the only thing keeping him on his feet. He turned his bloodshot eyes back to me. "This is my vocation, but it's Jacque's advocation."

"Here you are!" Jacque came up and linked arms with the DA. "I've made a connection for us. I think he can help us with the issue of grandparents' rights . . ."

Her voice faded as she steered Morse away into the crowd. He shot me a smile that told me Jacque did this all the time. I returned the smile and watched her deposit the district attorney into an ongoing discussion across the room. Kaysie was already there, talking animatedly to two men in suits and name tags.

Donna Raley was standing nearby. "We do have a little Internet of our own, and Jacque is one of the primary connections."

She laughed and shook her head. "That woman is connected to everybody in the world."

"I'm starting to understand that," I answered.

During the entirety of the trip, I watched in amazement as Jacque marched her troupe of survivors through the halls of the Capitol, using her award to pry open doors and shove her friends at the politicians, staffers, and reporters inside.

"Good Lord, Jacque," I exclaimed over dinner. "I've never seen anybody push their way into a room like you do and end up making the person inside think they invited you in the first place." I smiled at her. "It's pretty impressive."

She waved aside the praise. "Angela, I had to learn not to let myself be embarrassed. If I was going to do Debi or anybody else any good, I had to stop standing next to the wall and get into the center of the room. I try not to push, but I get there."

On the last evening of our visit, I met Jacque at the Ronald Reagan Building on Pennsylvania Avenue for the opening ceremony of Crime Victims' Rights Week. Later, we stood hand in hand during the candlelight vigil. It was the first time we had mourned Debi's death together.

But we were both mourning so much more.

Jacque carries the grief of others with her at all times. I felt almost suffocated by it after three days, but through her outreach to others, Jacque has lived it for the past two decades.

My own grief centered on my father. While conducting research for this book, I discovered all the things my father had never told me about the events surrounding Debi's murder. And I finally understood why he had hidden them from me: he could not risk seeing in my eyes the disappointment and condemnation he constantly directed at himself.

There are answers I will never have. Why did Debi say my father was home that night? Who was breathing in the master bedroom? What happened to the guest towels? And there are answers that I think I know: that my father accidentally left the back door unlocked that night, just hours before Scott Fizzell tested it to see if he could get inside ("I used that door all the time."); that Debi had let her life insurance lapse because she was in the middle of divorcing my father and hadn't yet set up the trust necessary to make Jessie her beneficiary; that for roughly an hour at the time of his wife's murder, my father was sitting in his car somewhere, lost in thought and booze as he was so often during his divorce from my mother, and on that night outside of Callie Smallwood's house, and on the night he died. But underlying all of these things is the one answer I am absolutely sure of: my father did not in any way orchestrate Debi's murder. Instead, he was a victim of bad decisions, worse luck, and a community's need to hold someone accountable for the death of a lovely, successful young mother.

I will never be able to tell my father that I believe his innocence. He never gave me that chance.

My mind whirled with all these thoughts as I stood next to Jacque during the victims' candlelight vigil. After we blew out our candles and the lights came back up, Jacque and I hugged each other for a long time.

"I'm so sorry about Debi," I told her.

By this time, Jacque could read people's sorrow like tea leaves. "I'm sorry about your father," she replied. "And I'm glad you're here."

We watched silently as the sound crew dismantled the stage recently vacated by a gospel choir. The area had to be clear for the award ceremony the next day. Finally, Jacque spoke. "You know, Angela, I haven't done any of this alone. I can only do what I do because of all those people who help me." She turned to face me. "When Debi was killed, there was a time when I thought I couldn't go on. Then my friend Mari Mackus said something that changed my life. She told me, 'Jacque, you can either die with Debi, or you can live. And where there's life, there's always hope.' And she was right."

Her words revealed a truth in our family. My father traveled one of those paths; Jacque, the other. And the hope that Jacque discovered on her path was a hope she continues to share with others.

She seemed to guess my thoughts. "I'm not a hero. I'm just an ordinary mother who loved her daughter. And nobody was going to kill my kid and get away with it."

A MESSAGE FROM JACQUE MacDONALD

To Debi Anne, daughter, wife, mother, hero, a joy for all seasons. From her family who will forever love and miss her.

To my husband, Dennis: a true example that it is love, not blood, that makes a family. In gratitude for putting his life on hold and making it possible for me to turn tragedy into triumph. I will forever love you.

To my daughter, and Debi's best friend, Karen: for telling me she was proud of me when others said I should give up. You have made my life easier. I love you.

To all still seeking justice: never give up. Remember, where there is life, there is hope.

To all those who touched our lives while seeking justice for Debi: I will never forget you.

RESOURCES

If you or a loved one becomes a victim of crime, contact your local district attorney's office. The following national organizations are also eager to help.

National Organization of Parents of Murdered Children
Phone Toll Free: 1-888-818-POMC
www.pomc.com

Mothers Against Drunk Driving
24-Hour Victim Services Helpline: 1-877-MADD-HELP (1-877-623-3435)
www.madd.org

National Center for Victims of Crime
Victim Helpline: 1-800-FYI-CALL (394-2255)
Monday–Friday, 8:30 am–8:30 pm ET
www.ncvc.org

U.S. Department of Justice Office for Victims of Crime
www.ojp.usdoj.gov/ovc/

Rape Abuse and Incest National Network
24-Hour Confidential Victim Helpline: 1-800-656-HOPE
www.rainn.org

National Domestic Violence Hotline
24-Hour Confidential Victim Helpline: 1-800-799-SAFE (7233)
www.ndvh.org

National Organization for Victim Assistance
24-Hour Helpline: 1-800-TRY-NOVA (1-800-879-6682)
www.trynova.org

Carole Sund/Carrington Memorial Reward Foundation
1-888-813-8389
www.CaroleSundFoundation.com

Citizens Against Homicide
1-415-455-5944
www.MurderVictims.com

Polly Klaas Foundation (missing children)
24-Hour Hotline: 1-800-587-4357
www.PollyKlaas.org

For more information about Jacque MacDonald's show, *The Victim's Voice*, go to http://mercedcountysmostwanted.org/victimsvoice.html

"*No Room for Doubt* is a compelling account of a 'real-life' homicide and its aftermath. Angela Dove writes about her stepmother's brutal murder in March 1988, meticulously recreating the course of the investigation and its chilling effect on those whose lives were tainted by this crime."
—Sue Grafton,
bestselling author of *'T' Is for Trespass*

"This book will bring light to its readers, showing them the reality of what one person can do when they take away the joy and life of another . . . This book clarifies that the ramifications of murder run deeply."
—Susan Levy, mother of murder victim Chandra Levy
and founder of Wings of Protection

"*No Room for Doubt* is an accurate and fascinating account of the painstaking search to catch a sexual killer who terrorized a community. Meticulously researched and highly readable, Angela Dove writes from inside the investigation with skill and compassion. She captures the intricacies and details of the forensic and behavioral evidence in a way that makes you feel like you were there . . . one of the most gripping true crime books I've read in years . . . the resolution will stun you."
—Mark E. Safarik M.S., V.S.M. (FBI Ret.)
Executive Director, Forensic Behavioral Services International

"A compelling true story of a loving mother's determination to seek her daughter Debi's murderer. While law enforcement struggles to solve the mystery, Jacque MacDonald is inspirational as she courageously uncovers the horrifying truth. Jacque MacDonald is a true inspiration to victims of crime. Her perseverance to seek justice when law enforcement had nearly given up is a true testimony of a mother's love and devotion."
—Debra Puglisi Sharp, author of
Shattered: Reclaiming a Life Torn Apart by Violence

"With Angela Dove's steady hand, every page is a gripping read and every word is factual. *No Room for Doubt* is a remarkable, almost cinematic, achievement." —Dawna Kaufmann,
true crime investigative journalist
and co-author of *A Question of Murder*

"This is a must-read for every victim of crime who feels helpless or hopeless. Jacque MacDonald is a role model and hero; she proves that one determined victim, who never gives up, can overcome enormous obstacles and bring a murderer to justice. Angela Dove has crafted an exciting, real-life book that should be read by every victim of violent crime and shared with their family, friends, and associates. Bravo, Jacque! Bravo, Angela!" —Genelle Reilly, mother of
murder victim Robin Reilly and board member of
Security on Campus and Justice for Homicide Victims